Joy's
Simple Food Remedies

Also by Joy Bauer

From Junk Food to Joy Food:
All the Foods You Love to Eat . . . Only Better*

The Joy Fit Club: Cookbook Diet Plan & Inspiration

Your Inner Skinny: Four Steps to Thin Forever

Slim & Scrumptious: More than 75 Delicious,
Healthy Meals Your Family Will Love

Joy Bauer's Food Cures: Eat Right to Get Healthier,
Look Younger, and Add Years to Your Life

*May be ordered by visiting:

Hay House USA: www.hayhouse.com®
Hay House Australia: www.hayhouse.com.au
Hay House UK: www.hayhouse.co.uk
Hay House India: www.hayhouse.co.in

Joy's
Simple Food Remedies
TASTY CURES FOR WHATEVER'S AILING YOU

JOY BAUER, M.S., R.D.N., C.D.N.

HAY HOUSE, INC.
Carlsbad, California • New York City
London • Sydney • New Delhi

Published in the United States by: Hay House, Inc.: www.hayhouse.com® • **Published in Australia by:** Hay House Australia Pty. Ltd.: www.hayhouse.com.au • **Published in the United Kingdom by:** Hay House UK, Ltd.: www.hayhouse.co.uk • **Published in India by:** Hay House Publishers India: www.hayhouse.co.in

Nutritional analysis for recipes courtesy of Genesis® R&D

Indexer: Jay Kreider
Cover design: Celia Fuller • *Interior design:* Celia Fuller
Photography of the recipes and Joy Bauer by:
    Photography: Lucy Schaeffer • *Food stylist:* Leslie Orlandini • *Prop stylist:* Paige Hicks
All other photography is used under license from Shutterstock.com

Cataloging-in-Publication Data is on file at the Library of Congress

Hardcover ISBN: 978-1-4019-5567-0
E-book ISBN: 978-1-4019-5568-7

10 9 8 7 6 5 4 3 2 1
1st edition, October 2018

Printed in the United States of America

SUSTAINABLE FORESTRY INITIATIVE
Certified Chain of Custody
Promoting Sustainable Forestry
www.sfiprogram.org
SFI-01268

SFI label applies to the text stock

To my family . . . the ultimate remedy to all of life's stresses.

CONTENTS

INTRODUCTION

Food, at the most basic level, is nourishment. It fuels us, giving us the energy we need to power through the day, whether that means nailing a big presentation, getting the kids to and from various after-school events, working through the jitters of a first date, acing a test, winning an Olympic gold medal, or simply having a productive and fulfilling day.

But, of course, food is so much more than that. It's social—think hors d'oeuvres at a cocktail party or drinks with co-workers at happy hour. It's celebration—going for an ice cream sundae after a big team win or enjoying cake at a birthday gathering. It's fun—exploring new ethnic cuisine while traveling or planning an afternoon picnic with someone special. It's comfort—digging into a creamy bowl of mac and cheese or a soothing, hearty chili. And if you choose wisely, food can also be healing. Take, for example, a bowl of chicken soup. Studies show this classic really does help with cold symptoms. Research also suggests that blueberries may boost brain health, ginger can ease aches and pains, and cocoa powder can help with blood pressure. Lucky for us, science is moving in the direction of utilizing food as medicine as we discover more about the curative properties of certain nutrients.

But which items deserve a spot in your medicine chest . . . errr . . . I mean your fridge and pantry? There are so many powerful and positive foods that you should be incorporating into your diet each and every day. When diving into the research, there seemed to be limitless options that contributed to alleviating ailments, boosting energy, and promoting overall health. That being said, I worked hard to really focus on the best of the best, while also keeping in mind versatility (what good is a food if you can only find it in the most remote of grocery stores or have to wait weeks for its arrival at your door?) and universal appeal (for instance, there was some interesting research on asparagus for hangovers . . . but I just couldn't see someone enjoying this power green the morning after too many cocktails; lucky for us, it does make an appearance in the seasonal allergies chapter). And I also opted for variety and tried to spread the love. Take vitamin C as an example: It's helpful for fighting colds, wrinkles, anxiety, and a few other issues. Instead of repeating guava and bell peppers (which are among the richest sources of C) for each of the ailments, I chose to alternate between other vitamin-C-rich picks, like strawberries and oranges. But you'll know that the other vitamin-C superfoods fit the bill, too.

To make this book both user-friendly and easy to follow, I narrowed it down to the top five foods for each ailment—believe me, this was no easy task. There were literally handfuls of contenders for each chapter. I settled on five because it's manageable, digestible (pun intended), and gets the job done.

In addition to the descriptions of each of the five foods, you'll learn easy ways to prepare and enjoy them. (You'll also find quick recipe suggestions and delicious prep methods on my website—**Joybauer.com**—for easy access.) Plus, I've included three mouthwatering recipes for each condition. The recipes are simple to make and scrumptious and in most cases, incorporate three or more of the medicinal foods featured. For example, the next time you're nursing a cold, suck on my Feel-Good Pops, which are rich in vitamin C and beta-carotene. Or whip up a batch of my Hangover Muffins and stash them in the freezer so you're prepared the next time you have one too many cocktails. Looking to blast belly fat? Make my Roasted Salmon and a bowl of Creamy Broccoli Soup to help whittle your middle.

A quick comment on salt: Some recipes call for coarse, kosher salt while others call for a finer type of salt (like fine sea salt or table salt). The sodium amount given within each recipe's nutritional information is based on the specific type of salt indicated in the ingredients. That being said, either type will work in any recipe and you can always increase or decrease the amount depending on your preference. Keep in mind that a recipe will be less salty if you use the same amount of kosher salt instead of fine salt and vice versa (1 teaspoon of kosher salt contains less sodium than 1 teaspoon fine salt). If you don't have an issue with sodium, feel free to use whichever you prefer.

Now, get ready to flip through the pages to find ailments that affect you or your loved ones, or, if you're curious, browse all of them. Take out a pen and paper to make a shopping list and then be prepared to start feeling better, looking better, and living a happier and healthier life.

Note: It's important to point out that food should not take the place of medication. Medication is a vital way to manage and treat various conditions and diseases. However, food is a powerful complement to medication. And who knows, one day soon, food may very well be the ultimate go-to for preventing, managing, and reversing whatever's ailing you.

Read, eat, and be healthy!

5 FOODS TO
MINIMIZE BELLY FAT

Belly fat. It's probably one of the most Googled terms out there. (Sorry, Kardashians.)

And it's no wonder, because so many Americans are struggling with weight. More than 70 percent of adults aged 20 years and older are overweight (classified as having a body mass index, or BMI, of 25 to 30). Almost 40 percent of adults are considered obese (having a BMI of 30 plus).

As we get older, many of us carry this excess weight around our middle. Sigh! You can thank a slowing metabolism and changing hormone levels. But those extra pounds generally don't just settle underneath the skin right on top of the belly. The fat also settles deep within the skin, around the organs. This fat, known as visceral fat, is downright dangerous because it messes with hormone production and increases inflammation, which, in turn, heightens the risk for heart disease, type 2 diabetes, and certain cancers.

That means *everyone* needs to know where they stand and work to trim their midsection. Even if you have a normal BMI or have skinny legs and arms, it's possible to have high levels of belly fat. Your first step: Know your waist circumference. To correctly measure your waist, stand straight and place a tape measure around your middle, just above your hip bones and below your belly button. Measure your waist just after you breathe out.

Ideally, men should be *below* 40 inches and women should be *below* 35 inches. If your midsection registers significantly higher than the ideal number, here's an important fact: Trimming just 1 inch can significantly reduce your risk for dangerous conditions and give you a huge health boost.

Of course, eating less and moving more is by far the most effective way to whittle your middle. The good news is that belly fat mobilizes relatively quickly. Even better news: You can trim your middle not only by *removing* foods but by *adding* certain foods, such as the following slimming selections.

1. Salmon

It's time to reel in some swimmers for dinner, and salmon, in particular, is a real catch. In general, salmon is loaded with protein (about 37 grams per 5 ounces cooked). The nutrient is more satiating than either carbs or fat, so increasing your intake will help you feel more satisfied throughout the day and could help you eat less overall.

Salmon can specifically help burn belly fat because it's one of the richest sources of vitamin D (more than 500 IU, or international units, per 5 ounces cooked). Vitamin D is directly involved with producing hormones that regulate appetite. Consuming enough of the vitamin (the recommended intake is 600 IU daily) reduces the likelihood that you'll overeat. Also, several studies have shown that vitamin D is involved with signaling belly fat cells to burn off.[1]

There are a million ways to prepare the delicious fish: Try salmon grilled, baked, broiled, or even mashed into a salmon salad (in place of tuna fish). It's also delicious in tacos or topped with pesto or a lemon-dill yogurt sauce.

To minimize your exposure to toxins (including the organic chlorine compound polychlorinated biphenyl, also known as PCB), look for wild and/or Alaskan salmon (all salmon from Alaska is wild). About 75 percent of the salmon consumed in the United States is farmed; to date, wild salmon is more nutritious and tends to be lower in potentially harmful pollutants. Canned wild salmon can also be a budget-friendly option if you're looking to save some cash.

2. Greek Yogurt

Yogurt, particularly low-fat Greek yogurt, contains satiating protein (about 20 grams per cup, or 17 grams per single container), which is twice as much as traditional yogurt. It can keep you feeling fuller longer and help control your appetite, which can translate to less belly fat. Greek yogurt is a bit tangier than traditional, but it's also creamier, so there's a flavor trade-off.

Yogurt is rich in calcium (about 200 mg per cup), and two studies (one in *The Journal of Nutrition*[2] and the other from the journal *Obesity*[3]) have linked calcium to lower levels of abdominal fat. Of course, all the nutrients in food work synergistically, but calcium has been singled out for a few reasons: Experts believe it may help to increase fat burn, reduce fat absorption, and slightly rev metabolism.

Lastly, yogurt contains probiotics, the beneficial bacteria that help with digestion. And according to a study in *Nutrition and Metabolism*,[4] probiotics may also promote a healthy weight.

Make a yogurt parfait layered with chopped fruit and heart-healthy nuts. Greek yogurt makes a perfect substitute for sour cream in creamy salad dressings and dips, or as an alternate topper for a baked potato or bowl of chili. You can also use it in place of mayo in egg or tuna salad.

3. Artichokes

While yogurt has probiotics, artichokes are *prebiotics*. And prebiotics feed probiotics so they can do their job.

This creates a gut filled with good bacteria, which is so important when it comes to belly fat because the combination helps to play interference with fat storage as well as reducing inflammation.

Artichoke and artichoke hearts are both terrific. A cup delivers 9 grams of fiber (an impressive amount!). While a whole steamed "choke" is a fun and delicious treat to devour, the hearts tend to be more convenient and easier to work into your weekly menu rotation.

Don't be intimidated by a whole artichoke—the spiky leaves have a tendency to scare off home chefs. But prep is fairly easy. Start by rinsing the artichoke well, even using a veggie brush to help get rid of the film, which can create a bitter taste if left behind. Next, remove the stem (if necessary; you don't have to do this step as the stem is edible and delicious) and about an inch off the top using a serrated knife. You can clip the pointy tips on the bottom leaves . . . or not—user's choice. Then gently open the petals to allow your seasonings to get into each of the leaves, and simply boil, bake, steam, or microwave.

To eat, pull off individual leaves and use your teeth to gently remove the "meaty" flesh as you pull the leaf from your mouth. Artichokes have a mild, even slightly lemony flavor. Some people describe the taste as similar to brussels sprouts (but not at all bitter), while others liken it to an eggplant (soft and juicy).

You can also enjoy canned artichoke hearts; try tossing them into salads, soups, and sides. I personally love roasted artichoke hearts with olive oil, lemon, and some seasonings (ground black pepper, oregano, garlic, and a small dash of salt).

4. Broccoli

Broccoli can help burn belly fat for a few key reasons.

One study has shown a relationship between people who consume ample amounts of deep-colored veggies (specifically green, yellow, and orange) and lower levels of visceral fat, the dangerous fat around your organs.[5] Plus, these veggies were shown to help reduce inflammation.

I specifically chose to focus on *broccoli* of all the stellar deep-colored veggies out there because broccoli is one of the few veggies that contain calcium, which has been shown to increase fat loss, especially around the abdominal area. And interestingly enough, a large-scale observational study suggests that the calcium from food seems to be more effective than calcium from supplements, providing another good reason to eat your greens.

And, hey, consider this: Broccoli is one of the highest-volume, lowest-calorie foods around (1 cup is only 25 calories), so you can eat a great big amount and still drop pounds. So aside from the specific belly-fat benefits, it's one of the best foods for weight loss in general.

One of my favorite ways to enjoy broccoli is misting a large batch of florets with olive oil, sprinkling on some seasonings, and roasting them in the oven set at 420°F until the tops are brown and crispy (about 17 minutes).

You can also mix this versatile green veggie into omelets, soups, and stir-fry entrées. I like to make broccoli "bread crumbs" by pulsing florets in a food processor and combining them with herbs and spices. It's a fantastic topper for casseroles, soups, steamed veggies, and roasted fish—the tasty green "bread crumbs" crisp up in the oven to elevate your meal and boost your health.

5. Onions

Onions contain a type of soluble fiber called inulin, which acts as a prebiotic, just like artichokes.

This is important for good gut health and, according to preliminary studies,[6] may also help facilitate weight loss in the abdominal area.

Onions are an eeeeeeasy way to add loads of flavor to a variety of dishes—everything from soups to stews to sandwiches to tacos to burgers to pizzas, you name it—*without* adding calories, fat, sodium, or sugar. (One raw onion has just about 50 calories and offers around 2.5 grams of fiber.)

Browse the produce section and you'll notice three main onion colors: yellow, red, and white. Each has a different flavor with different uses. Yellow onions, the most common, make up about 87 percent of the U.S. onion crop and can be used in almost any dish, though they're known for taking the starring role in French onion soup. They tend to be the sweetest variety. Red onions are great grilled or roasted and are delicious on salads or sandwiches. White onions work well in salads or sauces but also lend a subtly sweet flavor to dishes when sautéed. Keep in mind that leeks, shallots, and scallions are part of the onion family and contain the same beneficial compounds as well.

Caramelizing onions is another tasty method of preparation because it helps to bring out a natural sweetness. Caramelized onions can be used to add flavor to a variety of foods, including turkey burgers, sandwiches, and omelets. And of course, don't forget about onion powder when you're in a pinch. Be creative and experiment to find your favorite kinds and ways to use the versatile veggie.

And no need to sob when slicing—a pair of onion goggles (or even a pair of ski goggles or thick glasses) can help protect your eyes from the sulfuric compounds that can trigger tears when cutting.

Roasted Broccoli-Artichoke Dip

MAKES ABOUT 5 CUPS

4 heaping cups chopped broccoli
  florets
4 garlic cloves, minced
  (or ½ teaspoon garlic powder)
1 tablespoon olive oil
Pinch of salt
¼ teaspoon ground black pepper
One 14-ounce can artichoke hearts,
  drained, rinsed, and chopped
1 to 2 scallions, thinly sliced

1 shallot or ½ yellow or red onion,
  finely diced
1 teaspoon fresh tarragon
  (or ½ teaspoon dried tarragon)
½ teaspoon cumin
¼ teaspoon paprika
½ cup nonfat plain Greek yogurt
¼ cup grated Parmesan cheese
Minced or chopped fresh parsley for
  garnish, optional

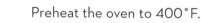

Preheat the oven to 400°F.

Mix the broccoli with the garlic, oil, salt, and pepper. Spread out the broccoli on a baking sheet covered with parchment paper. Mist the tops with oil spray and roast in the oven for about 10 to 15 minutes, until the broccoli is soft and slightly browned.

While the broccoli roasts, combine the artichokes, scallions, and shallot (or onion) in a large bowl.

Add the broccoli into the artichoke mixture. Add the tarragon, cumin, and paprika. Mix until everything is well combined.

Add the yogurt and Parmesan cheese and mix well.

Season with additional ground black pepper to taste and garnish with optional fresh parsley.

Note: You can finely chop veggies by hand or by pulsing in a food processor.

NUTRITIONAL INFORMATION *Per 2 tablespoons*
15 calories • 1 g protein • 0.5 g total fat (0 g saturated fat, 0.5 g unsaturated fat) •
0 mg cholesterol • 2 g carbs • 0 g fiber • 0 g total sugar • 75 mg sodium

HEALTHY HOME RUN This recipe includes four foods that may help fight belly fat. Serve with salmon to enjoy the ultimate belly-fat-blasting feast!

Creamy Broccoli Soup

MAKES 7 SERVINGS (about 1 cup each)

1 yellow onion, chopped

½ cup chopped celery (about 2 stalks)

1 garlic clove, minced (or ⅛ teaspoon garlic powder)

¼ teaspoon ground black pepper

4 cups reduced-sodium vegetable broth or stock

5 cups roughly chopped broccoli florets (one 12-ounce bag)

One 15-ounce can white beans, drained and rinsed (preferably low sodium)

¼ teaspoon nutmeg

½ cup nonfat or low-fat plain Greek yogurt

Liberally coat a large saucepan with oil spray and warm over medium heat. Add the onions and cook until softened and slightly browned, about 7 minutes.

Add the celery, garlic, and pepper and cook for 5 more minutes, stirring occasionally. Add more oil spray if the pan becomes too dry.

Add the broth, cover, and bring to a boil. Add the broccoli and reduce the heat to medium; cover and cook for about 5 minutes.

Add the beans and cook for 5 more minutes uncovered, stirring occasionally. Mix in the nutmeg.

Place an immersion blender into the soup and blend until the desired consistency is reached, or transfer the soup carefully to a blender or food processor. Add the yogurt for extra creaminess and continue to blend. You can make the soup completely smooth or leave some texture, depending on your preference. Also, you can certainly skip the yogurt if you follow a dairy-free diet (1 cup soup *without* yogurt is just 90 calories).

NUTRITIONAL INFORMATION *Per serving*
100 calories • 6 g protein • 0.5 g total fat (0 g saturated fat, 0.5 g unsaturated fat) • 0 mg cholesterol • 17 g carbs • 6 g fiber • 3 g total sugar (3 g natural sugar, 0 g added sugar) • 125 mg sodium

Roasted Salmon with Artichoke Hearts and Lemon-Dill Yogurt Sauce

MAKES 4 SERVINGS

Roasted Artichoke Hearts and Leeks

2 tablespoons olive oil
2 tablespoons lemon juice
3 garlic cloves, minced
½ teaspoon kosher salt
¼ teaspoon ground black pepper

Two 14-ounce cans quartered artichoke hearts, drained, rinsed, and patted dry (or use frozen, defrosted)
2 leeks, sliced and cleaned (or 2 large red onions, cut into wedges and separated)

Roasted Salmon

4 salmon fillets, about 5 ounces each
½ teaspoon kosher salt

¼ teaspoon ground black pepper

Lemon-Dill Yogurt Sauce

1 cup nonfat or low-fat plain Greek yogurt
1 tablespoon finely chopped fresh dill (or 1 teaspoon dried dill)

2 tablespoons lemon juice
¼ teaspoon garlic powder
Salt and ground black pepper to taste

For the artichokes and leeks:
Preheat the oven to 425°F. Combine the oil, lemon juice, garlic, salt, and pepper in a mixing bowl. Add the artichokes and leeks to the bowl and stir to coat evenly. Mist a baking sheet with oil spray and spread out the mixture in a single layer. Roast for about 20 minutes or until the vegetables are slightly browned and crispy. If using onions, they'll need about 5 more minutes in the oven.

For the salmon:
While the vegetables are roasting, place the salmon skin side down on a second baking sheet coated with oil spray. Mist the salmon tops with oil spray and sprinkle on salt and pepper. Roast in the oven alongside the veggies for 12 to 15 minutes or until desired doneness. (The general rule of thumb is 5 to 7 minutes per ½ inch of thickness.)

For the Lemon-Dill Yogurt Sauce:
Mix all the ingredients in a small bowl. (Add more dill, lemon, salt, and pepper to taste.) Top each salmon fillet with yogurt sauce and serve with the roasted vegetables on the side.

NUTRITIONAL INFORMATION
Per serving (1 salmon fillet, 2 tablespoons sauce, and 1 ¼ cups vegetables)
390 calories • 40 g protein • 15 g total fat (3 g saturated fat, 12 g unsaturated fat) • 65 mg cholesterol • 23 g carbs • 14 g fiber • 3 g total sugar (3 g natural sugar, 0 g added sugar) • 720 mg sodium

5 FOODS TO
BOOST ENERGY

There's no debating it—we are in an energy crisis. And I'm not talking about fossil fuels. Many of us regularly feel exhausted and experience frustrating fatigue or energy dips throughout the day.

It's estimated that up to 27 percent of us feel so pooped that we actually have to muster up the energy to visit the doctor. But before I get into the food fixes, let's talk about the most obvious—and most important—solution: Getting a good night's sleep. You're aiming for about seven to eight hours a night. Unfortunately, according to a report from the Centers for Disease Control and Prevention (CDC), more than a third of Americans fail to hit this mark on a regular basis.

Managing stress and getting regular exercise can help keep you feeling energized all day long. Working out increases levels of energy-lifting and mood-boosting neurotransmitters, making you feel recharged.[1] A good sweat session also offers the side perks of improving sleep,[2] calming your nerves, and keeping stress in check. It's a four-for-one deal—a total bargain.

Eating regular, appropriately sized, and well-balanced meals will keep your blood sugar steady. When blood sugar takes a dive, so do energy levels. Another cause of exhaustion is stuffing yourself. We all know how lethargic we feel after we eat way too much (um, hello, Thanksgiving nap).

Dehydration is another common cause of fatigue. Aim to drink at least half your weight in water ounces per day. And while a shot of caffeine can help rev your engine, too much caffeine can interfere with sleep.

Iron deficiency and anemia, a common blood disorder that is typically caused by a lack of iron in the diet, can cause tiredness too. Drowsiness can also be a side effect of some medications, such as antidepressants or antihistamines. Medical issues, such as chronic fatigue syndrome, fibromyalgia, sleep apnea, diabetes, depression, and hypothyroid, can also be linked with feelings of exhaustion.

The good news is that you can help recharge your battery with five energizing food fixes.

1. Purple Grapes

Grapes are great for more than just making wine. They're deliciously sweet and wonderfully hydrating. That's because they're made up of about 80 percent water. Even mild dehydration can cause fatigue . . . and the desire to do absolutely nothing but sit on the couch and binge-watch Netflix.[3] So grab a handful and hydrate.

Purple grapes also have another perk: They're a super source of resveratrol, a plant compound that's found in the skins of the grapes, which has been shown to help with a variety of conditions and disease. One animal study in the journal *Molecules* found it may help combat exhaustion.[4] Mice given a resveratrol supplement in varying doses were able to exercise longer and had lower levels of fatigue-related parameters than mice in the control group.

There's a big debate about organic versus conventionally grown food—I often say *any* produce is better than *no* produce. Not to mention, a good rinse can get rid of most pesticide residue. However, grapes are often found on the "Dirty Dozen" most contaminated produce list created by the Environmental Working Group, a nonprofit watchdog organization. So if you're able to go organic in this particular case, it might be worth the extra cash to minimize your exposure to pesticides.

Grapes are an easy, go-to snack. Simply pop them into your mouth and enjoy. For a more indulgent treat, try freezing them. They take on the consistency of an ice pop—sweet and refreshing. You can toss fresh, chopped grapes into a yogurt parfait, or add them to a green vegetable salad or even chicken salad. Or try slicing grapes thinly and using them on your peanut butter sandwich in place of sugary grape jelly or jam. It's a super delicious upgrade.

2. Dark-Meat Poultry

When it comes to boosting energy, the dark side offers some real benefits. Dark-meat chicken (specifically skinless drumsticks and thighs), as well as turkey, provides nutrients that can help fight fatigue. Similar to white meat, dark-meat poultry is a terrific source of lean protein (about 21 grams for a 3-ounce drumstick or thigh without the skin, not accounting for the weight of the bone), which provides the body with a sustained source of energy. Dark-meat turkey offers similar amounts (23 g of protein per 3 ounces). When it comes to protein, aim for about half your weight in grams each day—more if you're a serious exerciser.

Dark-meat poultry also contains a good amount of iron (roughly double the amount of white meat), a mineral that enables the body to produce hemoglobin, a substance in red blood cells that carries oxygen throughout the body. When you don't get enough iron, your red blood cells don't produce enough hemoglobin, and therefore can't transport enough oxygen. The result: You can feel fatigued. Indeed, fatigue is a common symptom of iron deficiency anemia, but even if you don't have anemia, adding iron to your diet (through food not supplements) can help improve your energy.[5]

Many people prefer dark meat chicken and turkey because it's more moist, tender, and flavorful. While some people worry about the extra fat and calories, the difference isn't significant. Dark-meat turkey, not including skin, will only cost you an extra 25 calories and about 1 g saturated fat per 3 ounces. The swap for chicken is even less—about an extra 10 calories and less than .5 g saturated fat per 3 ounces.

You can use thighs for all sort of delicious recipes. Scrap the skin if you're managing your weight or watching your saturated fat intake. Ground turkey and chicken are perfect for meatballs, chili, burgers, and tacos—93 percent lean ground turkey or chicken is the perfect balance of white and dark meat. The 99 percent extra-lean ground poultry option is all white meat, offering less iron and tending to be substantially drier.

A note to red-meat lovers: Lean beef is another great source of iron and protein, but because so many people are limiting their intake for health and environmental reasons, I thought it best to focus on chicken and turkey instead. But you can certainly feel free to include moderate amounts of lean beef in your diet.

3. Swiss Chard

Swiss chard often finds itself in spinach's shadow. The leafy green doesn't always get a lot of love, but I'm calling out the colorful veggie because it packs a one-two punch against fatigue. Swiss chard contains a good amount of plant-based iron (called non-heme iron). It's different from the iron found in animal products, such as beef and dark-meat poultry, because it's not as easily absorbed. But not to worry, the second power nutrient found in Swiss chard is vitamin C, which increases the absorption of its plant-based iron.[6] You'll get about 4 mg of iron in 1 cup of cooked chard and an impressive 32 mg of C. Men need 8 mg iron daily; women of childbearing ages need 18 mg, and after the age of 50, they need 8 mg. (Spinach contains more iron but just about half the vitamin C. So while it's another terrific pick-me-upper, Swiss chard wins the coveted spot.)

Just like spinach, you can eat Swiss chard leaves raw in salads (mix them in with other greens to give your salad base an energy boost) or use the leaves in place of bread or a tortilla to cut back on carbs when making sandwiches or wraps. You can also fill raw Swiss chard leaves with seasoned ground poultry meat (a.k.a. chicken lettuce wraps) for a double hit of fatigue-fighting foods.

Or serve it up as a tasty side. Sauté chard in a little olive oil, minced garlic, salt, and ground black pepper—it tastes amazing. You can also steam or microwave Swiss chard—it works perfectly served alongside any protein source, such as lean beef, pork, chicken, fish, or even seasoned lentils. (By the way, lentils are loaded with non-heme iron and protein, too.) You can also toss chopped, raw leaves into simmering soups, pasta dishes, poultry, and lentil stews, or morning omelets to easily kick up the nutrition. It's a wonderful spinach swap in just about any dish, including lasagna.

4. Tofu

I confess: I'm a total tofu fan. Tofu—curd made from mashed soybeans—offers a double dose of fatigue-fighting power. It's a terrific source of plant-based protein, which helps steady blood sugars and provides the body with a sustained source of energy. Tofu contains roughly 20 grams of protein per 1 cup (or 8 ounces)—and really, it's easy to eat double that amount when it's prepared in a flavorful way. That 1-cup amount also delivers non-heme iron—more than 20 percent of your daily needs. Serve it with a vitamin-C-rich food, such as Swiss chard, spinach, broccoli, or kale, to increase the absorption.

While some people complain that tofu is bland, its neutral flavor is actually one of its great assets because it takes on the tastes of whatever you cook it with. Plus, there are so many different varieties. Silken tofu (which is sold in soft, firm, and extra-firm consistencies) is smooth and custard-like, making it ideal for sauces, soups, smoothies, dressings, and even desserts. Then there's regular tofu, which has a spongy texture. Soft tofu can be crumbled into vegan "egg" scrambles or in dishes that call for ricotta or cottage cheese. Firm or extra-firm tofu holds its shape as blocks or cubes and can be used in stir-fries or crumbled. Super-firm is quite dense and dry. You can also find sprouted and baked tofu (these come in a bunch of different flavors).

I know some people have been scared off soy because of its supposed connection to breast cancer, but research has alleviated that concern by showing moderate consumption of whole soy foods (including tofu) are safe for healthy people. And in fact, some research, including one study of more than 18,000 breast cancer survivors in the United States and China published in the *American Journal of Clinical Nutrition*, suggests whole soy foods may help reduce the risk of a recurrence.[7]

Try baked tofu tossed in a green salad or sauté it in an Asian stir-fry. I love to scramble it up with veggies and seasonings for a protein-packed vegetarian morning meal. Silken tofu also gives smoothies a good dose of vegetarian protein and iron and lends a thick, creamy texture. I make a strawberry-banana-tofu smoothie by combining ¾ cup milk with ½ cup silken tofu, ½ ripe banana, ½ cup strawberries, and 3 to 5 ice cubes in a blender until smooth and frothy.

5. Walnuts

Everyone knows I'm a nut . . . for nuts of all kinds. But walnuts, in particular, have a few tricks to help counter tiredness (as well as wrinkles, see page 102). They're the richest nut in plant-based omega-3 fats, which act as an anti-inflammatory. In one study, breast cancer survivors who followed a fatigue reduction diet (FRD) consisting of a variety of healthful foods, including one daily serving of omega-3-rich seeds and walnuts (two servings for vegetarians), for three months saw a significant improvement of cancer-related fatigue compared to those on a control diet—44 percent versus 8 percent. The FRD helped improved sleep quality by about 50 percent (another tried-and-true way to boost daytime energy).[8]

Walnuts also provide some magnesium. The mineral is required for energy production; it's used in the production of ATP or adenosine triphosphate, a coenzyme that transports energy within our cells and is used to fuel metabolism and other functions in the body. You'll score about 50 mg of magnesium per ¼ cup or handful. (Women need 310 to 320 mg per day, depending on their age; men need 420 mg daily.)

One small study found that mice given a walnut extract for two weeks were able to swim against a current for longer periods of time than those given a placebo.[9] Researchers say the high content of plant-based omega-3 (alpha-linolenic acid) plus the combination of its antioxidants helped delay fatigue. And another study from Belgium showed that people who had chronic fatigue syndrome with the worst fatigue symptoms had the lowest levels of omega-3 fats.[10]

Walnuts are great to snack on by themselves or to add to a homemade trail mix or yogurt parfait. Sprinkle them onto salads for a nice crunch. They're a great addition to sweet desserts, too, including muffins and cookies. Or try whipping up a batch of my Rosemary Walnuts. To make, liberally mist 1 cup walnuts with oil spray until well-coated. Toss with 1 tablespoon finely chopped fresh rosemary and ¼ teaspoon each kosher salt and ground black pepper. Spread nuts in a single layer on a baking sheet and bake in a 325°F oven for about 10 minutes or until the nuts are lightly toasted but not burnt. Let cool and add salt to taste.

Savory Chicken Meatballs with Roasted Grapes

MAKES 4 SERVINGS

1 pound ground chicken
1 cup finely chopped Swiss chard leaves
3 to 4 tablespoons finely chopped
   fresh basil
1 tablespoon finely chopped
   fresh chives
1 tablespoon finely chopped fresh
   parsley, plus extra for garnish

½ cup walnuts, ground into flour using
   a food processor
1 teaspoon kosher salt
½ teaspoon ground black pepper
½ teaspoon crushed red pepper
   flakes (optional)
2 cups red or purple grapes, washed
   and patted dry
Walnuts for garnish (optional)

Preheat the oven to 350°F. Line a rimmed baking sheet with parchment paper.

Combine all the ingredients except for the grapes in a large bowl. Do not overmix. (You may want to use your hands here; lightly mist them with oil spray beforehand so the mixture doesn't stick.)

Form the meatballs into 16 golf-ball-size balls, keeping them light and fluffy. If necessary, reapply oil spray to your hands to prevent sticking. Place on the prepared baking sheet and bake for 15 to 20 minutes.

While the meatballs are cooking, add the grapes to a separate bowl and mist with oil spray, tossing to coat evenly. Sprinkle with a dash of optional salt and pepper. Set aside.

During the last 10 to 12 minutes of the meatballs cooking in the oven, remove the baking sheet, and scatter on the seasoned grapes. Place back into the oven until the meatballs are finished cooking and the grapes are roasted and slightly puckered.

Garnish with chopped parsley or basil and walnuts.

NUTRITIONAL INFORMATION *Per serving (4 meatballs and ½ cup roasted grapes)*
290 calories • 29 g protein • 11 g total fat (1 g saturated fat, 10 g unsaturated fat) • 65 mg cholesterol • 17 g carbs • 2 g fiber • 13 g total sugar (13 g natural sugar, 0 g added sugar) • 570 mg sodium

GET SAUCY! For an Italian spin, transfer meatballs to a pot of your favorite marinara sauce and simmer for 15 more minutes. Serve over sautéed Swiss chard or zucchini noodles!

Asian Tofu and Veggie Stir-fry

MAKES 4 SERVINGS

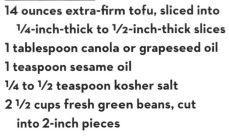

For the stir-fry

14 ounces extra-firm tofu, sliced into
¼-inch-thick to ½-inch-thick slices
1 tablespoon canola or grapeseed oil
1 teaspoon sesame oil
¼ to ½ teaspoon kosher salt
2 ½ cups fresh green beans, cut
into 2-inch pieces

½ to 1 cup finely chopped, shredded,
or thinly sliced carrots
3 cups roughly chopped Swiss chard
(thick stems removed)
¼ cup walnut pieces
Toasted sesame seeds for garnish
(optional)

For the sauce

3 tablespoons reduced-sodium
soy sauce
2 tablespoons water
1 tablespoon rice wine vinegar
1 tablespoon honey
1 tablespoon cornstarch
1 tablespoon sesame oil

1 ½ tablespoons grated fresh ginger
(or 1 ½ teaspoons ground ginger)
4 cloves garlic, minced (or ½
teaspoon garlic powder)
¼ teaspoon crushed red pepper flakes
(optional)

Remove excess water from the tofu by placing the pieces on a bunch of folded paper towels. Place a second batch of folded paper towels on top, followed by a plate or heavy book and let set for 20 minutes to 1 hour. When the tofu is drier, cut into small cubes or rectangles.

Whisk all the sauce ingredients in a bowl until smooth.

Heat a large skillet over medium-high heat and coat with the canola and sesame oils. Add the tofu, sprinkle the salt over the top, and cook for 6 to 8 minutes. Gently flip and toss the tofu until it is slightly browned and crispy, scraping the bottom of the pan with a spatula so the tofu doesn't break apart. Mist the pan with oil spray if it becomes too dry. Add 2 tablespoons of the previously prepared sauce and cook for 1 minute, tossing occasionally. Transfer the tofu to a plate with the bottom glaze.

Liberally coat the same pan with oil spray and return it to the heat. Add 1 tablespoon of the sauce and the green beans and carrots. Toss occasionally for about 3 minutes. Add the Swiss chard and remaining sauce and sauté for

2 to 3 more minutes until the sauce thickens and the chard cooks down.
Add the tofu back to the pan and toss everything to coat. Top each serving
with 1 tablespoon walnuts and optional sesame seeds.

NUTRITIONAL INFORMATION *Per serving (about 1 ¼ cups)*
230 calories • 12 g protein • 13 g total fat (1 g saturated fat, 12 g unsaturated fat) •
0 mg cholesterol • 17 g carbs • 3 g fiber • 7 g total sugar (3 g natural sugar, 4 g added sugar) •
620 mg sodium

Energizing Waldorf Salad/Wrap

MAKES 6 SERVINGS

6 chicken thighs (or any leftover cooked poultry, white and dark meat)

1 ½ cups chopped celery, about 3 to 4 stalks

1 large red apple, chopped

1 ½ cups seedless purple grapes, halved

1 cup nonfat or low-fat plain Greek yogurt

1 tablespoon Dijon mustard

1 tablespoon apple cider vinegar

1 tablespoon honey

½ teaspoon kosher salt

¼ teaspoon ground black pepper

4 to 8 cups any preferred lettuce leaves for serving

½ cup walnuts, halved (toasted, if desired)

To roast the chicken thighs, preheat the oven to 400°F.

Place the chicken, skin intact, on a baking tray lined with parchment paper and mist with oil spray. (You'll ultimately discard the skin, but leaving it on while cooking will result in moister and more delicious meat.)

Roast for about 40 to 45 minutes or until the chicken is cooked through and reaches an internal temperature of 165°F. Remove from the oven, cover, and let the chicken rest for about 10 minutes. Remove and discard the skin. Shred the chicken off the bones using two forks or your fingers. Cut into bite-size pieces and add to a large mixing bowl, along with the celery, apple, and grapes.

To make the dressing, whisk together the yogurt, mustard, apple cider vinegar, honey, salt, and pepper in a medium bowl.

Add the dressing to the large bowl with all the other ingredients and toss to coat thoroughly. Cover and chill in the fridge. Serve on a bed of fresh lettuce and sprinkle with walnuts.

For an Energizing Waldorf Wrap:
Mix the walnuts into the dressing with the other ingredients. Then, layer a whole-grain tortilla with lettuce leaves, 1 cup chicken-apple-walnut salad, and roll it up (320 calories, 27 g protein, 8 g fiber, 12 g total fat, 570 mg sodium).

NUTRITIONAL INFORMATION *Per serving*
260 calories • 22 g protein • 10 g total fat (0.5 g saturated fat, 9.5 g unsaturated fat) • 70 mg cholesterol • 19 g carbs • 3 g fiber • 14 g total sugar (11 g natural sugar, 3 g added sugar) • 380 mg sodium

5 FOODS TO
EASE ANXIETY
AND STRESS

Bitten-down fingernails, sweat circles around the armpits, dark bags under the eyes; these visible signs of anxiety and stress are worn by many. In fact, 40 million adults—that's more than 18 percent of us—suffer from anxiety disorders every year in the United States. It's the most common psychological disorder in this country.

Anxiety causes changes in the brain and in the body. When we're feeling nervous or worried, neurotransmitters (chemicals that transport messages) signal to the sympathetic nervous system to increase breathing and heart rate and to contract muscles. It affects blood flow and the sweat glands, and can cause lightheadedness, nausea, and other symptoms. It's this fight-or-flight reaction that prepares us to deal with a "stressor"—our boss asking us for that project we haven't finished yet, a honking car, or a screaming toddler.

Of course, it's important to make a distinction between these everyday stresses, which we all feel—and are totally normal—and chronic worry and apprehension, which can overwhelm you and leave you feeling out of control and paralyzed. The latter is what may be recognized as a more serious disorder, an actual diagnosable medical condition. This often goes hand in hand with depression and should be treated by a doctor.

The encouraging news is that anxiety—whether it's occasional, low-grade, or a more definitive disorder—is treatable. Medication, therapy, positive self-talk, meditation, and exercise are all effective tools. Diet can soothe stress, too—calming foods can help by stabilizing blood sugar and increasing levels of serotonin, a feel-good hormone. While we don't know the exact mechanism yet, the results from research thus far are compelling.

If you're feeling a little stressed, give these anxiety-easing eats, all of which are healthful and delicious, a try.

1. Fatty Fish

The omega-3s in fatty fish make them a feel-good standout. Whether you're reeling in salmon, sardines, Atlantic mackerel, or Arctic char, you're sure to get a beneficial boost. Numerous studies show that omega-3s are helpful in fighting depression, and one study found them to be particularly useful in combating anxiety, too. The research, done at Ohio State University, suggests that the good fats helped reduce inflammation and anxiety by 20 percent in younger adults who experienced an everyday stressor that would typically cause an anxiety-ridden response.[1] That's encouraging because if it works for occasional and expected anxiety, imagine how useful it could be for people who suffer from more involved anxiety disorders.

Fatty fish are also among the best dietary sources of vitamin D. Research shows that low levels of this vitamin have been linked to depression, a condition that's closely related to anxiety.

Salmon is wonderful on the grill or baked. Add bite-size pieces to pasta dishes, casseroles, omelets, and frittatas. You can enjoy it mashed up as a salad served over greens or on whole-grain bread. Or you can make scrumptious patties by combining it with eggs, lemon juice, seasonings, and bread crumbs or rolled oats.

Arctic char has a milder, more delicate flavor than the stronger-tasting salmon. But just like salmon, it's tasty cooked on the grill or in the oven. Finish it with a generous squeeze of fresh lemon juice for a mood-boosting dose of vitamin C.[2] As for mackerel, you can swap it for tuna or salmon in most recipes—it has a strong flavor and is very oily. It works well with a simple preparation: Bake with a little salt and pepper and a squeeze of citrus.

And don't forget about sardines. Ounce for ounce, sardines contain just as much heart-healthy omega-3 fat as salmon. They're extremely low in contaminants, eco-friendly (no need to worry about overfishing), packed with high-quality protein, and super affordable. If you buy canned sardines with the bones, you'll get a hefty dose of calcium, too. If you're a sardine lover, consider this yummy open-faced sandwich: Spread 2 slices of whole-grain bread with a little bit of low-fat mayo or herb-infused extra-virgin olive oil and top each half with a couple of canned sardines, a slice of tomato, and a few fresh basil leaves.

2. Chickpeas

It doesn't matter if they're called chickpeas or garbanzo beans—they can spell relief for people who are feeling frazzled. Some research suggests that tryptophan depletion might be linked to anxiety.[3] And fortunately, the little legume is rich in tryptophan, an amino acid that your body uses to help make serotonin, a feel-good chemical in the brain.

L-tryptophan (its full, scientific name) is just one amino acid in food that competes to get into the brain—and it's one of the least abundant. To give it a competitive advantage to help cross the blood-brain barrier, it requires some carbohydrate. Doing so causes the body to release insulin, which helps move this powerful amino acid along. As it turns out, chickpeas are one-stop shopping: They contain tryptophan and slow-burning carbs, a winning combination for destressing. Another small study found that men who consumed foods containing tryptophan with a dose of carbs had slightly lower anxiety scores than those who ate foods without tryptophan.[4]

Chickpeas also contain folate, a B vitamin that helps regulate mood (a 1-cup serving of cooked chickpeas provides more than 70 percent of the daily recommended intake). Low blood levels of folate have been linked to an increased risk for depressive symptoms. Plus, the high protein (14.5 g per cooked cup) and high fiber (12.5 g per cooked cup) content can help steady blood sugars and stabilize mood.

You can easily add a scoop of this uplifting food to salads. You can also dunk veggies in hummus, a Mediterranean dip made from mashed chickpeas.

I love to mix chickpeas with another stress-squasher, salmon, in my Wild Salmon and Chickpea Salad: Mash 6 ounces of cooked wild boneless, skinless salmon. Mix with 1 can of garbanzo beans (drained and rinsed), ½ cup chopped red onion, and ½ cup chopped red pepper. In a separate bowl, whisk together 2 tablespoons each extra-virgin olive oil and red wine vinegar and season with preferred herbs and spices. Pour the dressing over the salmon mixture and stir. This simple recipe makes about 3 servings, and each portion comes packed with protein, fiber, omega-3s, tryptophan, and folate. Enjoy over greens or in a whole-grain pita.

3. Steel-Cut Oats

A cozy, soothing bowl of oatmeal is pure comfort food on a chilly morning. But it's not just comforting in a physical, warm-your-bones sense. The whole-grain carb also contains the amino acid called tryptophan in almost the same amount as turkey. This dynamic duo helps stimulate the production of serotonin, the relaxation-promoting hormone, so it works on a physiological level, too.

All varieties of oats are great, but I particularly love the steel-cut type for anxiety and depression issues because they're minimally processed, and they cause a slower, steadier rise in blood sugar, meaning they have a lower glycemic index compared to traditional and instant oats. Oats also contain some magnesium, and a deficiency in this mineral may be linked with depression (some people with anxiety will often go on to develop depression).

Steel-cut oats take about 30 minutes to cook because they're not rolled flat like quicker cooking oats. I realize that's more time than most of us care to—or are able to—dedicate to breakfast during the morning rush, but I have two super-speedy solutions. First, you can make steel-cut oats overnight in a slow cooker. Simply combine 1 cup of steel-cut oats with 4 cups of water and add the toppings of your choice, including fresh or dried fruit; chopped nuts; nut butter; spices like cinnamon, nutmeg, or pumpkin pie seasoning blend; and vanilla extract. Then, before hitting the sack in the evening, set on low for about 6 to 8 hours to cook overnight. When you rise, combine the tasty and comforting contents in the slow cooker and get ready for a breakfast that's all set to be devoured. For guests, I serve optional sweeteners like brown sugar, honey, or maple syrup with additional fruit, nuts, and seeds on the side, so they can customize their own bowl.

Option two for the morning rush: Prepare steel-cut oats in advance (on the stove top or using the slow-cooker method) and then freeze them in individual 1-cup portions. In the morning, just pop a container out of the freezer, microwave (you may need to add a splash of water or milk to thin it out again), and it will be ready in minutes, just like regular oatmeal.

If you have the luxury of time, you can prepare it fresh and enjoy it warm off the stove top. Add your favorite toppings and dig in.

4. Orange

Orange you glad to see a mention of everyone's favorite citrus fruit in this chapter? Getting your day started with a juicy orange or enjoying one for a snack may be a great way to help alleviate anxiety. That's because the citrus star is rich in vitamin C—one orange contains 70 mg of the vitamin, filling almost your entire day's needs. Women need 75 mg daily and men need 90 mg.

One study of 120 people found that those who took vitamin C for two weeks and had to face a nerve-racking task (public speaking combined with a mental math test . . . aah!) showed fewer signs of stress. They reported feeling less frazzled, had lower blood pressure, and saw their levels of the stress hormone cortisol return to normal faster than those who took a placebo. Researchers explained that the vitamin worked on multiple fronts. Not only did it have a subjective effect on participants (subjects reported feeling better), but it also worked on a cardiovascular (heart) and neuroendocrine (brain and hormones) level as well.[5] Other research has shown a similar stress-soothing effect of the vitamin, which is better known for boosting your immunity.

Enjoy an orange with your breakfast or as a tasty afternoon snack paired with almonds or yogurt. Slice one up and add it to your salad for a bit of tart sweetness, add diced to salsa, or use as a topper for chicken or fish. You can also add orange sections to smoothies—it's great paired with other vitamin-C-rich fruits, such as strawberries, lemon, mango, pineapple, papaya, kiwi, or grapefruit. All are terrific mood-boosting choices. In fact, all vitamin-C-rich produce (including bell peppers) work great, but I chose oranges because they're universally loved, available year-round, and are budget-friendly.

Also, try my "stress-free soda": Cut orange juice with naturally flavored seltzer for a fun and fizzy beverage.

5. Chamomile Tea

Feeling stressed? Turn to a little herbal help. Chamomile appears to act as a mild sedative and may help relieve muscle tension and ease anxiety and irritability. One study showed that those who received a chamomile extract for eight weeks scored lower on an anxiety test than those who were given a placebo. The researchers suggested that chamomile can help with mild to moderate anxiety.[6]

The herb has been around for centuries—it's one of the most commonly used and well-documented medicinal plants in the world. Tea and extracts are made from dried flowers of the plant, which has been shown to have antioxidant and anti-inflammatory properties, in addition to reducing anxiety. It's estimated that more than 1 million cups of chamomile tea are sipped every day.

So pour yourself a cup of calm when you begin to feel a little tense; I often enjoy a mug of naturally caffeine-free chamomile tea before bed. I find it's a perfect way to relax and unwind before hitting the sack. Or, if you'd like more flavor, you can whip up my "Chaos Calmer," which features a few seasonal ingredients: Combine ½ cup of apple cider and ½ cup of water in a mug and heat in the microwave for 2 minutes, or until boiling. Add 1 chamomile tea bag, 1 strip of lemon peel, 1 cinnamon stick, and steep for 5 minutes. Remove the tea bag, lemon peel, and cinnamon stick, take your first sip . . . and breathe a sigh of relief.

If you are allergic to ragweed or certain flowers, you may be more likely to be allergic to chamomile. It may also interact with certain medications so make sure to check in with your M.D. before trying this soothing remedy.

Salmon Salad with Avocado and Chickpeas

MAKES 6 SERVINGS

One 15-ounce can chickpeas, drained and rinsed

1 avocado

One 15-ounce can salmon, drained and skin removed (or 15 ounces cooked salmon fillets)

¼ cup nonfat plain Greek yogurt

2 celery stalks, diced

1 tablespoon chives

2 tablespoons orange juice

1 tablespoon orange zest

½ teaspoon kosher salt

¼ teaspoon ground black pepper

Combine the chickpeas and avocado in a large bowl. Mash with the back of a fork or a potato masher until the avocado is smooth and creamy and about half the chickpeas are mashed.

Add all the remaining ingredients and mix to combine. Season with additional salt, ground black pepper, and chives to taste.

Serve with vegetable dippers or whole-grain crackers, on a whole-grain piece of toast, or as a sandwich.

NUTRITIONAL INFORMATION *Per ¾ cup*
210 calories • 23 g protein • 9 g total fat (1.5 g saturated fat, 7.5 g unsaturated fat) • 60 mg cholesterol • 14 g carbs • 6 g fiber • 3 g total sugar (3 g natural sugar, 0 g added sugar) • 530 mg sodium

Orange-Glazed Salmon with Confetti Chickpeas

MAKES 4 SERVINGS

For the orange glaze
1 ¼ cups fresh orange juice, divided
2 chamomile tea bags
1 tablespoon cornstarch
1 teaspoon orange zest

½ tablespoon chopped fresh thyme
   leaves (or ¼ teaspoon dried thyme)
1 tablespoon honey
¼ teaspoon kosher salt

For the salmon
4 salmon fillets (about 5 to 6
   ounces each)
½ teaspoon kosher salt

¼ teaspoon freshly ground black
   pepper

For the Confetti Chickpeas
1 yellow onion, diced
4 garlic cloves, minced
   (or ½ teaspoon garlic powder)
1 red bell pepper, diced
2 medium carrots, diced
2 small or 1 large green zucchini, diced
One 15-ounce can chickpeas,
   drained and rinsed

1 tablespoon fresh thyme leaves
   (or 1 teaspoon dried)
¾ teaspoon smoky paprika
¾ teaspoon kosher salt
Ground black pepper to taste
½ teaspoon dried red pepper flakes
   (optional)

For the glaze: Bring 1 cup orange juice to a boil in a small saucepan over medium-high heat. Add the chamomile tea bags and reduce the heat to simmer. Remove the tea bags after 5 minutes and discard. In a small bowl, mix the remaining ¼ cup orange juice and cornstarch until the cornstarch is completely dissolved. Add the mixture to the heated saucepan with orange juice. Add the zest, thyme, and honey to the pan. Increase the heat to medium-high and cook until the sauce thickens, stirring consistently for about 5 minutes. Remove from the heat and add salt, mixing until the glaze has slightly thickened and reduced to about ½ cup.

For the salmon: Preheat the oven to 400°F. Mist the salmon fillets with oil spray and season with salt and pepper. Place the salmon (skin side down) on a baking sheet lined with parchment paper and bake for 12 to 15 minutes or until

desired doneness. (The general rule of thumb is 5 to 7 minutes per ½ inch of thickness.) Remove from the oven and cover to keep warm.

For the confetti chickpeas: Liberally coat a large skillet with oil spray and warm over medium heat. Sauté the onion until translucent, about 5 minutes. Add the garlic and cook for about 30 seconds. Add the bell pepper, carrots, and zucchini; mist with oil spray; and cook until the veggies are just beginning to brown, about 5 minutes. Add the remaining ingredients and cook for 5 more minutes, stirring occasionally. Season with ground black pepper and optional red pepper flakes.

To assemble: Scoop a generous portion of chickpea confetti on each plate. Place a piece of salmon on top, and spoon on orange-chamomile glaze.

NUTRITIONAL INFORMATION

Per serving of Orange-Glazed Salmon (1 salmon fillet with 4 tablespoons glaze): 270 calories • 31 g protein • 9 g total fat (2 g saturated fat, 7 g unsaturated fat) • 65 mg cholesterol • 14 g carbs • 0 g fiber • 11 g sugar (7 g natural sugar, 4 g added sugar) • 430 mg sodium

Per serving of Confetti Chickpeas (1 ¼ cups): 140 calories • 7 g protein • 1 g total fat (0 g saturated fat, 1 g unsaturated fat) • 0 mg cholesterol • 24 g carbs • 6 g fiber • 4 g total sugar (4 g natural sugar, 0 g added sugar) • 410 mg sodium

Orange-Chamomile Blondies

MAKES 16 SQUARES

One 15.5-ounce can chickpeas,
  drained and rinsed

½ cup almond butter

⅓ cup honey

2 teaspoons vanilla extract

2 tablespoons dried chamomile (about
  5 chamomile tea bags)

1 ½ to 2 tablespoons orange zest
  (from 1 orange)

1 tablespoon canola oil

½ teaspoon salt

¼ teaspoon baking powder

¼ teaspoon baking soda

⅓ cup semisweet chocolate chips

⅓ cup chopped pecans (optional)

Preheat the oven to 350°F. Spray an 8-inch square pan with oil spray.

Place all the ingredients except for the chocolate chips (and pecans, if using) in a food processor or blender and process until the batter is smooth and creamy.

Fold in the chocolate chips and optional pecans. (The batter should be thick.)

Bake for about 25 to 30 minutes, or until a toothpick inserted into the center comes out clean and the edges are a tiny bit brown. Let the blondies cool in the pan for at least 20 minutes before slicing.

Note: You can enjoy these delicious treats immediately—they're like a warm and gooey cross between brownies and cookie dough! Or, let them firm in the pan (on the counter or in the fridge) a few hours or overnight for a more traditional chewy blondie texture.

NUTRITIONAL INFORMATION *Per square**
160 calories • 4 g protein • 9 g total fat (1.5 g saturated fat, 7.5 g unsaturated fat) •
0 mg cholesterol • 18 g carbs • 3 g fiber • 10 g total sugar (1 g natural sugar, 9 g added sugar) •
150 mg sodium

*Note: If using pecans, add about 15 calories per square.

5 FOODS TO
BANISH BLOATING

Bloating. The word alone is enough to conjure up feelings of pressure, gassiness, and discomfort. Typically, bloating refers to the *sensation* of fullness or heaviness in the abdominal area. Swollen fingers and feet sometimes come along for the ride, too. But it's bloating's evil cousin *distention* that relates to the actual visual expansion of the belly area. The two conditions are separate, though they are most likely related and people often use the term *bloating* to refer to both.

As many as 30 percent of the general population are impacted by "functional bloating," or bloating not accompanied by any disease or condition. And up to 96 percent of those who deal with gut disorders report suffering from bloating, and it affects women more than men. Although bloating is usually a benign condition, make sure to see a doctor if bloating is accompanied by other symptoms, such as weight loss, severe pain, fever, blood in the stool, or nausea and vomiting.

Theories about its causes are varied—it can be exacerbated by diet, fluid retention, the stomach not emptying properly, an imbalance of gut bacteria, pain in the pelvic area (a common symptom of irritable bowel syndrome, or IBS), or something else entirely. PMS is another well-known contributor. And lactose intolerance can also cause bloating.

Although bloating is quite common, the research behind it is pretty limited. Medications are available, but experts seem to be most excited by a specific eating plan called the low-FODMAP diet. (The acronym stands for fermentable oligosaccharides, disaccharides, monosaccharides, and polyols.) FODMAPS are a type of poorly absorbed carbohydrate; reducing intake of them seems to alleviate bloating and other digestive issues in some people. Taking probiotic supplements may also be beneficial, such as *Bifidobacterium infantis*, or *B. infantis*, particularly for IBS symptoms. Avoiding carbonated drinks, sugar alcohols (think sorbitol and mannitol), and salty foods; eating smaller meals; and increasing your physical activity can also help.

I selected the following five foods because they check a lot of boxes: They're low in salt, easy to digest, low(ish) in carbs, and low-FODMAP (except for kefir, which is only low-FODMAP if it's lactose free). Dig in and de-bloat.

1. Skinless Chicken Breast

Looking for a filling protein source to help beat the bloat? Skinless chicken breast is best. It's a FODMAP-free food. In fact, when someone starts out on a strict exclusion version of a low-FODMAP plan, only a few foods are allowed, and skinless chicken breast is one of them—that's how easy it is for the body to digest.[1]

Here's another reason chicken breast can help you beat bloating: Carbs cause water retention, and lean poultry is virtually pure protein sans carbohydrate. So by swapping starchy carbs like bread, pasta, potatoes, and rice with an equal portion of chicken breast, your body will hold on to less water and your stomach may feel flatter and more comfortable. Another protein perk: The nutrient helps keep you feeling fuller longer than carbs or fat because it takes longer to digest. This benefit can help curb your overall eating, which automatically makes you feel less bloated. And while all food helps increase metabolism (this is referred to as the thermic effect of food, meaning you get a slight uptick in your metabolism after eating), protein turns your calorie-burning furnace up the most—more so than fat and carbs. Bottom line? Eating skinless chicken breast can help you feel fuller longer, slightly rev your metabolism, and enable your body to release extra water.

There are so many simple and delicious ways to prepare skinless chicken breast—boiled, poached, or grilled, it's perfect atop a salad. You can chop it up and mix it with low-fat mayonnaise to create a tasty chicken salad. Add it to reduced-sodium chicken broth to make a comforting soup with some of your favorite easy-on-the-stomach veggies, including carrots, celery, and zucchini. Toss it into a flavorful stir-fry or curry dish with light coconut milk. You can even use chicken breasts as a replacement for pizza crust. To make, pound a chicken breast very thin using a mallet or heavy can (alternatively, you can ask your butcher to cut a large chicken breast into two to three thin slices), mist with oil spray, sprinkle on preferred seasonings, and then bake in the oven for about 15 minutes at 375°F, or until fully cooked. Top your chicken breast "crust" with reduced-sodium marinara sauce, sautéed veggies of choice, and if you're not dairy sensitive, a sprinkling of cheese for a scrumptious personal pizza.

2. Peppermint

Peppermint is typically associated with toothpaste, mouth rinse, and chewing gum, delivering refreshing flavor and breath. For that reason, it makes an appearance in the bad breath chapter (page 200). And to add to its might, peppermint also appears to have some brawn over bloating. In fact, there are several studies that show it can help alleviate symptoms of IBS, including feeling swollen. In one small study of more than 70 IBS patients, those who were given a peppermint oil supplement for four weeks reported less abdominal bloating and distension than those who took a placebo pill.[2] And according to a meta-analysis looking at the preponderance of research, peppermint was found to have a significant positive effect on IBS symptoms, including bloating, compared to a placebo in five of eight different studies.[3]

—The easiest and most soothing way to enjoy peppermint is with a nice cup of peppermint tea. You can enjoy it hot or cold, using either tea bags or the leaves. Peppermint tea is considered a low-FODMAP food.

Or incorporate peppermint extract into your food. It's potent, so start with just a drop or two. You can add it into any flavor tea or try it in a smoothie.

Peppermint chewing gum is another story. While it can help combat bad breath, gum chewing is *not* a good habit if you suffer from bloating and gas because it can cause you to swallow air and potentially make you more uncomfortable. Not to mention, sugarless gum often contains sugar alcohols, which can further worsen stomach issues—and can be counterproductive for people who are looking to de-puff.

3. Zucchini

When it comes to veggies, it pays to be picky—some produce (think broccoli and brussels sprouts) can make bloating worse. Fortunately, zucchini comes loaded with water and is naturally low in salt and packed with potassium, so it fills you up without making you feel puffed out.

A cup of zucchini contains nearly 300 mg of potassium (adults need 4,700 mg daily). Potassium is like the anti-sodium. While sodium causes you to retain water, potassium causes the body to release excess water and can help you feel and look less bloated. Plus, zucchini is considered a low-FODMAP food that is easy on the digestive tract (when eaten in moderation, up to one serving per day), so it gets the green light for people with gut problems like IBS.

Slice zucchini and enjoy it hot off the grill, misted with oil spray, and sprinkled with plenty of ground black pepper, seasonings, and a *small* dash of optional salt, if you must. Or whip up my delicious Ribbon Pasta Salad: Use a vegetable peeler to create long pasta-like zucchini strands, and toss with a squeeze of lemon juice, a touch of grated Parmesan (if you're not sensitive to dairy), and preferred seasonings to taste.

I also use zucchini to make zucchini noodles or "zoodles," a bloat-minimizing way to enjoy pasta. Pasta is rich in carbs, and for every gram of carb you consume, you temporarily hold on to 3 to 4 grams of water—this just adds insult to injury when you're dealing with bloating. One cup of cooked pasta provides about 35 grams of carb, while 1 cup of zucchini noodles provides just 4 grams of carb. And fewer starchy carbs equals less temporary water retention.

To make zoodles, cut off the ends of the zucchini and julienne using a spiral slicer to create spaghetti-shaped strands. (You can peel the zucchini or leave the skin intact, eater's choice.) If you don't have a spiral slicer, use a vegetable peeler or knife. Many stores sell zucchini already spiralized in the produce section and a few companies sell them frozen. Wrap noodle strands in a few layers of paper towels and squeeze to remove some of the moisture. Sauté them in a large skillet coated with oil spray for about 2 minutes over medium heat. Add preferred seasonings and dig in. You can also toss with some low-salt marinara, pesto, or meat sauce.

4. Cantaloupe

Cantaloupe is a lot like zucchini, but on the fruit side. It's rich in water, made up of 90 percent H_2O. It's also a good source of potassium; a cup delivers about 475 mg. And it's a low-FODMAP food (if you enjoy up to ½ cup per day), so it completes the trifecta for bloat-beating bites. (Honeydew is another good choice, as it's equally hydrating, although it does contain a little less potassium with about 400 mg per cup.)

Slice it up and enjoy a serving for breakfast or as a snack when you're feeling bloated and uncomfortable. Cut cantaloupe up into cubes or get fancy with a melon baller and serve as a refreshing fruit salad along with breakfast. You can also slice one in half and stuff it with a scoop of low-fat cottage cheese (another low-FODMAP food) for a filling snack or light lunch. During the summer months, I like to stick melon cubes on skewers along with grapes and pineapple and freeze for a chilly treat.

Mix cantaloupe chunks with other low-FODMAP fruit (such as blueberries, grapes, kiwi, honeydew, orange, and papaya) and a bit of yogurt or kefir to make a creamy and luscious smoothie. You can even freeze the smoothie contents in ice pop molds to create tasty treats.

Cantaloupe can easily be incorporated into salsa for a hit of sweetness: Mix diced cantaloupe with other traditional ingredients like chopped tomatoes, scallions (green part only), cilantro, lime juice, and preferred seasonings. You may want to swap the traditional white, yellow, and red onions for scallions, as according to a strict low-FODMAP plan, the green part of scallions is considered easier on the GI tract.

You can also whip up a cantaloupe and cucumber salad, tossing in pumpkin seeds for a nice crunch, topped with a vinaigrette dressing. Or try grilling cantaloupe: Peel and slice into wedges or chunks. You can either place the chunks on skewers or you can throw thick wedges on the warmed grill by themselves. Spritz with cooking oil and sprinkle on cinnamon before heating. Cook until you see grill marks, about 3 to 5 minutes. Flip and cook on the other side. You can use other flavorings, including lime juice, mint, cayenne, or a dash of maple syrup.

5. Kefir

Aside from increasing your flat water intake when you're feeling bloated (it seems counterintuitive, but it can help move food and fluid buildup through your system), there's another bevvy you may want to sip: kefir. While the cultured, fermented milk drink is not low-FODMAP (unless it's *lactose-free* kefir, which *is* considered low-FODMAP), it's a worthy boon for bloating sufferers. The creamy drink tastes a bit like yogurt with a tangier, tart flavor and contains probiotics: beneficial bacteria that aid in digestion and have historically been used to treat gastrointestinal problems, including IBS.

In one study of more than 100 adults with IBS who suffered abdominal pain and bloating, half were given a multi-strain probiotic treatment and the other half were given a placebo. Those who received the probiotic noticed significant improvements in bloating and other symptoms within four weeks. After finishing treatment, 85 percent of those in the probiotic group reported satisfactory relief—compared to just 47 percent taking a placebo. Moreover, nobody taking the probiotic suffered any adverse effects.

Probiotics have an anti-inflammatory effect in the gut, and they help create a more normal bacterial balance by boosting "good" bacteria and preventing the overgrowth of "bad" ones. And kefir, regular or lactose free (as well as yogurt), is a terrific source of probiotics.

Kefir also contains vitamin D—about 100 IU per cup (the goal is 600 IU daily for adults). A recent study showed people who have IBS are often deficient in the vitamin, and they experienced relief when they took a D supplement. Their bloating and abdominal pain eased and their quality of life improved.

You can sip a plain or flavored kefir drink. Look for lactose-free kefir if you're lactose intolerant or prefer to adhere to an exclusive low-FODMAP plan. You can use it much like you would milk or yogurt—add it to smoothies or use it to make parfaits, ice pops, dressings, and sauces. You could also use it to soak whole grains. For example, try combining about 1 cup of kefir with about ⅓ cup of old-fashioned rolled oats in a mason jar or other sealable container. Add some chopped fruit or berries and 1 to 2 teaspoons of chia seeds and let it sit in the fridge overnight. Then enjoy a yummy and healthy breakfast the following morning.

Mediterranean Zucchini Boats with Kefir-Mint Topping

MAKES 8 BOATS

For the Mediterranean Zucchini Boats

4 medium zucchini, each cut in half lengthwise

1 carrot, diced

1 bell pepper (red, orange, or yellow), diced

½ cup cherry tomatoes, quartered

1 pound boneless, skinless chicken breast, chopped into tiny pieces

2 to 4 tablespoons chopped fresh chives

2 to 3 teaspoons smoked paprika

1 to 2 teaspoons dried oregano

⅛ to ¼ teaspoon crushed red pepper flakes (optional)

Dash of kosher salt (optional)

For the Kefir-Mint Topping

½ cup plain low-fat kefir*

⅓ cup finely chopped fresh mint leaves

2 teaspoons lemon juice

¼ cup chopped cucumber (optional)

Choose a lactose-free variety if you are lactose intolerant.

Preheat the oven to 400°F.

Scoop out the center of the zucchini halves with a spoon. Save the insides and chop them into small pieces. Set aside the zucchini shells.

Liberally coat a large skillet with oil spray and warm over medium-high heat. Add the carrot, bell pepper, chopped zucchini centers, and tomatoes. Cook for about 5 minutes, stirring occasionally, until the veggies become soft.

Add the chicken pieces to the skillet and cook until they are no longer pink. Stir in the chives, paprika, oregano, and optional red pepper flakes and salt.

Place the zucchini boats open side up on a baking sheet. Spoon the chicken-vegetable mixture evenly into each zucchini boat, mist the tops with oil spray, and bake for 30 minutes on the middle rack.

To prepare the Kefir-Mint topping: Combine all the ingredients in a small bowl. Serve alongside the zucchini boats for a flavorful sauce.

LEFTOVERS TO LOVE If you're using small zucchinis, you'll have extra vegetable-chicken filling leftover. Stash in the fridge and serve over a fresh green salad, use for lettuce wraps and omelets, or eat straight out of the container. You can also save any leftover Kefir-Mint Topping for all these options. It adds just 10 calories per tablespoon.

NUTRITIONAL INFORMATION
Per 2 zucchini boats: 160 calories • 27 g protein • 3.5 g total fat (0 g saturated fat, 3.5 g unsaturated fat) • 85 mg cholesterol • 4 g carbs • 2 g fiber • 2 g total sugar (2 g natural, 0 g added sugar) • 65 mg sodium

Chicken Spinach Salad with Cilantro-Lime Dressing

MAKES 4 SERVINGS

For the poached chicken (or use any type of cooked chicken breast)

1 carrot

1 parsley sprig

5 peppercorns

½ lemon, sliced

2 boneless, skinless chicken breasts
(about 6 ounces each)

For the zucchini

1 medium (or 2 small) zucchini, sliced lengthwise or into discs

For the dressing

1 cup plain low-fat kefir*

¼ to ½ cup finely chopped fresh
cilantro leaves

1 tablespoon lime juice

¼ teaspoon kosher salt

Ground black pepper to taste

Herbs to taste

For the salad

4 to 8 heaping cups spinach leaves
(or any lettuce combo)

½ cup cantaloupe balls or cubes

*Choose lactose-free if you are lactose intolerant.

To poach the chicken: Fill a large pot with water and add the carrot, parsley, peppercorns, and lemon. Bring to a boil. Add the chicken and return to a boil. Cover, lower the heat, and simmer for 20 minutes or until the chicken reaches an internal temperature of 165°F.

For the zucchini: Liberally mist the zucchini tops with oil spray and sprinkle on any preferred no-salt seasonings. Cook on a hot grill until charred, or lay on a baking sheet lined with parchment paper and bake at 400°F for about 25 minutes.

For the dressing: Combine all the ingredients in a medium bowl. Season with extra herbs to taste.

To assemble the salad: Divide the spinach among 4 bowls. Top with equal portions of sliced chicken, zucchini, cantaloupe, and a few tablespoons dressing.

SALAD SAVVY This salad can be prepped ahead of time and assembled when you're ready to eat it. The chicken and zucchini can be warm or cool, depending on your preference.

NUTRITIONAL INFORMATION

Per serving of salad: 120 calories • 21 g protein • 2.5 g fat (0 g saturated fat, 2.5 g unsaturated fat) • 60 mg cholesterol • 4 g carbs • 2 g fiber • 2 g total sugar (2 g natural sugar, 0 g added sugar) • 85 mg sodium

Per 2 tablespoons dressing: 15 calories • 1 g protein • 0 g fat • 0 mg cholesterol • 2 g carbs • 0 g fiber • 1 g total sugar (1 g natural sugar, 0 g added sugar) • 70 mg sodium

Roast Chicken with Zucchini and Cucumber Salad

MAKES 4 SERVINGS

For the chicken

4 boneless, skinless chicken breasts
   (about 5 ounces each)
1 tablespoon olive oil
½ teaspoon paprika

1 to 2 teaspoons fresh chopped
   rosemary
Ground black pepper to taste

For the zucchini

2 zucchini, sliced lengthwise
   or into discs
½ teaspoon paprika

1 to 2 teaspoons fresh chopped
   rosemary
¼ teaspoon ground black pepper

For the cucumber salad

¼ cup low-fat kefir (regular or
   lactose-free)
1 tablespoon extra-virgin olive oil
1 tablespoon lemon juice
1 to 2 tablespoons finely chopped
   peppermint leaves

¼ teaspoon ground black pepper
Dash of salt (optional)
1 cucumber, diced
½ yellow or red onion, diced
   (optional)

Preheat the oven to 400°F. Coat the chicken with olive oil and place on a
baking sheet lined with parchment paper. Sprinkle on the paprika, rosemary,
and pepper. Roast for 25 to 40 minutes until the chicken reaches an internal
temperature of 165°F. Meanwhile, lay the zucchini on a baking sheet in a
single layer. Mist with oil spray, sprinkle with seasonings, and roast in the oven
alongside the chicken for about 20 minutes. For the salad, whisk together the
kefir, olive oil, lemon juice, mint, pepper, and optional salt in a medium bowl.
Mix in the cucumber and onion.

NUTRITIONAL INFORMATION *Per serving*
240 calories • 34 g protein • 9 g total fat (1 g saturated fat, 8 g unsaturated fat) •
80 mg cholesterol • 4 g carbs • 1 g fiber • 2 g total sugar (2 g natural sugar, 0 g added sugar) •
105 mg sodium

5 FOODS TO
CURE A HANGOVER

While there are probably hundreds of purported cures for a hangover (or *veisalgia*, pronounced vay-*sal*-gee-a), there's really a dearth of evidence to support their effectiveness. Some food fixes can help alleviate certain symptoms—including a pounding headache, insatiable thirst, low-grade nausea, or bloating—but they are not necessarily a complete fix. And the truth is that not many solid studies looking at treatments exist. One reason is that review boards won't approve studies where people get drunk enough to suffer a hangover.

Another big obstacle is that experts don't know exactly what causes a hangover. Once alcohol enters our system, enzymes in the liver break down ethanol (the actual "alcohol" in an alcoholic beverage) into toxic acetaldehyde. Acetaldehyde gets further broken down by another set of enzymes into a less toxic compound called acetate, which then gets broken down into water and carbon dioxide. This whole process takes time—the body can eliminate only about ½ ounce of alcohol per hour, which is why the morning after (or, in some cases, the whole day after) can be a crashing wave of misery. One study suggests that these symptoms are due to elevated levels of acetaldehyde.[1] Other research indicates that it's due to a buildup of acetate. Other possible causes include dehydration, hormonal changes, alcohol's toxicity, and the fact that alcohol alters cytokines (molecules responsible for cell communication). Or perhaps there are changes in the body that we just don't understand yet. The bottom line: It's difficult to find a cure when you don't know the exact cause.

Even so, there are a few tricks. First, ensure there's food in your system beforehand to help slow the absorption of alcohol by the body. Also, opt for clear alcohol. Dark-colored alcohols, like rum and whiskey, contain congeners, compounds that are often associated with hangover symptoms. Most important, drink plenty of water or load up on water-rich foods to keep yourself hydrated, including the morning after. Caffeinated coffee or tea can help ease headaches for some, but for others, it can make symptoms worse. Stocking the following five foods in your fridge or pantry can help to ease symptoms and reboot your system.

1. Broth

You wake up in the morning, dry-mouthed and dehydrated, and look for something to quench your thirst. (Alcohol is considered a diuretic, which basically means it increases the output of urine.) You could grab a nice, cold glass of water, but a better (less obvious) option is chicken or vegetable broth. Not only is it a clear liquid that's easy on the stomach, but it's also super hydrating. And it contains sodium, which will replenish lost electrolytes and help you hold on to water, which is exactly what you need after a night of drinking.

A study presented at a meeting of the American Chemical Society showed that a soup called Yak-a-mein, which consists of a salty broth base, helped relieve symptoms of a hangover. The soup also typically contains other ingredients, including a carb source such as noodles; a protein such as beef, chicken, or shrimp; onions or chopped scallions; and sliced hard-boiled egg. Feel free to jazz up your bowl if you can handle it. If not, no worries—sipping on plain old broth should still do the trick.[2]

Pop open a can or carton of store-bought broth for convenience. Another speedy and simple option is a bouillon cube, which is dehydrated and powdered or granulated stock. All you have to do is add it to boiling water.

Or you can make your own broth ahead of time and stash it in the fridge or freezer for weekend recovery. I whip up a delicious bone broth by placing the bones from 1 whole chicken (skin and fat removed); 6 carrots, peeled and chopped; 2 onions, peeled and chopped; 4 celery stalks, chopped; 6 garlic cloves; 1 tablespoon whole peppercorn; 1 bay leaf; 1 handful of parsley; and 24 cups (1 ½ gallons) of water in a large pot and bringing it to a boil. Once the mixture is boiling, turn the heat to the lowest setting and simmer for 12 to 24 hours. Add 2 to 4 cups of water every 6 hours. (It sounds like a lot of work but it's actually quite simple.) When the broth is done, strain it through a fine mesh strainer into a bowl or container. This recipe makes about 5 cups. Let it cool in the refrigerator and remove any fat that has risen to the top. Then stash it in the freezer in 1-cup servings to use as your go-to hangover Rx.

Of course, you can also take the easy way out; hit the market and stock up on ready-to-eat cubes, cans, and/or cartons.

2. Banana

Peel a banana for some easy hangover relief. It's loaded with potassium (more than 400 mg per banana), which helps replace lost electrolytes that typically happens with dehydration. A banana can also help increase blood sugar thanks to its natural fruit sugar and possibly alleviate that pounding headache. Plus, this beloved yellow pick is gentle on an unsettled stomach.

And there's an extra perk. In one study, when people were given a dose of vitamin B_6 before, during, and after a party where people drank, their hangover symptoms were reduced by 50 percent.[3] Stellar sources of vitamin B_6 include bananas and chickpeas.

To boost your B_6 intake, grab a banana and enjoy it before going out and again when you wake up. You can have it as is for a quick and simple snack or incorporate it into recipes. For instance, you can slice up a banana and add it to a soothing bowl of oatmeal the morning after a night out drinking. You can mash or chop them, and then mix them into whole-grain pancake or muffin batter. You can also whip up a hangover smoothie by combining a banana with other fruits and some yogurt, milk, or fruit juice.

One of my favorite treats—hungover or not—is my PB-Banana Freeze. Split 1 peeled banana lengthwise into 2 halves. Spread 1 half with nut butter. Sandwich the 2 banana halves together and wrap the entire banana in plastic wrap. (Or you can cut the bananas into 1-inch wheels and place them in a plastic bag or container.) Freeze for a few hours until solid or semisolid. It's a tasty treat that is both soothing and indulgent at the same time.

Or make your own Banana Cream Pie Pudding: Microwave a peeled banana for 20 to 30 seconds to bring out the sweetness. Mash the microwaved banana in a bowl and mix in a small single container of vanilla yogurt, about 5 to 6 ounces (use traditional for a milder flavor or Greek if you like a tangier taste) and ¼ teaspoon vanilla extract. Cover, chill in the refrigerator, and then enjoy. To give it some extra pizzazz, you can top it with crushed graham cracker and a squirt of aerated whipped topping—so delicious!

3. Mango

There is no miracle cure for a hangover, but sweet mango comes pretty close. A cup of the juicy fruit delivers big-time in the recovery department. You'll get nearly 300 mg potassium to replenish lost electrolytes, some vitamin B_6, and as an extra benefit, a hit of fiber. Plus, the natural sugar in fruit can raise your blood sugar back to a normal level (many people experience a drop in blood sugars during or after imbibing) and give you a shot of energy to help battle fatigue. Not to mention, it may also help metabolize alcohol.[4]

One Korean study found that mice who were given mango fruit extract were better able to break down ethanol, the actual *alcohol* in alcohol, an hour after being "served" compared to mice that were given a control liquid of water with salt. The fruit increased the activity of the two enzymes that degrade alcohol. The result: The mice had a lower blood alcohol content.[5]

Take advantage of fresh mango when it's in season. It's available year-round—but most varieties peak in the summer months. Slice one up and enjoy it as a snack, toss cubes into a smoothie, or dice it up and add it to a salsa recipe. It's also a delicious topping for waffles or pancakes . . . and I love it mixed with some cottage cheese or part-skim ricotta and a pinch of cayenne and lime juice. There's something to be said for "sweating it out"—while some people don't like the heat, others feel *cleansed* after enjoying a little spice.

I stash bags of frozen mango chunks in my freezer year-round. Most grocery stores stock them in the freezer section along with the other bagged frozen fruit varieties. Whether you go for fresh or frozen mango, you'll be on the road to recovery.

4. White Potato

One potato, two potato, three potato, score! White potatoes can help with a hangover for many of the same reasons a banana can. Potatoes are a good source of vitamin B_6, which can help reduce hangover symptoms. They are also rich in potassium, with more than 900 mg per 1 medium baked potato, and you can enjoy both the flesh and the skin. These two nutrients can help replace electrolytes and tame an aching head.

And because potatoes are starchy, they have the benefit of being gentle on the stomach in the same way as toast or crackers, but they deliver a bit more nutrition than these alternative carb sources. This is key after a night of too much revelry.

Enjoy a baked potato when you roll out of bed around lunchtime (ahem). Nuke your spud in the microwave for a quick pick-me-up: Poke with a fork a few times, and then cook on high for about 5 minutes; flip (careful, it's hot!) and cook for another 3 to 5 minutes. Or bake in the oven at 425°F for 45 minutes to an hour, depending on the size of your potato, or until fork tender, flipping every 20 minutes or so.

Enjoy a baked potato plain or with some warm marinara sauce and a sprinkle of grated Parm. Of course, you can also get fancy with an assortment of toppings—black beans; colorful, water-rich veggies such as chopped red bell pepper and broccoli florets; avocado; low-fat Greek yogurt; and some reduced-fat shredded cheese (full-fat dairy can be harsher on your stomach after a night out). Or cut potatoes into thin strips, spread them out on a baking sheet, liberally coat with an oil spray, and sprinkle on some salt to make oven-baked "fries." Bake in a 450°F oven until golden and crispy, about 30 minutes.

5. Pineapple

Pineapple, known as the "king of fruits," is a symbol of welcome, and let's just say it will be a welcome addition to your plate the morning after a boozy bender. It's rich in water, with an 87 percent H_2O content, and can help rehydrate you after a night of drinking. Not only that, but it contains a mixture of enzymes called bromelain that can aid digestion and ease inflammation, which helps a pounding headache or sore muscles after a night of dancing.

Pineapple is delicious plain, chopped and sprinkled into oatmeal, diced and added to a tasty salsa, or blended up in a smoothie or milkshake with other hangover helpers (mango and banana, anyone?). Try whipping up my scrumptious Vanilla-Pineapple Milkshake: In a blender, add ½ ripe banana, peeled and frozen; ½ to 1 cup frozen pineapple chunks; ½ cup milk; 1 teaspoon vanilla extract; and 3 to 5 ice cubes and process until smooth and frothy. To save time and energy, go for canned pineapple (chunks or crushed in its own juice), and feel free to mix with yogurt, cottage cheese, or cucumbers to create a refreshing salad.

Or be creative and use it as a base to create "pineapple pizzas." Use a pineapple slice as your crust or base, top it with a thin layer of yogurt, and then add other fruit toppings, such as blueberries or chopped strawberries. Sprinkle on chopped nuts, seeds, shredded coconut, or granola and dig in.

To cut a fresh pineapple, lay it on its side and cut off both the spiky top and bottom. Stand the pineapple up and use a sharp knife to cut off the skin from top to bottom, trying not to take off too much because the flesh closest to the outside is usually the sweetest and juiciest. It's okay if the eyes remain—you will remove those next. The eyes follow a diagonal path around the pineapple. You'll use a small paring knife to dig these out, starting on one side and carving until you hit the middle, then tackling the other side. You'll be creating V-shaped trenches, following a diagonal path all the way around.

You can then cut the pineapple into rounds, rings, spears, or chunks. You can keep the core in or remove it, whatever you prefer. Alternatively, you can also look into buying a handy pineapple slicer, which does the job in no time. If you have the kitchen space and eat pineapples regularly, it's a great investment. You can find it at most home-goods stores for about $20.

Hangover Helper

MAKES 1 SMOOTHIE

½ heaping cup chopped ripe mango
   (fresh or frozen)
½ ripe banana
½ heaping cup chopped pineapple
   (fresh, frozen, or canned and
   drained)

½ to ¾ cup unsweetened vanilla
   almond milk*
3 ice cubes

If using fresh fruit, add ½ cup vanilla almond milk and 3 ice cubes for a frothier smoothie. If using frozen fruit, use ¾ cup vanilla almond milk and skip the ice. If either variation becomes too thick to blend, add a splash of extra milk.

Add all the ingredients to a blender and puree until smooth.

Note: To pump up the protein, add a scoop of protein powder to the blender with the fruit and milk for an extra 100 calories and 20 g protein.

NUTRITIONAL INFORMATION
Per smoothie: 170 calories • 2 g protein • 2.5 g total fat (0 g saturated fat, 2.5 g unsaturated fat) • 0 mg cholesterol • 37 g carbs • 4 g fiber • 19 g total sugar (19 g natural sugar, 0 g added sugar) • 130 mg sodium

SMOOTHIE BOWL RX You can easily convert this refreshing beverage into a more substantial meal by blending ½ heaping cup frozen mango chunks, ½ fresh or frozen banana, ½ heaping cup frozen pineapple chunks, ½ to ¾ cup unsweetened vanilla almond milk, 1 tablespoon of nut butter (peanut or almond), and 3 ice cubes until thick and creamy. Pour the mixture into a bowl and top with 1 tablespoon chopped nuts, 1 tablespoon coconut flakes, ¼ cup chopped mango, and 1 teaspoon of optional honey.

Per smoothie bowl: 330 calories • 8 g protein • 16 g total fat (3 g saturated fat, 13 g unsaturated fat) • 0 mg cholesterol • 48 g carbs • 7 g fiber • 25 g total sugar (25 g natural sugar, 0 g added sugar) • 85 mg sodium

Banana Muffins with Mango-Pineapple Jam

MAKES 12 MUFFINS AND ABOUT 1 CUP JAM

Mango-Pineapple Jam
1 cup mango chunks, fresh or frozen
   and thawed

½ cup pineapple chunks, fresh
   or frozen and thawed
1 tablespoon chia seeds

Banana Muffins
1 ½ cups whole-grain flour*
1 teaspoon baking soda
¼ teaspoon kosher salt
3 medium ripe bananas, mashed**
¼ cup honey
1 teaspoon vanilla extract

1 large egg, lightly beaten
1 tablespoon melted butter or canola oil
½ cup nonfat plain Greek yogurt
1 cup Mango-Pineapple Jam (see
   recipe above)
Toasted pecans (optional for garnish)

Note: Whole-grain flour can sometimes result in a tougher finished product. For a softer and lighter texture, it's typically best to use whole-wheat pastry flour, white whole-wheat flour, or a mix of all-purpose flour and traditional whole-wheat flour.

***If the bananas aren't ripe, then peel, slice, and microwave for 30 seconds to soften.*

For the jam: Puree the mango and pineapple with a food processor or blender for a few seconds until well combined. Stir in the chia seeds. Set aside for at least 30 minutes at room temperature.

For the muffins: Preheat the oven to 375°F. Line a muffin tin with baking cups or liberally coat the tin with oil spray. Combine the flour, baking soda, and salt in a large bowl. Mix the bananas, honey, vanilla, egg, butter, and yogurt in a separate bowl. Add the wet mixture to the dry and stir until just combined. Fill each muffin cup halfway (batter will be sticky). Make a small well in the center of each with the back of a spoon (or your finger) and fill with about 1 tablespoon of Mango-Pineapple Jam. Use the remaining batter to top off the muffin cups. Bake for about 18 to 20 minutes. You can wrap the muffins and freeze for up to 2 months.

NUTRITIONAL INFORMATION *Per muffin*
120 calories • 3 g protein • 2 g total fat (0 g saturated fat, 2 g unsaturated fat) • 0 mg cholesterol • 25 g carbs • 3 g fiber • 12 g total sugar (7 g natural sugar, 5 g added sugar) • 160 mg sodium

MAKE-AHEAD MUFFINS Make a big batch and stash them in the freezer. Then they will be ready to defrost and devour on mornings (or afternoons) when you need 'em most. Or whip up a batch of the Mango-Pineapple Jam and use it for whole-grain toast or to sweeten up your oatmeal. Simply add the jam mixture to a mason jar and refrigerate for 30 minutes to overnight in order to set. It should keep for a week in the fridge.

Perk-You-Up Pancakes

MAKES ABOUT 16 PANCAKES AND 1 ½ CUPS COMPOTE

Tropical Compote

1 ½ cups mango chunks, fresh or
    frozen and thawed
1 ½ cups pineapple chunks, fresh,
    canned, or frozen and thawed

3 tablespoon orange juice
    or lemon juice

Perk-You-Up Pancakes

1 ¾ cups nonfat or low-fat milk*
1 tablespoon lemon juice*
1 ½ cups whole-grain flour
1 tablespoon baking powder
1 teaspoon cinnamon
½ teaspoon nutmeg

¼ teaspoon salt
2 ripe bananas, mashed
1 egg
1 tablespoon maple syrup
½ teaspoon vanilla extract
1 tablespoon melted butter or canola oil

Alternatively, use 1 ¾ cups low-fat buttermilk instead of the milk and lemon juice.

For the compote: Cook the fruit and juice in a small saucepan over medium heat. Once bubbling, reduce the heat slightly and cook for 10 to 12 minutes more, occasionally stirring. Remove from the heat and set aside.

For the pancakes: Whisk together the flour, baking powder, cinnamon, nutmeg, and salt in a large bowl and set aside. Combine the milk and lemon juice in a medium bowl. (If using buttermilk, skip this step.) Add the bananas, egg, maple syrup, vanilla, and butter. Mix these wet ingredients into the dry.

Coat a large skillet with oil spray and warm over medium heat. Ladle about ¼ cup batter per pancake onto the skillet and cook for about 1 to 2 minutes on each side until golden brown. Reapply oil spray to skillet between batches. Serve the pancakes with the Tropical Compote on top, or instead, garnish with pineapple, mango, and pecans, or mix them into the batter right before cooking.

NUTRITIONAL INFORMATION

Per 3 pancakes: 220 calories • 9 g protein • 4 g total fat (0.5 g saturated fat, 3.5 g unsaturated fat) • 30 mg cholesterol • 42 g carbs • 5 g fiber • 11 g total sugar (9 g natural sugar, 2 g added sugar) • 150 mg sodium

Per 2 tablespoons compote: 25 calories • 0 g protein • 0 g fat • 0 mg cholesterol • 6 g carbs • 1 g fiber • 3 g total sugar (3 g natural sugar, 0 g added sugar) • 0 mg sodium

QUICK FIX! You can add chopped mango, pineapple, and banana into any boxed, whole-grain pancake mix. Simply follow the directions on the package (add egg, water, etc), then fold in the "feel-better" fruit and cook 'em up on the skillet.

5 FOODS TO COMBAT COLDS AND FLU

Millions of us miss work because of a cold or the flu every year. Or we walk around trying to plug away at all the responsibilities on our to-do list while feeling less than par, carrying around a bag of tissues and pack of cough drops.

You know the feeling all too well—it starts with watery eyes, a scratchy throat, a runny nose. Then it often progresses to sneezing and coughing. It may also include a headache and body aches. On average, adults suffer through two to three cases of the common cold per year, and children even more. It can take a good week or longer to get over a cold. No one is safe because the cold virus is super contagious, spreading from an infected person through the air, close contact, or contaminated surfaces. (I'm looking at you, stuffy elevator, germy doorknob, and bathroom sink handle.)

The flu is even worse. Depending on the year, between 9.2 million and 35.6 million cases are reported. And we're not talking about just a case of the sniffles and a few missed days of work. Up to 710,000 people are hospitalized, and as many as 56,000 deaths each year are attributed to the flu. It's like a cold on steroids—not only do you get the cough, sore throat, and runny nose, but you're also struck with fever, unbelievable fatigue, muscle and body aches, and in some cases, diarrhea and/or vomiting.

You can catch a cold at any time of year, but cold and flu season typically peaks in the cooler winter months because we spend most of our time indoors in close quarters. And catch this: There are more than 200 viruses that can cause a cold.

Your best defenses against these super contagious bugs: staying clean by washing your hands and keeping your hands away from your face. Regular exercise has been shown to help boost your immunity as can logging adequate sleep (aim for seven to eight hours a night). And, of course, most health experts agree that getting a flu shot is helpful against the flu (though not against colds).

And there's one more component that you can control: your diet. Certain nutrients and foods have a direct relationship to boosting our immune system and/or suppressing symptoms once we're struck with a cold.

1. Chicken Soup

Chicken soup is good for more than just the soul. This homemade remedy has been shown to offer a myriad of benefits against cold symptoms.

Hot fluids in general (think tea as well as soup) help to keep nasal passages moist. They increase the movement of mucus (the hot liquid causes blood vessels to dilate, which boosts blood flow and helps to flush out mucus—hello, open nostrils!). Fluids help prevent dehydration. And they can help soothe a sore throat. Soup provides psychological comfort that can have a placebo effect for those who are feeling under the weather.

But there's something special about chicken soup in particular—and the staple has some solid scientific backing. The tried-and-true cold remedy may contain substances that function as an anti-inflammatory, which may ease the symptoms of upper respiratory tract infections, including congestion, stuffy nose, cough, and sore throat. For instance, research indicates that a homemade chicken soup with its powerful combo of chicken and veggies helps control the movement of neutrophils, a type of white blood cells, which then decreases the flow of mucus and therefore protects against these common upper respiratory symptoms.[1]

Yes, your mom *was* right (again). Enjoy plenty of chicken soup with veggies when you feel a cold coming on or when one has already struck. Homemade or store-bought (canned and frozen) versions both seem to help, so pick your favorite, grab a spoon, and dig in.

2. Guava

Oranges may be the poster fruit for vitamin C, but the real C standout is guava, which tastes almost like a mix of strawberry and pear. One guava has twice the amount of immune-boosting vitamin C as an orange. You'll score 125 grams of vitamin C in a single guava, which is more than you need in an entire day!

Vitamin C helps boost immunity by stimulating the production and function of white blood cells that attack viruses in the body that can cause the cold or flu. In one review of studies involving nearly 600 people, researchers found that those who regularly exercised intensely (in this case, marathoners and skiers) were less likely to catch a cold when they took in ample amounts of vitamin C.[2] And while these findings didn't translate to the general population, we do know that the vitamin can help cut the frequency and severity of symptoms once a cold has been caught—by 8 percent in adults and 14 percent in children.

Enjoy guava straight up as a delectably juicy snack when it's in season (the cooler months before the chilly winter weather kicks in). You can also add guava to fruit and vegetable smoothies for a refreshing, *feel-good* beverage. And try mixing diced guava into yogurt and cottage cheese or tossing it into a mixed green salad to elevate its taste and nutrient status.

3. Mushrooms

When it comes to keeping your immune system strong and healthy, vitamin C gets a lot of well-deserved love. Guavas, strawberries, oranges, and other citrus picks and even bell peppers get tossed into your cart whenever the temperature starts to dip. But there are a lot of other players when it comes to boosting immunity.

Take one of my favorite fungi: the mushroom. It's rich in beta-glucans and chitosans, which can help protect against colds, flu, and other infections. One study in *The Journal of Nutrition* found that white button mushrooms, which make up about 90 percent of the type consumed in the United States, have antiviral properties.[3] Researchers found there was an increase in the production of killer cells—a type of white blood cell that fights infection—in mice that were fed a supplement of white button mushrooms. They're also a great source of selenium, which prevents inflammation in general.

All types of mushrooms are fantastic, whether you like the basic white button; smaller, brown cremini (a.k.a. baby bella); rich shiitake; or meaty portobellos. They are low in calories and very versatile, working as a delicious addition to main entrées or as a stand-alone side dish.

Add sautéed white button mushrooms to salads, pizza, or on top of a turkey burger. Or use a portobello as a replacement for meat to create a tasty vegetarian burger. And for a simple side dish, take a large container of cremini mushrooms, cut each into 4 pieces, drizzle with low-sodium soy sauce, and roast at 400°F until they're soft and browned. You can even use mushrooms to create a low-cal, low-carb "pizza" using this simple recipe: Layer a roasted or grilled portobello cap (stem removed) with marinara sauce, a sprinkling of shredded part-skim mozzarella cheese, some oregano and other preferred seasonings, and broil until the cheese is melty and slightly browned. It is amazingly addictive!

4. Carrots

Carrots are loaded with beta-carotene, the plant pigment that gives carrots (and sweet potatoes) their bright orange color. Beta-carotene is converted by the body to vitamin A. In fact, ½ cup of raw carrots (about 6 baby carrots) provides more than 200 percent of your daily needs for vitamin A.

Vitamin A has many functions in the body, but one of its most noteworthy jobs is as an antioxidant that can help boost immunity. Vitamin A also plays a role in keeping the mucous membranes that line the nose, sinuses, and mouth healthy. It's no coincidence that carrots are among the ingredients in chicken noodle soup.

Enjoy raw carrot sticks or baby carrots as a snack with hummus or salsa—they make the perfect dipper. Or slice up carrots and add them to lentil stews and soups as well as chicken soup (of course). Another delicious soup spin: Boil carrots in vegetable broth with some minced ginger until they're nice and soft. Then puree everything using an immersion (or traditional) blender for a comforting bowl. (Bonus: Cooked carrots provide you with a bigger dose of beta-carotene than raw because cooking makes carotenoids more available for the body to absorb.[4])

You can also serve them as a simple side, roasted with a few spritzes of oil spray and the seasonings of your choice. (I like to roast them with cumin, turmeric, paprika, thyme, salt, and pepper, but really, anything goes.) One of my absolute favorite sides: Burnt carrot "fries." Slice carrots into sticks, spread them out on a baking sheet, mist with oil spray, sprinkle with salt and pepper, and roast until browned. It's a scrumptious side with immune-boosting benefits.

You can add grated carrots into muffin batter or potato latkes. Or try adding shredded carrots into coleslaw. You can even juice carrots to make a refreshing and nutrient-packed beverage or add it as part of a medley of juiced fruits and veggies for a hint of sweetness and beta-carotene.

Beware of supplements that contain vitamin A as it is possible to get too much from these forms. However, food sources are safe, so enjoy as many crunchy carrots as you'd like.

5. Pink Grapefruit

Get a one-two punch of immune-strengthening power from beta-carotene and vitamin C in a single food: pink grapefruit. One whole grapefruit (which is roughly a cup of grapefruit sections) delivers about 75 milligrams of vitamin C—a full day's worth for women (men need 90 mg). It also contains 3,450 micrograms of beta-carotene and 2,645 IU of vitamin A.

Note that while white grapefruit is terrific, it doesn't provide much vitamin A, so upgrade your grapefruit game by going for pink.

Both of these nutrients (think two for the price of one) bolster your immune system and may help you ward off cold and flu viruses. Vitamin C plays a key role in immune function; deficiencies can make you more susceptible to catching a bug. Plus, once you have a cold, vitamin C can help dampen symptoms. You get an extra immune boost with beta-carotene, which is converted to vitamin A, because it helps to protect the mucous membranes in your nose and mouth.

Pink grapefruit is in season from October through early spring. You can leave grapefruits on the counter for a week; if you're going to keep them longer, stash them in the fridge.

Pink grapefruit is a great side dish with eggs or yogurt for breakfast. Or add it to a fruit salad with other delicious produce options. You can also grill it or broil it (add a dash of cinnamon and sugar to the tops of each half, then broil or grill for 2 to 4 minutes). And you can make a grapefruit salsa by combining grapefruit and orange sections with jalapeño, green onion, basil, salt, and other preferred seasonings.

I also love shredding it: Slice the grapefruit in half. Using a knife, cut between the membrane and flesh to separate each triangular segment. Then use a fork or spoon to scoop out the flesh into a bowl; the inside should just fall apart and appear somewhat shredded. Serve chilled with some chopped mint and dig in.

Other fuss-free prep tips: Toss pink grapefruit sections into a vegetable salad with feta cheese or mix it into vanilla Greek yogurt or cottage cheese.

Easy Chicken Noodle Soup

MAKES ABOUT 12 CUPS

1 yellow onion, diced

3 celery stalks, diced

1 cup diced or shredded carrots

3 garlic cloves, minced

8 cups reduced-sodium chicken or vegetable broth

1 pound chicken breasts, cut in bite-size pieces

8 to 16 ounces sliced cremini or button mushrooms

2 whole carrots, peeled and chopped into large chunks

1 parsnip, peeled and chopped into 3-inch pieces (optional)

1 teaspoon dried basil

1 teaspoon oregano

½ teaspoon kosher salt

2 cups whole-grain rotini pasta, cooked

Salt and pepper to taste

2 sprigs fresh dill (optional)

Liberally coat a large pot with oil spray and warm over medium-high heat. Add the onion, celery, and diced carrots and sauté for about 5 minutes, stirring occasionally, until the vegetables are soft. Add the garlic and cook for another 30 seconds until fragrant.

Add the broth, chicken, mushrooms, carrot chunks, optional parsnip, basil, oregano, and salt. Stir everything together. Bring to a boil, then reduce heat and simmer for about 20 minutes. Add cooked pasta. Season with salt and pepper to taste. Garnish with optional fresh dill.

NUTRITIONAL INFORMATION *Per cup*
110 calories • 14 g protein • 2 g total fat (0 g saturated fat, 2 g unsaturated fat) •
20 mg cholesterol • 10 g carbs • 2 g fiber • 2 g total sugar (2 g natural sugar, 0 g added sugar) •
320 mg sodium

Portobello Burgers with Grapefruit Relish and Carrot "Fries"

MAKES 4 SERVINGS

Portobello Burgers

4 portobello mushroom caps, cleaned
    with stems removed
½ teaspoon kosher salt
½ teaspoon freshly ground black pepper

1 teaspoon garlic powder
4 to 8 lettuce leaves
4 whole-grain hamburger buns
    (optional)

Grapefruit Relish

½ large pink grapefruit, peel and pith
    removed, chopped into small pieces
½ red bell pepper, diced
¼ red onion, diced
¼ cup chopped mint leaves
¼ cup chopped cilantro

1 tablespoon extra-virgin olive oil
1 garlic clove, minced
1 teaspoon honey (optional)
1 to 2 teaspoons lime zest
⅛ teaspoon kosher salt
⅛ teaspoon ground black pepper

Carrot Fries

8 medium carrots, peeled and sliced
    into sticks

1 teaspoon kosher salt

For the mushrooms: Mist both sides of the mushroom caps with oil spray and sprinkle with seasonings. Grill the mushrooms, bottom side down, for 10 minutes per side or until they soften and grill marks appear. Alternatively, you can cook in the oven for 20 minutes at 425°F.

For the relish: Combine all ingredients in a bowl and toss to coat.

For the carrot fries: Preheat the oven to 425°F. Lay the carrots in a single layer on a baking sheet. Liberally coat with oil spray and sprinkle on salt and pepper. Roast for about 25 minutes, until some of the edges start to burn. Finish under the broiler for 1 to 2 minutes, watching closely to ensure they don't become overly burnt.

To assemble: Place each portobello burger on top of a lettuce cup (and a bun, if desired). Top each burger with 2 to 3 tablespoons of Grapefruit Relish. Pair with the Carrot Fries and enjoy!

NUTRITIONAL INFORMATION *Per serving**
110 calories • 4 g protein • 4 g total fat (0 g saturated fat, 4 g unsaturated fat) •
0 mg cholesterol • 19 g carbs • 5 g fiber • 10 g total sugar (10 g natural sugar, 0 g added sugar) •
750 mg sodium

*Note. If using a bun, add about 150 calories.

Feel-Good Pops

MAKES 13 POPS

1 grapefruit (pink when available for
   added sweetness), peel and pith
   removed*
1 orange, peel and pith removed*
1 cup guava juice

1 cup carrot juice
½ teaspoon ground ginger
1 teaspoon lime juice
1 tablespoon honey

*When prepping the grapefruit and orange, discard any obvious pits, but there's
no need to remove all of them.

Combine all the ingredients in a food processor or high-powered blender until
completely pureed. Pour the mixture into a set of standard ice pop molds,
using about ⅓ cup mixture per pop. Freeze until the pops are firm and solid, at
least three hours.

An alternative method if you don't have ice pop molds: Pour the mixture into
small paper cups and wrap each top tightly with a piece of aluminum foil.
Carefully poke a wooden stick through the foil and into the cup to serve as a
handle, making sure each one is centered and straight. Place in the freezer.

NUTRITIONAL INFORMATION *Per pop*
35 calories • 0 g protein • 0 g fat • 0 mg cholesterol • 8 g carbs • 1 g fiber • 6 g total sugar
(5 g natural sugar, 1 g added sugar) • 15 mg sodium

PERFECT POPS IN A FLASH! For easier prep, try this all-juice version: Simply combine 1 cup pink grapefruit juice, 1/2 cup orange juice, 1 cup guava juice, 1 cup carrot juice, 1/2 teaspoon ground ginger, and 1/2 teaspoon lime juice in a food processor. Pour the mixture into molds and freeze. Each pop is just 45 calories.

5 FOODS TO
LIFT BRAIN FOG

Where are my keys?
What did I do with my cell phone?
I could have sworn I parked my car down this row—did it get stolen?
Why did I walk into this room again . . . and why am I holding a hair dryer?

Do any of these scenarios sound familiar? No doubt you've suffered one or more of these "senior moments" . . . that is, if you can even recall them. And despite the nickname, you don't have to have gray hair or an AARP card to have experienced them. They can occur at any age, at any point in your life.

These temporary slips of mental clarity are often referred to as "brain fog." Although forgetfulness is a primary symptom, it's not the only one. You may not feel mentally sharp; instead, there may be a bit of fuzziness, like when you can't recall a specific word (that frustrating tip-of-the-tongue feeling) or you don't process things as quickly as normal.

Indeed, brain fog is characterized by moments of cloudiness, difficulty focusing or thinking, trouble multitasking, and a general haziness in thought processing. These dips in brain function are likely caused by inflammatory molecules in the brain. And in case you're curious, you can actually find *brain fog* in the dictionary, defined as "a usually temporary state of diminished mental capacity marked by inability to concentrate or to think or reason clearly."

There are any number of triggers, from physical fatigue to a lack of sleep, from eating too much or too little, from feeling faint to dehydration, even prolonged standing (called orthostatic intolerance) and stress. People with certain medical conditions may be more prone to brain fog—for instance, those with celiac disease, chronic fatigue syndrome, obesity, and fibromyalgia. Some fibromyalgia sufferers refer to the condition as "fibromyalgia fog."

Exercise and adequate sleep can most definitely help you stay on your A game, as can eating a smart diet filled with certain nutrients to nurture your noggin and steady your blood sugars, including these brain-boosting bites.

1. Blueberries

Blueberries are pure brain food—plain and simple. These little blue orbs were ranked number one compared to 40 other fruits by the U.S. Department of Agriculture (USDA) for their antioxidant activity. It's no wonder they always claim a spot on most nutritionists' list of top superfoods (myself included).

This super fruit has the ability to help prevent or slow cognitive decline, among other health perks, thanks to its high antioxidant content. This is likely due to the berries' anthocyanins, the compounds that give them their blueish hue. These powerful compounds enter the brain and other organs, where they protect the memory-carrying cells (neurons) from the harmful effects of oxidation and inflammation.

A 2012 study from Harvard University found that women who ate at least one cup of blueberries and strawberries per week significantly sharpened their smarts; they experienced a sizable two-and-a-half-year delay in mental decline compared to women who rarely ate berries.[1]

Blueberries are delicious, fresh or frozen, as a snack—simply pop them into your mouth one after the other and enjoy. You can also add them to yogurt, oatmeal, whole-grain pancake or muffin batter, or smoothies. They're just as delicious in frozen desserts as they are in warm desserts. You can make tasty ice pops by pureeing a few handfuls in a blender with other fruits and milk, and then freezing the contents in ice pop molds. Or simply top fresh blueberries with a squirt of aerated whipped topping and a dash of cocoa powder for a simple indulgence with double brain benefits.

Here's a fun idea: Sprinkle them into your ice cube trays with water and freeze, and then add to your beverages for a *pretty* powerful addition. You can also put them on top of nut butter sandwiches in place of jelly or jam for a touch of strategic sweetness.

2. Coffee

Need a little jolt? A cup of joe might help bring back some mental clarity. The caffeine in coffee has been shown to increase alertness, improve mood, boost cognitive function, and make you feel less tired. In fact, up until 2004, caffeine was considered a performance-enhancing substance by the International Olympic Committee and its use by athletes was restricted during competition.

It's not just the caffeine that will perk you up. There are loads of protective antioxidants in the beneficial brew. One study reported that coffee is the main source of dietary antioxidants for Americans.[2] So the brain benefits are likely coming from a combination of its caffeine and antioxidant activity.

Studies suggest that a low to moderate intake of coffee—anywhere from about 38 mg caffeine per day (roughly ⅓ of a cup) up to 400 mg per day (equivalent to 4 cups)—is healthy and doesn't cause dehydration. And according to a meta-analysis (a thoughtful review of several studies), habitual drinkers saw greater cognitive and mood benefits than nondrinkers.[3] While the combo of caffeine and antioxidants seems to be most beneficial, decaf is a solid option for those who are sensitive to caffeine because it still offers the antioxidants.

A few caveats: Pregnant women and people who are sensitive to caffeine (those who exhibit shakiness, irritability, gastrointestinal distress, heart palpitations, and insomnia) should obviously avoid or limit their consumption. Also, consuming too much caffeine can cause symptoms similar to those of brain fog, including headaches, mood swings, and nausea. And everyone should steer clear close to bedtime, as caffeine can interfere with sleep, and a lack of shut-eye can lead to a case of brain fog.

I'm a huge fan of coffee. I wake up every morning to a cup of black coffee, but you can flavor yours with whatever you like. If you're trying to keep it low in calories and sugar, make your own vanilla creamer by adding a few drops of vanilla extract to ¼ cup low-fat cow's milk, soy milk, or unsweetened vanilla almond milk.

Another coffee hack: Freeze leftover joe in ice cube trays for future iced creations. You can add spices or flavorings liked cinnamon or nutmeg before freezing for extra zing. Add a few coffee cubes to your next cup of java to create iced coffee that doesn't become watered down.

3. Cocoa Powder

There are more reasons to be crazy for cocoa than you may already know. The flavanols in cocoa are associated with improved cognitive function, and in this case, it seems to be all about blood flow. Cocoa contains a compound called (-)-epicatechin, which appears to improve circulation and the growth of blood vessels. Better blood flow means more oxygen to the brain, and therefore, better brain function.

In a 2016 study in the journal *Appetite*, people who ate more chocolate (all types) performed better when it came to memory, organization, reasoning, and other measures of cognition than those who consumed less.[4] And another review of studies suggests that chocolate not only improved cognition but also helped boost mood.[5]

Unfortunately, the amount of chocolate—even dark chocolate—that you'd have to eat to get a beneficial amount of flavanols would bring a startling amount of calories and sugar along for the ride, so it's best to stick to cocoa powder. Check out these stats for comparison: 1 ounce of dark chocolate (60 to 80 percent cacao) has between 150 calories and 170 calories, 11 g total fat (6 of which are saturated), and 8 g sugar. On the other hand, 1 tablespoon of 100 percent cocoa powder has about 15 calories, 0.5 g total fat, and no saturated fat or sugar. Plus, cocoa powder is a super concentrated source of flavanols and even offers fiber and magnesium. Go for unsweetened varieties that haven't been "dutched" or processed with alkali (this is done to remove bitterness, but it destroys many of the flavanols). Ideally, look for varieties with at least 200 mg flavanols.

A simple way to get your fix is to add 1 to 2 tablespoons of cocoa powder to smoothies. I also like to whip up a quick and easy snack of chocolate protein pudding by stirring 2 teaspoons cocoa powder into traditional vanilla yogurt (not Greek yogurt, which tends to taste too tangy for this simple pudding recipe).

You can even satisfy a chocolate craving in the morning by making a batch of my dark chocolate oats. Mix ½ cup of rolled oats with about 1 cup water or milk and cook on the stovetop or in the microwave. Stir in 1 ½ teaspoons cocoa powder, 1 to 2 teaspoons sugar, and ¼ teaspoon vanilla extract—and top with lots of blueberries (for a double dose of smarts) and/or sliced banana.

4. Lentils

Lentils aren't shown a whole lot of love, but they certainly should be. They're packed with plant-based protein (about 18 g per cooked cup) and fiber (16 grams per cooked cup)—a stellar combo that helps steady blood sugar, and in turn, sharpens brain power and focus. Lentils deliver B vitamins and are free of saturated fat and cholesterol. They are also budget-friendly and incredibly versatile.

Not only that, lentils are rich in plant-based iron. Iron helps the brain produce neurotransmitters and is critical for brain function. One study from Idaho State University found that young women who ate iron-rich lunches for 16 weeks saw improvements in various markers of cognitive function, including planning speed, attention, and spatial working memory—that is, the ability to record info about your environment.[6]

When you think of good sources of iron, most people automatically think of beef, but lentils are a terrific source and significantly better for the environment. A cup of cooked lentils contains almost 7 grams of iron (that's about 40 percent of what adult women and about 90 percent of what adult men need each day). Note that this a different type of iron from the one found in meat. To increase the absorption of plant-based non-heme iron, pair it with some vitamin-C-rich foods like bell peppers, citrus fruits, tomatoes, strawberries, and broccoli. For instance, whip up a batch of seasoned lentils with chopped bell peppers or tomatoes and you're set.

You can add cooked cold lentils to a vegetable salad or mix them with beans to create a delicious bean-lentil pilaf. For warm meals, you can add them to soups, chilis, or stews or you can mix them into browned ground turkey meat to make the meal heartier and healthier.

I like to use lentils as a sub for ground turkey (or go 50-50) in dishes like sloppy joes, tacos, and even meatballs. To make a vegetarian swap, substitute 1 cup of dried, uncooked lentils for 1 cup of ground turkey meat. When you cook up the lentils, you'll end up with about 2 cups (or a little more). I like to use green or brown lentils because of their neutral flavor, which allows them to take on the delicious tastes of whatever ingredients and seasonings you're cooking them with. Plus, their texture more closely resembles ground turkey meat.

5. Celery

Celery contains a flavonoid called luteolin, which acts as an antioxidant and anti-inflammatory. Inflammation is a culprit behind many conditions, including dementia, Alzheimer's, and other brain diseases, and may also play a role in brain fog. Luteolin helps protect the brain and may increase memory, both of which are important when you're trying to ward off a dreaded mental dip.

One study showed that when older mice were given a luteolin-supplemented diet, signs of inflammation were reduced and brain function improved.[7]

While there are a few terrific sources of luteolin, I'm featuring celery because it's one of the best and most accessible. You can find this beneficial compound in other foods, including thyme, bell peppers, and chamomile tea. Another perk of the stalk: Celery is made up of 95 percent water, which makes it one of the most hydrating produce picks around. Dehydration can contribute to brain drain, so choosing foods that help you stay hydrated can help you think more clearly.

Celery is a go-to dipper because of its sturdiness and shape—its hollow middle allows for maximum scooping, whether you're dunking into salsa, hummus, or a Greek-yogurt-based dip. You can also fill celery sticks with peanut butter, reduced-fat cream cheese, or cottage cheese for a satisfying snack. Or try adding diced celery to tuna, chicken, and egg salad as an easy flavor enhancer that adds a bit of crunch.

Celery is one of the three staple ingredients of a vegetable stock base, along with carrots and onions. It's a standard addition to almost any soup, stew, or stir-fry, and a no-brainer on top of a tossed green salad.

Smart Smoothie

MAKES 2 SERVINGS

2 cups blueberries, fresh or frozen
½ ripe banana, fresh or frozen
2 teaspoons cocoa powder
¼ teaspoon vanilla extract

½ cup brewed coffee
  (room temperature or chilled)
1 teaspoon chia seeds
3 to 5 ice cubes

Place all the ingredients in a blender and puree until smooth.

NUTRITIONAL INFORMATION *Per serving (1 ¼ cups)*
120 calories • 2 g protein • 1.5 g total fat (0 g saturated fat, 1.5 g unsaturated fat) • 0 mg
cholesterol • 29 g carbs • 6 g fiber • 18 g total sugar (18 g natural sugar, 0 g added sugar) •
10 mg sodium

SMART SMOOTHIE BOWL Place the leftover smoothie contents
(or the entire double portion) in the fridge, covered, for a few hours
or overnight. The gelling effect of the chia seeds will transform your
smoothie into a pudding-like consistency that's perfect for a brainy
bowl of goodness. Top with extra berries and/or yogurt and enjoy!

Lentil Hummus

MAKES ABOUT 2 CUPS

2 cups lentils, cooked and cooled

2 garlic cloves, peeled and roughly chopped

3 tablespoons tahini (sesame seed paste)

2 tablespoons lemon juice

1 tablespoon extra-virgin olive oil, plus more for garnish

½ teaspoon ground cumin

½ teaspoon thyme

¾ teaspoon salt

¼ teaspoon freshly ground black pepper

Sweet paprika or crushed red pepper flakes for garnish (optional)

Celery sticks for dipping

Add lentils, garlic, tahini, lemon juice, oil, cumin, thyme, salt, and pepper to a blender or food processor. Blend until smooth, scraping down the sides as necessary.

For a thinner consistency, add a small bit of water, 1 tablespoon at a time, into the food processor and pulse until the hummus has reached your desired consistency. Do not add more than 3 to 4 tablespoons of water or it will become too thin.

Season with salt and pepper to taste and garnish with an optional drizzle of extra-virgin olive oil and a sprinkle of paprika or crushed red pepper flakes.

Serve with celery dippers. Keep in an airtight container in the fridge for up to 5 days.

NUTRITIONAL INFORMATION *Per 2 tablespoons*
60 calories • 3 g protein • 2.5 g fat (0 g saturated fat, 2.5 g unsaturated fat) • 0 mg cholesterol • 6 g carbs • 2 g fiber • 1 g total sugar (1 g natural sugar, 0 g added sugar) • 90 mg sodium

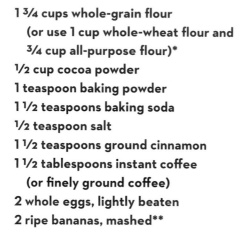

Mind Muffins

MAKES 20 MUFFINS

1 ¾ cups whole-grain flour
    (or use 1 cup whole-wheat flour and
    ¾ cup all-purpose flour)*
½ cup cocoa powder
1 teaspoon baking powder
1 ½ teaspoons baking soda
½ teaspoon salt
1 ½ teaspoons ground cinnamon
1 ½ tablespoons instant coffee
    (or finely ground coffee)
2 whole eggs, lightly beaten
2 ripe bananas, mashed**

½ cup plain nonfat or low-fat
    Greek yogurt
½ cup honey
¾ cup milk (preferably nonfat
    or low-fat cow's milk, soy milk, or
    unsweetened almond milk)
1 tablespoon canola oil
2 teaspoons vanilla extract
1 ¾ cups blueberries, divided
½ cup dark chocolate chips (optional)
20 banana slices (optional)
Dash of cocoa powder (optional)

*Note: Whole-grain flour can sometimes result in a tougher finished product. For a softer and lighter texture, it's typically best to use whole-wheat pastry flour, white whole-wheat flour, or a mix of all-purpose flour and traditional whole-wheat flour.

**If the bananas aren't ripe, then peel, slice, and microwave for 30 seconds to soften.

Preheat the oven to 400°F. Liberally mist muffin tins with oil spray.

Mix the flour, cocoa powder, baking powder, baking soda, salt, cinnamon, and instant coffee in a large bowl and set aside. Whisk the eggs, mashed bananas, yogurt, honey, milk, oil, and vanilla in a separate bowl until well combined.

Pour the wet ingredients into the dry, gently stirring until fully incorporated. Fold in 1 ½ cups blueberries and optional chocolate chips. Do not overmix.

Divide the batter evenly among 20 muffin cups (about ¼ cup batter per muffin) and top with remaining fresh blueberries and optional banana slices. Bake for 17 to 20 minutes, or until a toothpick inserted into the center comes out clean. Garnish with an optional dash of cocoa powder. You can freeze leftovers for up to 3 months.

NUTRITIONAL INFORMATION *Per muffin*
90 calories • 4 g protein • 2 g total fat (0 g saturated fat, 2 g unsaturated fat) • 15 mg cholesterol • 18 g carbs • 3 g fiber • 7 g total sugar (3 g natural sugar, 4 g added sugar) • 170 mg sodium

5 FOODS TO EASE ACHES AND PAINS

Sore muscles and achy joints can do more than sideline you from your regular workouts—they can interfere with your everyday life, making it difficult to go dancing with friends, haul groceries from the car, work at the computer, and even carry the kiddos around.

Sore muscles are extremely common—few of us have escaped the agony of achy muscles. Whether it's from an overzealous workout or an injury, muscle pain is just that . . . a *pain*! One survey of nearly 29,000 adults suggests that musculoskeletal pain is responsible for the largest amount of lost productive time—more than five hours per week—compared to ailments such as headache, back pain, and other issues.[1]

Arthritis is another serious and potentially debilitating problem. Although many may think of arthritis as a senior's disease, about 66 percent of cases occur *before* age 65. The condition that causes pain, swelling, stiffness in the joints, and a decreased range of motion is the nation's number-one cause of disability. It affects more than 50 million adults—that's somewhere between one in four to five people over the age of 18. There are more than 100 different forms of arthritis, but osteoarthritis and rheumatoid arthritis (an autoimmune disease) are two of the more common types. While physical activity is a recommended fix for both problems, it can sometimes be challenging to get off the couch and get moving when your muscles are tight and your joints are hurting.

Fortunately, there are some delicious food fixes that can help alleviate aches and pains. Try adding these beneficial bites to your weekly menu rotation.

1. Ginger

Forget looking in the medicine cabinet for a drug fix when you're feeling achy. The answer may very well be in your spice rack. Ginger contains compounds that work like an anti-inflammatory—similar to what you'd buy at the drug store.

A study in *The Journal of Pain* found that consuming 2 grams of ginger daily (about 1 teaspoon of fresh grated gingerroot or ¼ teaspoon of dried ginger powder) helped to relieve muscle soreness by 25 percent the day after a workout compared to those who were given a placebo.[2] Research suggests it can also help with knee pain in osteoarthritis sufferers.

Getting your daily dose can be as easy as making a soothing cup of ginger tea. To brew, cut 2 to 3 thin slices of fresh gingerroot and steep in 1 to 2 cups of simmering water for about 5 minutes. Pour the water into a mug and feel free to add a squeeze of lemon, if you'd like.

You can also try grating fresh ginger into stir-fries, curries, or marinades, or on top of sautéed veggies like broccoli or green beans. Or add a dash of ginger to smoothies, oatmeal, or a healthy muffin recipe.

I like to store fresh gingerroot (that knobby-looking thing you see stacked in crates at the grocery store) in the freezer; make sure to wrap it tightly in a plastic bag and cut off pieces as needed. It lasts for two months, which is a huge bonus when you're looking for a last-minute flavor fix.

If the fresh version is too much of a fuss, simply substitute with ground ginger. The dried, ground form of ginger still packs a powerful dose of anti-inflammatory compounds, and because it's so easy to use (you can sprinkle it on just about anything), you'll be likely to use it even more.

2. Turmeric

Another hidden gem in your spice cabinet that can help ease aches and pains is turmeric. This mustard-yellow spice, which is the main ingredient in curry powder, contains curcumin. It's this active ingredient that helps suppress inflammatory chemicals that contribute to pain and swelling in the joints.

One analysis from the *Journal of Medicinal Food* of several randomized controlled studies found that a curcumin extract helped relieve pain from osteoarthritis as well as over-the-counter pain relievers. Not only that, but it also improved function and mobility, which was gauged by joint stiffness, movement, and other measurements.[3]

To boost turmeric's pain-relieving powers, add a dash of ground black pepper. Black pepper contains a compound called piperine, which increases the bioavailability of curcumin by preventing it from being broken down in the gut and liver. Curcumin is also fat-soluble, meaning your body needs some fat to absorb it. So pair it with a healthy fat source—think avocados or olive oil in savory dishes. Or add it to cow's milk, unsweetened almond milk, soy milk, or light coconut milk to create a spicy golden milk latte. To make, bring 1 cup of milk to a simmer (do not boil). Turn off the heat and whisk in ¼ teaspoon turmeric, ¼ teaspoon cinnamon, ¼ teaspoon ginger, and a pinch of ground black pepper until thoroughly mixed. Add 1 to 2 teaspoons of your sweetener of choice, like honey, and stir. Pour into a mug and enjoy. (Add 1 to 2 tablespoons cocoa powder for a hot cocoa version.)

I like turmeric blended with other curry spices—cumin, coriander, mustard seed—but you can also try simply sprinkling some curry powder into chicken salad with green peas (or sliced purple grapes) for an easy and tasty lunch. Or whip up a chicken curry dish with cauliflower and brown rice for dinner. It also tastes delicious in egg salad and adds an interesting flavor twist to pancake or muffin batter. Another serving suggestion: Mix a dash into a tasty fruit smoothie. Bottom line: Aim to add ¼ to ½ teaspoon into appropriate recipes to score a few health perks.

3. Tart Cherry Juice

Pour yourself a cup of relief. Tart cherry juice has been shown to help reduce various markers of inflammation in the blood. Researchers have studied its effect on post-exercise soreness, as well as arthritis, gout, fibromyalgia, and other inflammatory diseases. In one recent review of studies, researchers found that cherries and their juice helped reduce oxidative stress and inflammation, which in turn, helped to lessen the effects of arthritis.[4] Encouraging news for anyone suffering from day-to-day discomfort due to a medical condition, injury, or aging!

Not only does it deserve a spot in your medicine chest, but you may also want to stash a bottle in your gym bag. Studies suggest it can help with recovery from a tough workout—tart cherry juice has been shown to help reduce pain and soreness in marathoners and other endurance athletes. In fact, some small studies have suggested the juice works as well as nonsteroidal anti-inflammatory drugs (NSAIDS), common over-the-counter (OTC) medications.[5] The pain-taming powers in tart cherries may come from the fruit's potent phytochemicals called anthocyanins.

According to research, the juice may help prepare athletes for an event as well as help promote recovery two to three days afterward, which relates to both strength and endurance exercise, according to a study in *Current Sports Medicine Reports*.[6] While the research shows promising results with high amounts of juice (8-plus ounces), I suggest experimenting with smaller doses to minimize calories and sugar (like all juice, tart cherry juice is rich in natural fruit sugar).

For instance, I create a delicious and healthy "soda" by mixing a shot of tart cherry juice with naturally flavored cherry seltzer. (I also add some grated fresh ginger for a double pain-fighting punch.) Other refreshing options include mixing tart cherry juice into a smoothie or making tart cherry ice cubes to add flavor to a nice tall glass of water or bubbly seltzer. Or use it to make a tart cherry vinaigrette to dress up your greens.

You can even incorporate it into your cooking. For example, mix a shot of the juice with water when preparing oatmeal or whole grains, like brown rice or quinoa. Feel free to experiment away!

4. Extra-Virgin Olive Oil

Aside from being rich in heart-healthy monounsaturated fat, the Mediterranean diet staple of extra-virgin olive oil boasts more than 30 phenolic compounds, which are powerful plant chemicals that help protect your health in a variety of ways. One of those compounds, oleocanthal, may help prevent arthritis-related inflammation because it blocks the same inflammatory pathways as anti-inflammatory pain meds found in the pharmacy.[7]

Extra-virgin olive oil is the highest-quality olive oil available and the only oil source of oleocanthal. It has a low smoke point, meaning it's not meant to be heated to high temperatures, or heated in general for a prolonged period of time. If it is, it can start to smoke, creating an off flavor and odor. In fact, some of the healthful pain-fighting compounds are diminished by heat, including oleocanthal, which becomes a little less bioavailable when the oil has been heated or cooked. (However, the heart-healthy fats remain intact.) That means when it comes to taming pain and inflammation, it's better used in cold dishes like pasta salads and chilled dips and salad dressings.

It's a mainstay in bruschetta (helping to make tomato's lycopene, a potent antioxidant, more bioavailable in the body), hummus, pesto, and bean dips. It's also a delicious and healthy replacement for butter that you can serve with a whole-grain sliced baguette. (Add some chopped herbs to jazz it up.)

You can also whip up a flavorful lemon vinaigrette by combining 1 minced garlic clove, 2 tablespoons fresh lemon juice, 1 to 2 teaspoons chia seeds, ½ teaspoon Dijon mustard, and ⅛ teaspoon honey in a bowl. Then slowly drizzle ¼ cup extra-virgin olive oil into the mix and add a dash of salt and pepper to taste.

Or try this light and tasty balsamic vinaigrette: Combine ½ cup good-quality balsamic vinegar with 3 to 4 tablespoons extra-virgin olive oil, 1 tablespoon Dijon mustard, 1 teaspoon honey, and 1 teaspoon garlic powder.

5. Broccoli

Beat pain with broccoli? This superstar veggie is loaded with so many beneficial nutrients, including vitamin K (it contains more than 90 micrograms per cup). Vitamin K may help protect against cartilage wear and tear and reduce the risk for arthritis. In one study, people with the highest blood levels of vitamin K showed up to 40 percent less osteoarthritis than those who had the lowest levels of the clotting vitamin.[8]

Another noteworthy nutrient in the super stalk: sulforaphane, an antioxidant that can help block inflammation and prevent cartilage damage. In one study, sulforaphane was found to reduce the production of an enzyme that's responsible for cartilage damage.[9] It also helped reduce the signs of arthritis in mice.

While some of this research is preliminary, meaning studies were conducted in the lab or on animals, there are so many good reasons to boost your intake of broccoli. It's low in calories, high in fiber, and loaded with nutrients. Basically, there's no reason *not* to enjoy it.

Serve it as a super side—it's delicious raw, steamed, or baked. (Although some studies suggest one of the active ingredients, sulforaphane, is more bioavailable when broccoli is raw or very lightly steamed compared to cooked or frozen; the enzyme responsible for forming the beneficial compound is sensitive to heat and freezing temperatures.) Definitely include broccoli florets on your crudité platter with dips rich in extra-virgin olive oil. I also love roasting broccoli with a little olive oil and garlic (burned and crispy is my fave; I suggest lightly re-misting the tops with extra-virgin olive oil when they're out of the oven to give your aches a double hit of relief). You can also grate or mince broccoli and mix it into a meatloaf or burger patties. Add a batch to simmering marinara sauce, or use it to make vegetable pancakes or veggie tater tots. I even use it to create broccoli "bread crumbs" (minced florets with optional Parm and seasonings) as a topper for baked spaghetti squash and delicious casseroles.

Try tossing broccoli florets or spears into stir-fries, adding onto your slice of pizza, or using as dippers for hummus (which involves another pain-fighter, extra-virgin olive oil), salsa, or bruschetta.

Ginger Turmeric Cherry Tea

MAKES 1 SERVING

1 tea bag, black or green (regular or decaf)
¼ teaspoon ground turmeric
¼ teaspoon ground ginger
Pinch ground black pepper
2 ounces tart cherry juice

Bring ¾ cup of water (about 6 ounces) to a boil. Place the tea bag, turmeric, ginger, and pepper in a mug, add the boiling water, stir, and cover. Let steep for 3 to 5 minutes.

While the tea is steeping, bring the cherry juice to a light boil, either on the stove top or in the microwave.

Add the boiling juice to the mug of tea and mix. Remove tea bag and discard. Mix the tea and enjoy.

NUTRITIONAL INFORMATION *Per serving*
35 calories • 0 g protein • 0 g fat • 0 mg cholesterol • 9 g carbs • 0 g fiber • 7 g total sugar (7 g natural sugar, 0 g added sugar) • 10 mg sodium

TEA TIME! In the mood for a refreshing chilled drink? Pour this hot tea into a glass with ice and sip away.

Chicken Curry with Broccoli

MAKES 4 SERVINGS

1 ½ pounds boneless, skinless chicken
    breasts, cut into 2-inch chunks
½ teaspoon kosher salt, divided
1 large yellow onion, finely chopped
2 garlic cloves, minced
    (or ¼ teaspoon garlic powder)
1 tablespoon minced fresh ginger
    (or 1 teaspoon ginger powder)
1 tablespoon curry powder

2 cups reduced-sodium chicken broth
1 tablespoon cornstarch
5 cups broccoli florets
1 medium carrot, roughly chopped
    or sliced into sticks (optional)
1 red pepper, roughly chopped or
    sliced into sticks (optional)
¼ cup nonfat plain yogurt
¼ cup chopped cilantro (optional)

Coat a large skillet with oil spray and warm over medium-high heat. Season the chicken with ¼ teaspoon kosher salt and cook in the skillet, stirring, 3 to 4 minutes, until it is partially cooked. Transfer the chicken to a plate, cover, and set aside.

Reapply oil spray to the skillet. Add the onion and cook over medium heat until soft and translucent, 3 to 4 minutes. Add the garlic, ginger, and curry powder and cook, stirring, 1 to 2 minutes, until the mixture becomes fragrant.

In a small bowl, mix the broth and cornstarch together until the cornstarch completely dissolves. Add the broth mixture, broccoli, and optional carrots and red pepper to the warm skillet and stir. Tightly cover and steam for about 2 minutes.

Return the chicken to the pan. Cook for about 4 more minutes, stirring occasionally, until the chicken is cooked through but still tender and the sauce is nice and thick.

Remove the skillet from the heat. Stir in the yogurt and season with the remaining ¼ teaspoon of kosher salt and black pepper to taste. Garnish with the optional cilantro. Serve the chicken with optional brown basmati rice or quinoa.

NUTRITIONAL INFORMATION *Per serving (about 2 heaping cups)*
260 calories • 45 g protein • 3.5 g total fat (0 g saturated fat, 3.5 g unsaturated fat) •
100 mg cholesterol • 13 g carbs • 4 g fiber • 4 g total sugar (4 g natural sugar, 0 g added sugar) •
450 mg sodium

Broccoli-Walnut Salad with Cherry Vinaigrette

MAKES 4 SERVINGS

Salad
½ cup roughly chopped walnuts

8 to 10 cups dark leafy greens, such as kale, baby spinach, or a combination of preferred greens

2 cups broccoli florets, roughly chopped

Half a red onion, very thinly sliced

Cherry Vinaigrette
⅓ cup tart cherry juice

3 tablespoons extra-virgin olive oil

2 teaspoons apple cider vinegar

2 teaspoons Dijon mustard

2 teaspoons reduced-sodium soy sauce

2 teaspoons minced fresh ginger (or ¼ teaspoon ginger powder)

¼ to ½ teaspoon wasabi (optional)

Toss the walnuts in a skillet warmed over medium heat for about 5 minutes or until fragrant. Arrange the walnuts in a single layer on a baking sheet and bake for 8 to 10 minutes at 350°F. Keep an eye on them; nuts burn quickly.

In a large bowl, toss together the greens, broccoli, walnuts, and onion.

Whisk together all the dressing ingredients in a separate bowl. Drizzle the dressing over the salad and gently toss. Serve with your favorite protein, such as chicken, fish, or chickpeas.

Single-serve salad: To prepare a single serving of salad, toss 2 cups of leafy greens with ½ cup chopped broccoli, 2 tablespoons toasted walnuts, and some sliced onion. Drizzle a few tablespoons of dressing over the salad. The dressing will keep in the fridge for about a week. Set the dressing on the counter for several minutes before using to allow it to become liquid again. Then whisk together to combine.

NUTRITIONAL INFORMATION *Per serving (3 cups salad with 2 tablespoons vinaigrette)*
210 calories • 6 g protein • 17 g total fat (2 g saturated fat, 15 g unsaturated fat) • 0 mg cholesterol • 11 g carbs • 5 g fiber • 3 g total sugar (3 g natural sugar, 0 g added sugar) • 210 mg sodium

5 FOODS TO
REDUCE WRINKLES

Crow's feet. Laugh lines. Frown lines. Computer face. Smoker's lines. Elevens. We certainly have a creative and diverse way of referring to all the different kinds of wrinkles that take up residence on our face. Here's one you probably *haven't* heard: *rhytides*, which is actually the scientific term. No matter what you call them, the unfortunate truth is that wrinkles are a fact of life.

While most 20-year-olds aren't too concerned about skin aging, that's roughly when the process starts. Around this point, collagen production begins to slow by about 1 percent a year. (This protein, which is found in connective tissue, helps keep skin firm.) The result: skin that's thinner and more sensitive. That's just one of the intrinsic causes of aging; there are other subtle changes. Sweat and oil glands don't function as well, which can leave skin dry and less resilient. We also experience a loss of elasticity and our fat pads begin to thin out. Without this underlying structure, skin sags, creases form, and—you guessed it—we get wrinkles.[1]

Of course, genetics play a role in when and how severe your wrinkles appear. But there are outside, or extrinsic, factors that can also make skin look and feel older, too. These external stressors can exacerbate skin damage and make wrinkles more prominent. The good news is that many of these are within your control. For example, one of the primary skin agers is the sun, and limiting your exposure is key. Staying out of the sun, wearing protective clothing and sunglasses, and slathering your skin in sunscreen can all help age-proof your skin. Quitting smoking and limiting your exposure to pollution as much as possible can also help prevent skin damage. And there's another tool for your antiaging arsenal: Eating a healthy diet that's rich in vitamins, minerals, antioxidants, and good-for-you fats, which can help nourish your skin from the inside out.

With that in mind, it's a great time to load up your plate with beautifying bites to help slough off old skin cells and reveal a new, healthy complexion. Then say hello to gorgeous, glowing skin.

1. Tomatoes

You say tomato, I say to-*mah*-to. No matter how you pronounce it, the popular garden delight (some call it a vegetable, some call it a fruit) is a serious skin saver. Thanks to their high content of lycopene, tomatoes have a photo-protective effect, meaning they protect against the sun's rays. Lycopene is the pigment that gives fruits and vegetables their red color and their headline-making status for protection against prostate cancer. It helps reduce inflammation, improves cell turnover, and inhibits DNA damage caused by UVB exposure. The result: It helps prevent collagen breakdown, the number-one cause of wrinkles.

In one study, people who ate 5 tablespoons of tomato paste, along with a bit of olive oil, daily for a period of 12 weeks, had 33 percent more protection from sunburn compared to a group that ate just olive oil. Lycopene is better absorbed when it's consumed with some fat because it's fat-soluble.[2] In another study, the tomato group also had much higher levels of procollagen, a precursor to collagen.[3] Of course, while tomatoes might help improve skin's natural sun protection factor (SPF), they are definitely not a replacement for sunscreen.

Tomatoes' other skin perks include helping to prevent reddening from UVA rays and improving pigmentation and brown spots. One study even suggests tomatoes may help cut the risk of skin cancer in half.[4]

Tomatoes are delicious sliced and added to sandwiches or tossed on top of salads. You can get an added bonus from cooking them, as lycopene becomes even more available once tomatoes are heated. That's because lycopene is housed within the tomato cell walls, and when heated, the cell walls break down and make lycopene easier to absorb.[5] They are fabulous chopped and lightly sautéed with fresh basil and then added to scrambled eggs. Or try roasting them for a delicious treat.

Of course, you can use tomatoes to make a yummy sauce. (Store-bought tomato and marinara sauces work great, too.) Use it as a topper for pasta, lower-carb vegetable "noodles," or chicken. Also, canned tomatoes can be easily used in stews or chilis. There are endless tomato-rich options.

2. Walnuts

Go ahead and get a little nutty—doing so may help protect your skin. Walnuts are rich in the plant-based form of omega-3 fats called alpha-linolenic acid (ALA). They're the only nut to deliver a substantial amount—an ounce contains 2.5 grams ALA (pecans come in second with a mere 0.5 grams per ounce). These compounds help maintain cell membranes so that they become an effective barrier, allowing in water and nutrients to help nourish and moisturize while keeping potentially harmful toxins out.

Omega-3s have also been shown to protect skin against sun damage. In one study in sunny, skin-scorching southeastern Arizona, people who ate diets rich in fish oils (think salmon, sardines, and Arctic char) and other plant-based omega-3 fats (think walnuts, chia seeds, and ground flaxseeds) had a 29 percent lower risk for squamous cell skin cancer than those who got very little omega-3s from food.[6] Omega-3 fats help reduce inflammation, protect DNA, and actually increase our sunburn threshold.[7]

Walnuts are a tasty snack on their own, though stick to a handful or two to keep calories in check. Or jazz up them up by combining walnuts with whole-grain cereal, dried fruit, and semisweet chocolate chips to create a DIY trail mix.

You can also work walnuts into meals. I'd recommend toasting them to bring out a richer, creamier flavor. I use toasted walnuts as a low-carb replacement for croutons on salads. Toasted walnuts are also delicious in sweet dessert dishes (like baked apples stuffed with an oatmeal filling) and sprinkled into pasta entrées and roasted vegetables. To toast, arrange walnuts in a single layer on a baking sheet and bake for 8 to 10 minutes in a 350°F oven. Be sure to keep an eye on them because nuts burn quickly. You can also add chopped walnuts to healthy cookie, muffin, and pancake batter or sprinkle onto yogurt, cottage cheese, or oatmeal to provide a dose of nutrition and satisfying crunch.

3. Green Tea/Matcha

It's teatime! Green tea offers a two-for-one benefit against wrinkles. For one, green tea is hydrating, and dehydration can increase the appearance of fine lines. And two, tea contains natural compounds known as polyphenols, which have antioxidant properties. One type of polyphenol, called a catechin, acts as a powerful protector against sun damage and helps to tame inflammation and keep skin looking smoother and more elastic. By the way, both regular and decaf green tea offer these benefits.

One of the most studied catechins is called epigallocatechin gallate (EGCG). In animal and lab studies, EGCG helped prevent sun-related skin cancers and improve immune functioning.[8] It also helps fight wrinkles and rejuvenate skin cells.

Brew up a warm and soothing cup of green tea, or try a different variety called matcha, which is a fine powdered form of green tea leaves that offers potentially even more antioxidants. That's because it entails consuming the ground-up tea leaves instead of just the brewed water. (Regular green tea leaves, which contain many of the beneficial compounds, are usually discarded.) Of course, regular green tea is still fabulous and simple, but matcha can give you as much as 10 times more antioxidants.

It's easy to make a cup of tea using matcha. Traditionally, it's done by first making a paste with the powder and a small amount of hot water, then adding more steaming water to the mug. But you can just as easily stir the powder into 6 to 8 ounces of boiling water.

You can use matcha powder (available in regular or decaf, both rich in beneficial compounds) in baked foods and smoothies, too. I add 2 teaspoons matcha powder dissolved into 1 tablespoon water to a scrumptious pound cake recipe (the addition of matcha powder gives it a slight green tint—fun twist). I also whip up a refreshing vanilla-mango smoothie by combining 1 tablespoon of the powder with ½ cup of hot water and letting it cool. Then I blend it with ½ cup nonfat vanilla yogurt, 1 cup fresh or frozen mango chunks, and a handful of ice cubes (optional) for a refreshing—skinsational—treat.

4. Strawberries

Strawberries are the pick of the patch because they're loaded with vitamin C. Vitamin C is a natural antioxidant that helps defend your skin against damaging free radicals, particles that can age your skin. Vitamin C also helps your body produce collagen, the protein that keeps your skin firm and elastic. The benefits don't end there. The superstar vitamin offers protection from the sun, helps promote wound healing, and controls inflammation.

One study suggests that people who consumed more vitamin C were less likely to have a wrinkled appearance and dry skin caused by aging.[9] In fact, a one-unit increase in vitamin C intake correlated with an 11 percent reduction in the chances of having a wrinkled appearance and a 7 percent drop in dryness associated with aging.

A cup of sliced strawberries delivers just about 100 mg of vitamin C, more than what you need for an entire day. (Other C-rich picks include guava, oranges, grapefruit, kiwi, and bell peppers, so feel free to incorporate all of them into your diet for some variety.)

You can enjoy them straight up as a sweet snack or pair them with a handful of walnuts for a double dose of age-defying goodness. Strawberries can make a healthier replacement for jelly or jam in PB&J sandwiches: Spread peanut butter on whole-grain bread (or pita), then layer sliced strawberries on top. Top with a second slice of bread or skip the top slice and enjoy open-faced for a lighter version of the childhood classic.

Try tossing fresh or frozen strawberries into smoothies (they're great with bananas, other berries, kiwi, or really any fruit you can think of), add them into oatmeal, or layer them in yogurt parfaits. You can pick up frozen bags year-round and keep them stashed in your freezer.

5. Kale

Kale is the super veggie that leaves other foods feeling green with envy when it comes to its wrinkle-fighting powers. The leafy green is rich in beta-carotene, which I often refer to as "nature's exfoliant." Beta-carotene promotes cell turnover, helping your skin slough off old cells and replacing them with healthy new ones so your complexion maintains that dewy, fresh, youthful look. Foods rich in beta-carotene, like kale, may help prevent sagging and wrinkling, and bonus, even clogged pores.

Beta-carotene is converted to vitamin A in the body, where it aids in the growth and repair of body tissues and acts as an antioxidant that may protect against sun damage. It helps protect skin from the sun, reduces the risk for skin cancer, boosts skin elasticity, and may help reduce wrinkling and skin sagging. In extremely high doses, straight vitamin A from supplements can be toxic, so I never recommend taking it this way. However, ample beta-carotene from food is entirely safe. Kale also contains vitamin C (as well as the antioxidants lutein and zeaxanthin) to make it an overall healthy, balanced superfood for your skin.

You can bake, steam, or roast kale or add it to soups and stews. You can also blend a handful into almost any fruit smoothie to add a boost of nutrients. Or try mixing raw kale leaves into your salad to kick up the nutritional value of your bowl. (Spinach is a suitable substitute, as it offers a number of the same nutrients and can be used in many of the same dishes.)

I love making amazingly addictive kale chips, which I like to call "beauty chips." Trim the stem ends off a large bunch of kale. Cut or tear the leaves into 2-inch pieces and spread them out in a single layer between two baking sheets that have been misted with oil spray. Liberally mist the kale tops with oil spray and sprinkle with kosher salt and any preferred additional seasonings. Bake for 8 to 10 minutes, until the kale is crispy and the edges begin to brown. Warning: Once you start snacking, you may not be able to stop!

Matcha Smoothie Bowl

MAKES 1 SERVING

1 ripe banana
1 cup fresh or frozen strawberries
½ cup fresh or frozen blackberries, blueberries, or mixed berries
1 cup fresh kale leaves, loosely packed
1 cup unsweetened plain or vanilla almond milk (or any other preferred milk)

1 teaspoon matcha powder
1 teaspoon lime juice
1 to 2 teaspoons honey (optional)
1 to 2 tablespoons chopped walnuts

Place all the ingredients in a blender (with the exception of the walnuts).

Note: If using fresh berries, add 1 cup of ice to the blender. (Skip the ice if using frozen berries.)

Blend the mixture until smooth and thick (do not overmix or it will become too thin). Pour into a bowl and top with walnuts and any other preferred extras, such as chia seeds, shredded coconut, fresh fruit (sliced strawberries, blueberries, raspberries, or bananas), and so on.

NUTRITIONAL INFORMATION *Per serving**
270 calories • 7 g protein • 8 g total fat (0 g saturated fat, 8 g unsaturated fat) • 0 mg cholesterol • 49 g carbs • 8 g fiber • 27 g total sugar (27 g natural sugar, 0 g added sugar) • 180 mg sodium

*Note: If using honey, add 20 calories per teaspoon.

Kale Pasta Pesto

MAKES 5 SERVINGS AND 1 CUP PESTO SAUCE

3 cups loosely packed kale, stems removed
1 cup loosely packed fresh basil leaves
1/2 cup Parmesan cheese, grated
1/4 cup reduced-sodium vegetable broth
1/4 cup toasted walnuts
3/4 to 1 teaspoon kosher salt

2 tablespoons matcha powder
2 garlic cloves, roughly chopped (or 1/4 teaspoon garlic powder)
1/4 cup extra-virgin olive oil
10 cups whole-grain pasta, cooked
16 ounces grape tomatoes, halved
Ground black pepper to taste

Add the kale, basil, Parmesan, broth, walnuts, salt, matcha, and garlic to a food processor and pulse until the the greens are finely chopped. Scrape down the sides as needed to ensure everything is incorporated and well blended. Then drizzle in the olive oil while you continue to pulse until everything is evenly blended. Season with additional salt, ground black pepper, and garlic to taste. (Mix in 1 to 2 tablespoons extra broth if a thinner texture is desired.)

Toss the kale pesto sauce with cooked pasta and tomatoes.

NUTRITIONAL INFORMATION *Per serving (2 cups pasta pesto)*
520 calories • 20 g protein • 21 g total fat (3 g saturated fat, 18 g unsaturated fat) • 5 mg cholesterol • 74 g carbs • 10 g fiber • 3 g total sugar (3 g natural sugar, 0 g added sugar) • 560 mg sodium

Matcha Pancakes

MAKES 2 SERVINGS

1 cup whole-grain flour (or use a mixture of ½ whole-grain and ½ all-purpose flour)
2 tablespoons matcha powder
1 teaspoon baking powder

1 cup unsweetened almond milk (or any other preferred milk)
1 teaspoon vanilla extract
½ cup strawberries, sliced
⅓ cup walnuts, chopped

Stir together the flour, matcha powder, and baking powder in a mixing bowl.

Add the milk and vanilla and stir everything together.

Liberally coat a skillet with oil spray and warm over medium heat. Pour about ¼ cup batter to form a pancake, then drop in the strawberries and walnuts. Reapply oil spray between pancakes as needed to prevent sticking.

Flip the pancake after 3 to 4 minutes, or when the batter begins to bubble. Repeat until all pancakes are cooked. Top each pancake with optional yogurt, a drizzle of maple syrup, or additional strawberries and walnuts.

NUTRITIONAL INFORMATION *Per serving (3 pancakes)*
380 calories • 18 g protein • 16 g total fat (1.5 g saturated fat, 14.5 g unsaturated fat) • 0 mg cholesterol • 50 g carbs • 8 g fiber • 3 g total sugar (3 g natural sugar, 0 g added sugar) • 330 mg sodium

5 FOODS TO LOWER CHOLESTEROL

More than 70 million American adults have high cholesterol—and this specifically refers to LDL cholesterol, the bad type that increases our risk for heart disease, according to leading cardiologists and the CDC.

Most of us think of cholesterol as a four-letter word because of its connection to heart disease, but believe it or not, we need some of the waxy, fat-like substance—our bodies use cholesterol to make hormones, vitamin D, and even bile for digestion. That being said, you *can* have too much of a good thing. That's the case with cholesterol—some is good, but excessive amounts, not so much.

Of course, we all know that cholesterol comes from food (animal products including meat, poultry, full-fat dairy, egg yolks, as well as shellfish—years back, shrimp was practically tossed back to sea for its high cholesterol content). But our liver also makes it. In fact, your body produces all the cholesterol you need.

When you eat a diet that's high in saturated fat, *trans* fat, refined carbs, and sugar, your liver produces even *more* cholesterol. The result: Your levels creep higher. If they get too high—more than 100 to 130 milligrams per deciliter (mg/dl) for LDL cholesterol, according to the American Heart Association—you're considered at risk for heart disease.

Enough of the heartbreaking news! Let's focus on some uplifting information instead: Studies show that making smart food choices and exercising can help reduce LDL cholesterol by up to 15 percent. And while it's true that some folks are genetically predisposed to produce excessive amounts of cholesterol—regardless of how well they eat—everyone with elevated numbers can benefit from these five power foods.

Note: For some people, cholesterol-lowering medication may also be needed. Make sure you know your numbers and chat with your doctor about the plan that works best for you.

1. Apples

It's a cliché, but it's true: An apple a day just may keep the doc away. The beloved fruit is a nutritional powerhouse and has specific cholesterol-lowering capabilities.

This is in part because apples contain pectin, a type of carbohydrate found in the cell walls of plants. The majority of pectin is buried within fruit peels, which gives apples an advantage over other fruits (such as oranges, bananas, and melons) because we tend to eat apples with the skin on.

How does the cholesterol-lowering effect work? We're unable to properly digest pectin, so it binds to cholesterol and helps to carry it out of the body, preventing cholesterol from being absorbed into the bloodstream and clogging up our blood vessels.

Some additional apple assets worth noting: One medium apple is just 80 calories and provides 4 grams of filling fiber. Plus, an apple comes perfectly portioned, is easy to tote, and is so versatile.

I love that there are so many delicious ways to enjoy it. Slice it up and serve it with nut butter. Chop it up and add it to chicken salad, hearty stews, and healthy pancake and muffin batters for a surprising burst of sweetness. Bake it with a sprinkle of cinnamon for a good-for-you dessert. Or try whipping up your own homemade apple sauce on the stove top or in a slow cooker.

2. Lentils

It's time to show lentils some long-overdue love—these fiber-rich pulses are taking over the plant-based food scene. Why? They're tasty, easy to prepare, budget-friendly, and loaded with the good stuff, including 18 grams of satiating protein per cooked cup.

Furthermore, lentils contain an impressive amount of fiber (16 grams per cooked cup), and they also can take the place of animal protein. Thus they replace a food that provides some dietary cholesterol and is often high in saturated fat (in the case of marbled, fatty beef and pork), a double whammy when it comes to blood cholesterol levels.

One Canadian study found that people who enjoyed a ¾-cup daily serving of lentils or other legumes (beans, chickpeas, or peas) experienced a 5 percent drop in LDL cholesterol within a few months. This led researchers to note a strong association between legumes and improving this heart-health marker.[1] Whether you're cooking with red, yellow, brown, green, or black lentils (user's choice!), there are so many delicious ways to incorporate them into your diet. Try making a heartwarming lentil soup or chili. Sprinkle a seasoned and chilled batch onto your salad as a tasty topper. Serve warm, seasoned lentils as a side dish.

3. Avocado

Gaining loads of attention and respect lately, avocado can help to normalize high cholesterol numbers. That's because this creamy green fruit (yes, it's actually considered a fruit) contains fiber and monounsaturated fat, which helps raise good cholesterol and lower bad cholesterol. Bonus: Avocado contains beta-sitosterol, a specific plant-based fat shown to reinforce cholesterol-lowering capabilities.

One study found that an avocado a day as part of an overall healthy diet led to a significant reduction in LDL cholesterol versus a comparable diet without avocado.

While most people enjoy avocado in the form of guacamole, it's incredibly versatile. You can use it as a healthier replacement for mayo in tuna or chicken salad. It also adds creaminess to smoothies, puddings, and mousse. I personally love it as the star ingredient on avocado toast—there are so many fun spins. After spreading some mashed avocado on a slice of whole-grain toast, you can add mango and pomegranate seeds or sliced tomato, cucumber, sea salt, and ground black pepper. Or try topping your smashed avocado with scrambled egg whites that have been sautéed with spinach and jalapeños—or whatever healthy toppings you prefer!

4. Chia Seeds

Chia seeds have certainly moved beyond those kitschy pottery pets from the early '80s. In fact, I refer to them as "nutrition sprinkles" because they have the ability to boost the health quotient of just about any meal or snack.

One tablespoon provides 60 calories, 3 grams of protein, and an impressive 4 grams of fiber.

They're a type of soluble fiber, which absorbs water and acts like a gel in the body. You can think of soluble fiber as a "cholesterol-magnet," latching on to circulating plaque particles and escorting them out of the body before they can do any damage.

Chia seeds, which come from a desert plant that's a member of the mint family, also contain omega-3 fats, shown to significantly reduce artery-clogging triglyceride levels in the blood. Win-win.

You can use chia seeds, which are virtually tasteless, just like you would other seeds or chopped nuts. (Ground flaxseeds have similar properties and are another great option. However, unlike flaxseeds, you don't need to grind chia seeds first because they're completely digestible in whole form.) Try sprinkling a tablespoon into cereal, yogurt, oatmeal, cottage cheese, or a smoothie recipe. You can mix them into dips, sauces, or salad dressings. Or add a few tablespoons to any pancake or muffin batter. You can even try using chia seeds as a vegan alternative to eggs in most recipes (1 tablespoon of chia seeds to 3 tablespoons of water; let sit for about 10 minutes until the mixture thickens). Then substitute a chia seed "egg" for a regular egg in some of your healthy creations.

5. Oats

Oatmeal is a breakfast staple that continues to rise and shine on so many levels—health, yumminess, and convenience.

Take a look at these impressive stats: A half cup of dry oats (traditional or quick) provides about 150 calories, 5 grams of protein, and 4 grams of fiber. Oats specifically contain a fermentable soluble fiber called "beta-glucan." Enjoy a nice warm bowl of oatmeal for breakfast, where the fiber dissolves to form a gel, which binds to cholesterol, preventing you from absorbing it. The cholesterol is then excreted out of your body, so your cholesterol levels stay nice and healthy. Good morning, indeed!

Top your morning bowl of oatmeal with chopped apples and cinnamon for a double dose of cholesterol-lowering magic (add 2 teaspoons of chia seeds for a tasty trifecta). Too rushed in the A.M. to whip up a quick breakfast? Avoid the morning rush by making oatmeal the night before. To make overnight oats, simply place about ½ cup rolled oats and other desired ingredients—about ½ to ¾ cup skim or almond milk; chopped fruit; spices like nutmeg, cinnamon, and vanilla extract; and other mix-ins, including 1 to 2 teaspoons of chia seeds—in a mason jar or other container you can seal and refrigerate. Then rise and dine. You can even take it to go—just don't forget your spoon.

You can also use rolled oats (instead of refined, white bread crumbs) as a binder for meatloaf/meatballs. And here's another trick: Make oat flour by pulsing old-fashioned rolled oats in a food processor until they're smooth and powdery. This is a perfect swap for up to half the amount of flour a muffin or pancake recipe calls for.

Lentil-Apple Burgers with Creamy Avocado Sauce

MAKES 6 LARGE BURGERS AND 1 CUP SAUCE

Lentil-Apple Burgers

1 cup uncooked lentils

2 cups reduced-sodium chicken or
vegetable broth or stock

1 small red onion, finely diced

1 apple, skin on and finely diced

2 tablespoons lemon juice

1/2 teaspoon salt

1/4 teaspoon ground black pepper

8 ounces (about 5 cups) fresh
spinach leaves

2 garlic cloves, minced

1 tablespoon fresh rosemary
(or 1 teaspoon dried rosemary)

2 tablespoons chia seeds

1 cup rolled oats, pulsed in a food
processor to create a fine flour

Arugula leaves

Creamy Avocado Sauce

1 ripe avocado

1/2 cup nonfat plain Greek yogurt

3 tablespoons lemon juice

1/4 teaspoon salt

For the burgers:

Add lentils and broth or stock to a pot. Bring to a boil and allow to simmer for 30 minutes over low to medium heat until the lentils are soft. Transfer the lentils with the leftover liquid to a separate bowl and mash with the back of a fork or a potato masher (no need to fully mash everything; about halfway is fine). Alternatively, you can put the mixture in a food processor and pulse until it's mostly smooth. (Both techniques work well.)

Liberally coat a large skillet with oil spray and warm over medium heat. Add the onion, apple, lemon juice, salt, and pepper and cook until the onion is soft, about 5 minutes. Add the spinach, garlic, and rosemary. Stir until the spinach is wilted, about 3 minutes.

Add the spinach-apple mixture, chia seeds, and oat flour to the lentils and combine thoroughly. Using your hands, shape the mixture into 6 large patties. If the mixture feels too dry and crumbly, add 1 to 2 tablespoons broth and mix well before shaping into patties.

Liberally coat the same skillet with oil spray, and cook the patties for about 5 minutes on each side, applying extra spray between flips so the patties don't stick. Serve each burger topped with arugula and a dollop of Creamy Avocado Sauce.

For the sauce:
Combine all the ingredients in a food processor or blender and mix until smooth. Save any leftover sauce for future use. This sauce also tastes delicious on chicken, fish, and baked potatoes.

NUTRITIONAL INFORMATION

Per burger: 220 calories • 13 g protein • 3.5 g total fat (0.5 g saturated fat, 3.5 g unsaturated fat) • 0 mg cholesterol • 37 g carbs • 10 g fiber • 5 g total sugar (5 g natural sugar, 0 g added sugar) • 290 mg sodium

Per 1 tablespoon sauce: 20 calories • 1 g protein • 1.5 g total fat (0 g saturated fat, 1.5 g unsaturated fat) • 0 mg cholesterol • 1 g carbs • 1 g fiber • 0 g total sugar • 40 mg sodium

Lentil–Butternut Squash Stew

MAKES 10 CUPS

4 cups butternut squash, peeled and cut into 1/2-inch chunks (about 1 medium squash)

1 large apple, skin on, diced

1 onion, diced

2 large carrots, peeled and chopped

4 garlic cloves, minced (or 1/2 teaspoon garlic powder)

1 cup uncooked lentils

1/2 teaspoon kosher salt

1/2 teaspoon paprika

1/2 teaspoon chili powder

1/2 teaspoon cumin

1/2 teaspoon crushed red pepper flakes

3 tablespoons chia seeds

5 cups reduced-sodium vegetable broth

5 cups roughly chopped kale

1 tablespoon apple cider vinegar

1 avocado, chopped (optional)*

Nonfat or low-fat plain Greek yogurt (optional)

Chopped cilantro (optional)

For a slow cooker:
Combine all ingredients, from the butternut squash through the vegetable broth, into a slow cooker. Cover and cook on high for 5 to 6 hours or on low for 6 to 7 hours. When there are 30 minutes of cooking time left, carefully remove the lid, stir in the kale and vinegar, and replace the cover to complete cooking. When the stew is done, season with salt and pepper to taste. Top with chopped avocado, yogurt, and cilantro, if desired.

For the stove top:
Liberally coat a skillet with oil spray and warm over medium heat. Add the onion and carrots and cook until soft, about 5 minutes. Add the garlic, salt, paprika, chili, cumin, and red pepper flakes. Stir until fragrant, 1 to 2 minutes. Add the lentils, chia seeds, broth, and vinegar and bring to a boil. Turn down the heat to simmer and cook for 20 minutes, stirring occasionally. Add the squash, apples, and kale and continue to simmer for 25 more minutes, until the veggies and lentils are soft. Season with additional salt and pepper to taste. Garnish each serving with optional chopped avocado, yogurt, and cilantro.

NUTRITIONAL INFORMATION *Per serving (2 cups)**
250 calories • 12 g protein • 3.5 g total fat (0 g saturated fat, 3.5 g unsaturated fat) • 0 mg cholesterol • 47 g carbs • 13 g fiber • 11 g total sugar (11 g natural sugar, 0 g added sugar) • 380 mg sodium

Note: If topping with avocado, add 60 calories, 3 g fiber, and 5 g fat per serving.

Apple Protein Pancakes

MAKES 1 SERVING

½ cup quick-cooking oats
4 egg whites
1 teaspoon vanilla extract

½ apple, skin on, finely diced
½ teaspoon ground cinnamon
2 teaspoons chia seeds

Combine the oats, egg whites, vanilla, apples, cinnamon, and chia seeds in a small bowl and stir until thoroughly mixed. Set aside.

Liberally coat a skillet with oil spray and warm over medium heat. Pour or spoon the mixture onto the skillet, making about 5 small pancakes. Cook each side for about 1 to 2 minutes, until the pancakes are golden brown. Reapply oil spray between flips to ensure the pancakes don't stick to the pan.

Enjoy the pancakes plain or topped with yogurt or a drizzle of maple syrup or honey.

NUTRITIONAL INFORMATION *Per serving**
320 calories • 22 g protein • 7 g total fat (1 g saturated fat, 6 g unsaturated fat) • 0 mg cholesterol • 44 g carbs • 10 g fiber • 10 g total sugar (9 g natural sugar, 1 g added sugar) • 250 mg sodium

*Note: 2 tablespoons low-fat yogurt add about 20 calories; 1 teaspoon syrup or honey adds about 20 calories.

2. Turmeric

Turmeric is fast becoming the golden child (quite literally) of the spice rack. This is turmeric's second nod in the book. (It also snagged a spot in the aches and pains chapter; see page 90.) Its sneeze-busting powers are thanks to the spice's active ingredient, curcumin. Curcumin has been shown to help improve seasonal allergy symptoms—including sneezing, runny nose, and nasal congestion. The curcumin works on the immune system in a variety of ways; it suppresses a number of different allergy-causing substances while increasing the production of other compounds.[4]

You'll get a more potent punch from turmeric by combining it with a dash of ground black pepper. That's because black pepper contains a compound called piperine, which prevents curcumin from being broken down in the gut and liver. Fat also helps boost the absorption of curcumin, so you may want to pair your turmeric with a healthful fat source, like extra-virgin olive oil (double bonus!), nuts, or avocado.

I love adding turmeric to fruit smoothies because it's fast and fuss-free: Combine ¾ cup milk (I suggest using a milk with some fat like 2-percent low-fat cow's milk, soy milk, or light coconut milk), 1 ½ cups cubed pineapple, ½ teaspoon ground turmeric, optional honey, 2 to 3 ice cubes, and a pinch of ground black pepper in a blender until smooth. Add an additional splash of milk or water as needed to achieve your desired consistency.

Other tasty ways to enjoy the spice: Use it to make a flavorful chicken curry for dinner, mix it into yogurt or hummus for a tangy dip, or blend it into tuna and chicken salad for a nice earthy flavor. You can also use it to whip up a delicious golden milk latte (see page 90).

5 FOODS TO
RELIEVE SEASONAL ALLERGIES

Lush, green grass. Beautiful, blooming flowers. Buzzing bumblebees. Spring is in the air. And for millions of allergy sufferers, it's the start of consistently runny (or stuffy) noses, watery eyes, and scratchy throats that can last until mid-September. It's estimated that more than 8 percent of American adults suffer from hay fever, or *seasonal allergic rhinitis*, the scientific term for seasonal allergies.

Seasonal allergies occur because the immune system mistakes a normally benign substance—like pollen from a tree or grass—as an intruder. As a result, the immune system pumps out antibodies to fight these "foreign substances," and anytime you're exposed to them moving forward, the antibodies release chemicals such as histamines, which cause allergy symptoms. The most common allergy triggers include mold and tree, grass, and weed pollen. In the fall, ragweed, a wild plant that grows almost everywhere, is perhaps the most common offender.

It's important to get tested so you know what your specific triggers are and so that you can do your best to minimize your exposure to them. Part of that is knowing how weather and other factors, such as the time of day, affect you. For instance, tree, grass, and ragweed pollen levels are high on cool nights and warm days. Molds grow quickly in heat and high humidity. In spring and summer, tree and grass pollen levels are highest in the evening. In late summer and early fall, levels of ragweed pollen spike in the morning.

Other pollen protective moves include keeping windows and doors shut at home and while driving in your car, showering and washing your hair after working or exercising outdoors, taking allergy meds (over-the-counter or prescription), and going for allergy shots. Also, adding certain foods to your menu can help ease sneezes, wheezes, sniffles, and a scratchy throat.

1. Extra-Virgin Olive Oil

Olive oil is a staple of the Mediterranean diet, an eating pattern that is well-known for its health benefits—among them, a reduced risk for heart disease and stroke and a boost in longevity. You may now be able to add protection against seasonal allergies to this already impressive list. One study suggests that kids who most closely followed a Med diet experienced fewer allergy symptoms, including wheezing, sneezing, and itchy, watery eyes, compared to those who didn't.[1] It seems that pregnant moms who regularly used olive oil passed the allergy protection onto their babies-to-be—infants whose mothers cook with the oil or dressed salads with it were less likely to suffer wheezing during their first year of life, according to another study.[2]

The Mediterranean diet is loaded with tons of beneficial foods, so why single out extra-virgin olive oil? The healthy fat contains plant compounds called phenols (phenols are more concentrated in extra-virgin olive oil compared to regular olive oil). One in particular, hydroxytyrosol, seems to help suppress the immune response when people are exposed to allergens.[3]

Extra-virgin olive oil is one item you'll *always* find in my pantry, not only because I love the flavor but also because this type of oil is highest in nutrients compared to virgin olive oil and olive oil. I use it for all types of meal prep, but in the fight against allergies, it's much more effective when used for non-cooking needs like whipping up salad dressings, dips, hummus, and cold pasta salads. That's because the beneficial phenol compound, hydroxytyrosol, is affected by heat, and becomes a bit less potent when you grill, roast, bake, or stir-fry. If using for cooking, try to stick to low temps and short cooking times.

For pan sautéing and roasting, I usually pour oil into misters and spray it onto meats and vegetables (and pans) versus pouring it straight from the bottle. This trick helps me cut back on the amount of oil I'm using, while still delivering the key compounds for good health.

2. Turmeric

Turmeric is fast becoming the golden child (quite literally) of the spice rack. This is turmeric's second nod in the book. (It also snagged a spot in the aches and pains chapter; see page 90.) Its sneeze-busting powers are thanks to the spice's active ingredient, curcumin. Curcumin has been shown to help improve seasonal allergy symptoms—including sneezing, runny nose, and nasal congestion. The curcumin works on the immune system in a variety of ways; it suppresses a number of different allergy-causing substances while increasing the production of other compounds.[4]

You'll get a more potent punch from turmeric by combining it with a dash of ground black pepper. That's because black pepper contains a compound called piperine, which prevents curcumin from being broken down in the gut and liver. Fat also helps boost the absorption of curcumin, so you may want to pair your turmeric with a healthful fat source, like extra-virgin olive oil (double bonus!), nuts, or avocado.

I love adding turmeric to fruit smoothies because it's fast and fuss-free: Combine ¾ cup milk (I suggest using a milk with some fat like 2-percent low-fat cow's milk, soy milk, or light coconut milk), 1 ½ cups cubed pineapple, ½ teaspoon ground turmeric, optional honey, 2 to 3 ice cubes, and a pinch of ground black pepper in a blender until smooth. Add an additional splash of milk or water as needed to achieve your desired consistency.

Other tasty ways to enjoy the spice: Use it to make a flavorful chicken curry for dinner, mix it into yogurt or hummus for a tangy dip, or blend it into tuna and chicken salad for a nice earthy flavor. You can also use it to whip up a delicious golden milk latte (see page 90).

3. Lettuce

(Kale, Swiss Chard, Red Leaf, Radicchio, Green Leaf, and Chicory Greens)

While romaine and iceberg are standard salad bases, there's good reason to think outside the bowl. A variety of lettuce greens—including kale (page 105), Swiss chard (page 19), red leaf lettuce, radicchio, green leaf lettuce, and chicory greens—may help fight seasonal allergies. These greens contain quercetin, a flavonoid with strong anti-inflammatory and antioxidant powers, and anti-allergic properties. Multiple studies conducted in the lab and on animals have shown that quercetin blocks a number of substances involved in allergic reactions. In one study, animals given quercetin had fewer compounds, including substance P (SP), calcitonin gene-related peptide (CGRP), and nerve growth factor (NGF), involved in the allergic response.[5]

Histamine is another common allergy-causing substance that's released from mast cells (you've likely heard of antihistamine, an over-the-counter treatment for allergies). Quercetin also seems to be effective at blocking histamine.[6]

Mix up a salad using one or more of these types of greens to create a beautiful blend. For an additional super source of quercetin, add some chopped onions (they're rich in the allergy-fighter category, too), and drizzle on EVOO for added oomph. You can toss a cup of loosely packed kale or Swiss chard into a smoothie with your favorite fruits. Add a handful of greens into warm soups or your morning omelets. Or sauté the lettuce greens in extra-virgin olive oil, a dash of turmeric, and salt and ground black pepper for a nutrient-packed side dish to serve alongside fish, chicken, or another entrée.

Try this spicy and tasty spin on my favorite Kale Chips. To make, simply tear kale into small pieces, spread out in a single layer on a baking sheet, mist the tops with extra-virgin olive oil, and sprinkle with salt and 1 teaspoon turmeric powder for a triple dose of allergy-fighting power. Bake in a 400°F oven for about 8 minutes to 10 minutes until crispy and brown around the edges. It's an incredibly addictive snack—and one for which you don't have to feel guilty going back for seconds.

4. Asparagus

It's time to talk about the stalk: asparagus. The vegetable that's notorious for leaving a strong scent in restrooms (that not all people are able to smell, by the way) is loaded with allergy-fighting quercetin. As mentioned earlier, quercetin helps combat seasonal allergy symptoms by suppressing the release of multiple allergy-causing compounds—including histamine—in lab and animal studies.

Not a fan of asparagus? No worries, I'm about to convert you. There are a lot of great ways to incorporate the green into other delicious foods. Asparagus pairs perfectly with eggs. Chop up asparagus (feel free to include the leaves), sauté in olive oil, and add to your morning omelet. Or include asparagus in your favorite frittata or quiche recipe.

You can also add chopped asparagus to a wrap or salad for a satisfying crunch. Or try this simple, tasty side dish: Lightly sauté asparagus with extra-virgin olive oil and garlic, and then season with salt, pepper, and freshly grated Parmesan. You can finish it off with a little bit of lemon juice, if you'd like.

Another easy suggestion: Add cooked (whole or chopped) asparagus into pasta dishes. It's an easy way to pump up the nutrition of your penne and possibly stifle some sneezes, too. You can even whip up your own cream of asparagus soup.

Thin spears tend to be a little more tender and sweet, while thicker ones are a bit meatier and more strongly flavored. To preserve freshness, keep them rubber-banded and trim an inch from the bottom once you get them home. You can keep them in a glass cup or jar with about an inch or so of water at the bottom, loosely covered with a plastic bag, for about a week. Although you can buy them year-round, they are best in the spring.

5. Capers

Capers may be little, but they deliver *big* on taste. What exactly are these tiny flavor pods? They're unripened edible flower buds that have been staples in Mediterranean cuisine, particularly Italian and Spanish dishes, for centuries. They're used in Spanish tapas and Italian piccata and puttanesca dishes.

After capers are harvested—by hand!—they're dried in the sun, and then pickled in a liquid or sometimes salted. They have a vinegary, olive-y, earthy flavor and can be used to top chicken and fish dishes; tossed into soups, stews, and sauces; or added to salad dressings (paired with lemon, which works as a delicious complement). They're an ingredient in tartar sauce and often served alongside lox and cream cheese. They range in size from small (about the size of a pea) to large (the size of an olive), with the smaller varieties costing more.

Capers make an appearance in this chapter because they're among the richest sources of quercetin. You'll score 14.8 mg per tablespoon, or about 5 mg per teaspoon. As a refresher, quercetin is a flavonoid that has been shown to help block the release of allergy-causing compounds—including histamine. Quercetin, like many other antioxidants, does not have a set daily requirement, so it's impossible to quantify how impressive these numbers are. But compared to other food sources, capers rank top of the top.

Use capers to punch up cold pasta salad dishes. Serve them with grilled or baked salmon and finish the dish off with a squeeze of lemon. However you incorporate capers into your meals and snacks, it's a good idea to rinse, or even soak them before using, as they're often high in sodium and can taste super salty, too. If you have high blood pressure or are worried about bloating, you may want to use them sparingly.

Honey-Turmeric Chicken with Roasted Asparagus

MAKES 4 SERVINGS

⅓ cup whole-grain flour or almond flour

1 tablespoon ground turmeric

1½ pounds boneless, skinless chicken breasts, cut into large pieces

1 tablespoon extra-virgin olive oil

1 pound asparagus

2 garlic cloves, minced

3 tablespoons honey

¼ cup capers, drained and rinsed

½ to 1 teaspoon kosher salt

¼ teaspoon ground black pepper

2 to 4 tablespoons white wine or reduced-sodium chicken broth

Preheat the oven to 400°F.

Combine the flour and turmeric in a bowl. Place the chicken into the mixture and coat on all sides. Set aside. Discard extra flour.

Heat oil in a large oven-safe skillet. Transfer the chicken to the skillet and pan-fry for about 2 minutes on each side.

Add the asparagus and garlic to the skillet with the chicken. Lightly drizzle the honey over the chicken and asparagus. Sprinkle the capers on top. (It may seem like the skillet is overflowing, but the asparagus will reduce in size.)

Place the skillet in the oven and allow to cook for about 20 minutes, turning the chicken and asparagus at the 10-minute mark.

Remove the skillet from the oven. Add 2 tablespoons white wine or chicken broth and let it sizzle to soak up the flavors on the bottom of the skillet. When you are transferring to serving plates, be sure to deglaze the bottom of the skillet to elevate the taste.

Sprinkle the entire dish with salt and ground black pepper before serving.

NUTRITIONAL INFORMATION *Per serving*
330 calories • 42 g protein • 8 g total fat (1.5 g saturated fat, 6.5 g unsaturated fat) • 125 mg cholesterol • 22 g carbs • 3 g fiber • 12 g total sugar (4 g natural sugar, 8 g added sugar) • 530 mg sodium

Asparagus, Swiss Chard, and Feta Frittata

MAKES 8 SLICES

6 whole eggs
6 egg whites
½ cup light sour cream
¼ teaspoon kosher salt
1 teaspoon cumin
½ teaspoon ground black pepper
½ teaspoon paprika
1 ½ tablespoons fresh thyme leaves
   (or 1 ½ teaspoons dried thyme)
1 to 2 tablespoons extra-virgin olive oil
1 garlic clove, minced

1 yellow onion, diced
3 cups sliced asparagus, cut into
   1-inch pieces (about 1 bunch)
½ bunch Swiss chard or kale, about
   4 cups, stems removed, roughly
   chopped
¼ to ½ cup (or 1 to 2 ounces)
   crumbled feta cheese
   (may substitute with any
   preferred cheese)

Preheat the oven to 350°F. Blend the eggs and egg whites with the sour cream in a large bowl using a whisk or hand mixer. Add the salt, cumin, pepper, paprika, and thyme, and set aside.

Heat the olive oil in a large oven-safe skillet with oil spray and warm over medium heat. Add the garlic and cook for about 30 seconds, until it starts to lightly brown and smells fragrant. Add the onion and asparagus, and sauté about 5 minutes, until the onion starts to brown. Add a drop more oil to the pan and toss in the leafy greens. Continue to sauté, stirring occasionally, until the greens are cooked down, about 5 more minutes. Try to spread out the veggies evenly in the skillet. (It will look like a lot.)

Pour the egg mixture on top of the veggies and make sure everything is nicely dispersed throughout the skillet. Sprinkle the cheese over the top. Transfer the skillet to the oven and bake until the sides are golden brown and the eggs no longer run if a fork is poked through them, about 35 minutes.

NUTRITIONAL INFORMATION *Per slice*
120 calories • 10 g protein • 7 g total fat (2.5 g saturated fat, 4.5 g unsaturated fat) • 115 mg cholesterol • 6 g carbs • 2 g fiber • 2 g total sugar (2 g natural sugar, 0 g added sugar) • 270 mg sodium

Kale Caesar Salad

MAKES 6 SERVINGS

For the salad

1 pound asparagus, chopped into
   2-inch pieces (about 2 cups)

4 cups curly or Tuscan kale leaves,
   ribs removed and torn into bite-size
   pieces*

4 cups chopped romaine lettuce

¼ cup capers, drained and rinsed

For the dressing

½ ripe avocado, mashed

1 clove garlic, minced (or 1/8 teaspoon
   garlic powder)

2 tablespoons fresh lemon juice

2 teaspoons Worcestershire sauce

½ teaspoon Dijon mustard

¼ cup grated Parmesan cheese

¾ teaspoon kosher salt

½ teaspoon freshly ground black
   pepper

1 teaspoon anchovy paste (optional but
   adds a nice umami flavor)

4 tablespoons water

2 tablespoons extra-virgin olive oil

Bring a medium pot of water to a boil and prepare a large bowl of water with ice cubes. Blanch the asparagus by gently placing it into the boiling water for 2 to 3 minutes. Immediately submerge the asparagus in the ice water bath. Drain and set aside.

To prepare the dressing, place all the ingredients in a food processor or powerful blender and mix until throughly combined and smooth.

*See note in tip box about massaging kale leaves before preparing the salad.

Add the kale, romaine, capers, and blanched asparagus to the mixing bowl. Pour on the dressing and toss to combine. Serve immediately. The dressing will keep in the fridge for about a week.

NUTRITIONAL INFORMATION

Per serving of salad with 2 tablespoons dressing: 110 calories • 5 g protein • 8 g total fat (2 g saturated fat, 6 g unsaturated fat) • 5 mg cholesterol • 7 g carbs • 3 g fiber • 3 g total sugar (3 g natural sugar, 0 g added sugar) • 490 mg sodium

MASSAGE MAGIC Kale is a tougher green compared to spinach and other leaves, so it requires a little massaging if you're going to enjoy it raw. To do so, spritz with a bit of fresh lemon juice or extra-virgin olive oil and gently massage the leaves with your hands (almost kneading it like dough) for about 3 to 5 minutes. The leaves will wilt a bit and become a slightly darker green color. Don't skip this step; it makes kale leaves more tender and tasty.

5 FOODS TO
PREVENT
HEADACHES
AND MIGRAINES

Headaches are a significant problem for many people. According to one study in the journal *Headache*, 14 percent of American adults report having suffered through a serious headache or migraine in the past three months. In fact, headache or pain in the head was the fourth leading cause of visits to the emergency room in 2009–2010, and it accounts for nearly 53 percent of all primary care visits.[1]

What's the difference between an everyday "tension" headache and the more ominous-sounding migraine? A tension headache is a dull, aching pain, sometimes accompanied by pressure or tenderness in the temples, forehead, or scalp. It may also be paired with tightness in the neck or shoulders. It can often be relieved with simple lifestyle changes, including drinking more water (aim for at least half your weight in ounces daily), more sleep (a good goal is seven to eight hours a night), and eating regularly (particularly food rich in high-quality carbs, protein, fiber, and healthy fat) so you don't experience blood sugar dips. Over-the-counter meds, like ibuprofen and acetaminophen, can also help ease regular headache pain.

A migraine is more debilitating and complicated than a regular old headache, affecting one in seven people. Symptoms include a throbbing or pulsing pain in the head (usually on one side, but it can spread to both sides). Migraines can be associated with aura, which includes visual manifestations such as seeing spots or flashes of light and loss of peripheral vision. Migraines may also include a sensitivity to light or sound, a pins-and-needles sensation, difficulty speaking, and weakness or numbness in the arms and/or legs. Some people also suffer from lightheadedness, nausea, or vomiting.

Over-the-counter medications may help if taken at the onset of symptoms, but in an ironic twist, they may also *cause* migraines if taken too frequently. For chronic migraine sufferers, doctors may prescribe preventive medications in addition to acute drugs that may be taken once an episode does occur.

The causes of migraines aren't fully understood—possibly because there may very well be thousands of genes responsible. Doctors have multiple theories; they suspect that abnormal brain activity or a hyperexcitable brain due to changes in blood flow, brain chemicals, and/or nerve signals may play a role. Recently, experts have called into question the causal connection between migraine and blood flow, once a commonly held theory. The thinking now is that fluctuations in blood flow are an effect of migraine rather than a cause. Other migraine theories have recently emerged and I'm curious to see how the science develops.

One thing virtually all experts agree on is that there's a genetic component—if one or both of your parents suffers migraines, you will be more likely to suffer as well. And women are two to three times more likely than men to be struck. But even though you may be predisposed, you still need to be exposed to a trigger, so figuring out your personal triggers and avoiding them when possible is key. Some triggers are obviously out of your control (weather changes, hormonal fluctuations, external stress); however, you can control others (diet, sleep, hydration, and the amount of time spent staring at your computer).

When it comes to diet, some of the more common food triggers include wine, chocolate, processed meats, aged cheese, fermented soy, cold foods like ice cream, and coffee. Start a food journal to help narrow down any personal culprits, and then do your best to avoid them. At the same time, give the following five foods a shot since they contain beneficial nutrients that may help prevent both tension headaches and migraines.

Note that in some rare cases, certain people may find these foods to be a trigger. If you notice a connection between one of these low-risk foods and headaches, obviously avoid it.

1. Pumpkin Seeds

Pumpkin makes a few appearances throughout this book (see page 186 in the blood pressure chapter and page 211 in the boost libido chapter), and now it's time for the seeds to take center stage. What's so special about the seeds? They're packed with magnesium, a mineral that seems to prevent the wave of brain signaling that causes the visual changes associated with aura. Magnesium also seems to block the transmission of pain chemicals in the brain. One study suggests that half of all migraine sufferers may actually be deficient in the mineral.[2] Magnesium seems to work best for people who suffer migraines with aura and for those whose migraines strike around their menstrual cycles.

You'll find about 160 mg of magnesium per ¼ cup of roasted pumpkin seeds, which is about half of what adult women need. (Sunflower seeds are a pretty close second, with about 130 mg per ¼ cup.) The recommended dietary allowance for women ages 19 to 30 is 310 mg; for women 31 and older, it's 320. Men need 400 mg up to age 40, and 420 mg from 31 on.

Pumpkin seeds also chip in protein (nearly 9 g per ¼ cup of kernels out of the shell), healthy fat, and fiber (about 2 g per ¼ cup) to help steady blood sugar, so they do double duty.

Snack on roasted pumpkin seeds in or out of the shell between meals or sprinkle shelled kernels into cottage cheese, cereal, or oatmeal. You can also make your own granola with pumpkin seeds in the mix. They make an excellent addition to tossed salads and sautéed veggies; you can even mix ground pumpkin seeds into vinaigrettes and other salad dressings.

Another idea: Add some pumpkin seeds in with your usual ingredients for burger patties and meatballs (veggie, turkey, or lean beef—anything goes). Or add pumpkin seeds to whole-grain flour for healthy pancakes, muffins, and breads.

2. Beans

Beans are another magnesium megastar. Depending on the variety you choose, you could score anywhere from about 70 mg to about 130 mg per cup. White beans (that includes great northern, cannellini, and navy) are the real winners, with pinto beans not too far behind. Black beans and kidney beans are also good choices. Really, any starchy bean can be a boon for headache prevention because they're such a rich source of magnesium.

Beans are also high in fiber and protein—12 g and 19 g per cup respectively—a dynamic duo that helps keep blood sugar steady and satisfy appetite, two common headache triggers. Plus, you just can't beat the convenience and affordability; canned beans are so simple to add to recipes. Just rinse under cold running water to get rid of the excess sodium, or look for low-sodium or no-salt-added varieties, and then dump them into your recipe and enjoy. Dried beans are an even more affordable option, though they require a little more work because they have to be soaked before using. Take advantage when these go on sale because they have a long shelf life; canned beans last for up to two years, and dried varieties for about a year.

The vegetarian protein source can be used to make a hearty game-day chili or a veggie burger base. I like to use white beans to whip up a delicious hummus instead of chickpeas, which also contain some magnesium but a much smaller amount than white beans. Beans are a perfect addition to salads, tacos, and burritos. Seasoned beans also make an amazing stand-alone side dish and can be incorporated into quinoa or amaranth, along with some spinach for a triple dose of headache-fighting power.

Pureed beans can even be used as a nutrient-rich alternative to butter or oil in baked goods. I sneak a white bean puree into my vanilla cupcakes to boost the nutrition a bit. It's a simple hack: I mix 1 can (15 ounces) of white beans (drained and rinsed) with 1 cup of water in a blender, puree, and combine with 1 box of vanilla cake. (This trick works just as well with a favorite homemade recipe.) Follow the baking instructions on the box or recipe and voilà! Delish baked goodies, for which I promise no one will ever notice the good-for-you swap.

3. Spinach

Spinach is a lean, green magnesium machine with more than 150 mg per 1 cup cooked. (Cup per cup, cooked spinach has about six times more magnesium than fresh simply because it's more condensed—spinach shrinks when it's cooked.) That means if you enjoy 2 cups cooked, you'd basically hit your daily needs in one shot, though men would need a little more to hit their quota.

Spinach offers a two-for-one benefit because it contains riboflavin, also called vitamin B_2. Riboflavin is necessary for the body's production of energy at the cellular level. Some research suggests that people with migraines may have a genetic defect that makes it difficult for their cells to maintain energy reserves, and this lack of basic energy could trigger the debilitating headaches.

While you'll score more magnesium and riboflavin from cooked (boiled, sautéed, or steamed—eater's choice), fresh spinach is great, too, so get your fix any way you prefer. One of my all-time favorite ways to prepare the great green is also one of the simplest—sautéed. I add a little olive oil, salt, pepper, shallots, and garlic. It's a simple but beloved side dish that you can serve with protein-packed chicken or fish.

Of course, fresh spinach is a great base for salads, but you can also toss a handful of baby spinach leaves into a fruit smoothie. Other scrumptious serving suggestions: Make a quick spinach-marinara sauce by wilting a bunch of spinach leaves into a pot of simmering tomato sauce, and then serve over whole-grain pasta or grilled chicken cutlets. Or add some leaves into an omelet or scrambled eggs for a great start to your day.

When it comes to convenience, frozen chopped spinach is a must-have. Try adding it to warm soup (canned or homemade) for a quick hit of nutrition. For a speedy snack or side, nuke a package in the microwave, drain the excess water, mix with cottage cheese and a can of drained, rinsed beans, and sprinkle on some preferred seasonings. Simple and delish!

4. Flaxseed

Flaxseed is a super seed when it comes to fighting headaches. It's a stellar source of the plant-based form of omega-3s, called alpha-linolenic acid, or ALA for short. A tablespoon has about 2 grams. (Chia seeds and walnuts are two other solid plant-based omega-3 options.) Note that flaxseed oil has nearly three times as much as ground flax, but it's also less versatile and significantly higher in calories. If you choose to use the oil, it's best in small amounts specifically for cold-prep recipes, such as salad dressings and even fruit smoothies, because of its low smoke point. Also, flaxseed oil may interact with certain medications, so talk to your doctor before incorporating it into your diet.[3]

Omega-3 fatty acids have been shown to reduce the frequency, duration, and severity of headaches.[4] (For that reason, I also recommend consuming omega-3-rich fish, like salmon and sardines, which contain the other forms of omega-3 fats, EPA and DHA, at least two times per week.) I selected flaxseeds for this chapter because of their versatility, neutral flavor, and the added benefit of magnesium. Ground flaxseeds contain about 30 mg of magnesium per tablespoon, which can help pump up your headache-fighting powers. Also, people who aren't fans of fish can still get a two-for-one benefit seamlessly by sneaking flaxseeds into many other meals and snacks.

Ground flaxseed is easier to digest than whole flaxseeds, which may pass through the body undigested, preventing you from reaping the beneficial nutrients. You can buy ground flax, which makes life easy since it's ready to use. Or purchase the whole seeds and grind them yourself using a coffee grinder, and then add them to meals whenever you can for a nutrient boost. You can store it in an airtight container and refrigerate for a few months.

Try mixing ground flaxseed into oatmeal, cereal, and if you've ruled out dairy as a trigger, cottage cheese. And try combining it with whole-grain flour for pancakes, muffins, and other baked goods. You can also blend a tablespoon into an energizing fruit smoothie or stir it into soups and sauces. For a vegan venture, try using ground flax to replace eggs in just about any recipe that calls for them: Swap each egg for a mixture of 2 tablespoons ground seeds and 2 tablespoons water, and get ready for a surprising discovery. (Chia seeds work just as well.)

5. Amaranth

Amaranth is an ancient grain that has quickly become a modern-day star. That's because it's loaded with health-boosting nutrients, including headache-busting magnesium. It contains about 160 mg per 1 cup cooked. It's also packed with protein—the most of any grain, in fact. It delivers nearly 10 g per 1 cup cooked and almost 6 g of fiber. This combo can help steady your blood sugar level and stabilize your appetite to prevent any blood sugar dips that may trigger a headache. Pretty impressive stats for a simple cereal grain once eaten by the Aztecs. (Oh, and it's also gluten-free for all those who must steer clear.)

Amaranth is easy to make—you can "pop" the grain, similar to corn, in a hot skillet. Or you can boil it like you would rice or quinoa. Amaranth absorbs plenty of water, so you want to use about 3 cups of water per 1 cup of amaranth. It takes about 20 to 25 minutes to cook—amaranth fluffs up and has a light and slightly nutty flavor. It can be used for a variety of dishes, from a simple side with veggies to a yummy fruit porridge (delicious with berries and nuts) to an ingredient in baked goods, like muffins, cookies, and breads. You can even add it to soups. Pretty much anything you can do with rice, you can do with amaranth, though amaranth has more of a porridge-like consistency. You can find it in the health food section in most supermarkets. And FYI: Quinoa is a close second, providing about 120 mg of magnesium, 8 g of protein, and nearly 6 g of fiber per 1 cup cooked. So feel free to swap it in if you prefer the texture and taste.

For an extra perk, add some ginger to your amaranth (or quinoa) side. In one study, ground ginger powder worked as well as a powerful migraine medication in treating the painful headaches and caused fewer side effects.[5] Try this easy and delicious ginger seasoning blend to spice up your recipe: Combine ginger, onion powder, garlic powder, paprika, salt, and red pepper flakes (or ground black pepper if you don't want it spicy).

Overnight Power Porridge

MAKES 1 SERVING

2 tablespoons cooked amaranth (or 2 tablespoons cooked quinoa)*

¼ cup dry oats (traditional or quick cooking)*

½ cup almond milk (or any other preferred milk)

1 teaspoon ground flaxseeds

1 teaspoon chia seeds

½ ripe banana, chopped and mashed

½ to 1 teaspoon ground cinnamon

¼ to ½ cup berries (any type)

1 tablespoon pumpkin seeds

Honey or maple syrup (optional)

Combine the amaranth, oats, milk, flaxseeds, chia seeds, banana, and cinnamon in a bowl. Cover and refrigerate overnight. Prior to serving, top with berries and pumpkin seeds. Feel free to add honey or maple syrup before the other toppings.

You can sub ½ cup of cooked quinoa for both the amaranth and oats for a scrumptious and speedy variation.

NUTRITIONAL INFORMATION *Per serving*
290 calories • 9 g protein • 10 g total fat (1.5 g saturated fat, 8.5 g unsaturated fat) • 10 mg cholesterol • 45 g carbs • 10 g fiber • 12 g total sugar (12 g natural sugar, 0 g added sugar) • 110 mg sodium

Spinach-Bean Dip

MAKES ABOUT 3 CUPS

One 10-ounce package frozen chopped spinach (or fresh baby spinach, chopped)
One 15-ounce can cannellini beans, drained and rinsed
1 teaspoon fresh lemon juice
2 garlic cloves, pressed (or ¼ teaspoon garlic powder)
3 tablespoons extra-virgin olive oil

1 tablespoon ground flaxseeds
¾ teaspoon kosher salt
¼ teaspoon ground black pepper
½ teaspoon onion powder
⅓ cup grated Parmesan cheese
½ teaspoon red pepper flakes (optional)
3 to 4 tablespoons toasted pumpkin seeds

Thaw the spinach in the microwave and allow it to cool for 10 to 15 minutes before squeezing out a majority of the water with paper towels or cheesecloth. Set aside.

Add the beans, lemon juice, garlic, oil, flaxseeds, salt, pepper, and onion powder into the bowl of a food processor or high-powered blender and process until the mixture is thick and creamy.

Spoon the mixture into a bowl and stir in the spinach, Parmesan, and red pepper flakes, if desired. Season with additional salt and pepper to taste. Top with the pumpkin seeds and serve warm or chilled with your favorite veggies. This dip also makes a delicious sandwich spread.

NUTRITIONAL INFORMATION
Per 2-tablespoon serving: 45 calories • 2 g protein • 3 g total fat (0 g saturated fat, 3 g unsaturated fat) • 0 mg cholesterol • 3 g carbs • 1 g fiber • 0 g total sugar • 100 mg sodium

Burrito Bowl

MAKES 6 SERVINGS

1 cup dry amaranth (or quinoa)
One 15-ounce can black beans, drained and rinsed
One 15-ounce can white beans, drained and rinsed
One 15-ounce can corn
4 tablespoons lime juice
1 ½ teaspoons paprika
1 ½ teaspoons chili powder
2 teaspoons ground cumin
½ teaspoon cinnamon

2 teaspoons kosher salt
1 teaspoon ground black pepper
8 to 10 cups baby spinach leaves
1 avocado, sliced
Toasted pumpkin seeds, shell off (optional)
Ground flaxseed (optional)
Salsa (optional)
Sliced lime (optional)
Greek yogurt or light sour cream (optional)

In a large saucepan, prepare the amaranth (or quinoa) according to the package directions. When it's done cooking and the water has been absorbed, add in the beans, corn, lime juice, and seasonings. Remove from over the heat and cover to keep warm.

Coat a separate skillet with oil spray and warm over medium-high heat. Add the spinach and sauté for about 2 minutes or until the desired texture is reached. Season with a dash of cumin, and salt and pepper to taste.

To assemble: Fill each burrito bowl with 1 cup amaranth-bean mixture and a generous portion of sautéed spinach. Then top with a few avocado slices, 1 to 2 tablespoons pumpkin seeds, and 1 to 2 teaspoons ground flaxseeds. Garnish with optional salsa, sliced lime, and Greek yogurt or light sour cream.

NUTRITIONAL INFORMATION *Per bowl*
370 calories • 18 g protein • 13 g total fat (2 g saturated fat, 11 g unsaturated fat) •
0 mg cholesterol • 50 g carbs • 15 g fiber • 3 g total sugar (3 g natural sugar, 0 g added sugar) •
800 mg sodium

TEXTURE TIP While amaranth provides a bit more magnesium than quinoa, both grains are terrific sources and can help fight migraines. The textures are very different, so select the one you prefer for the base of your bowl. Use amaranth for a porridge-like consistency or the same amount of quinoa for a drier consistency that resembles the texture of rice.

5 FOODS TO
ALLEVIATE GAS

Nothing brings on the LOLs like a good old fart joke or a well-placed whoopee cushion. No matter your age, passing gas, breaking wind, or cutting the cheese is as funny now as it was back in sixth grade.

Most people pass gas roughly 13 times a day, according to some estimates. ("Gas" includes belching, or *eructation*, in addition to farting.) Flatulence is one of the most common patient complaints, with up to about a third of Americans suffering. While it's totally natural to pass gas, some people excrete more than others. People with certain conditions, like irritable bowel syndrome (IBS), food sensitivities, reflux, celiac disease, and lactose intolerance, are more likely to suffer from excessive gas.

Lower intestinal gas is caused by unabsorbed dietary compounds that are fermented by bacteria in the colon. Because there are so many different kinds of bacteria, the amount and type of gas produced can vary. Some come with a distinct odor (those flatus contain more sulfur) while others are unscented (those flatus contain less). Upper intestinal gas may be caused by swallowing too much air. Inability to release excess gas can cause excruciating razor-sharp pain in the belly or chest. If this occurs frequently, it may be a sign of an underlying problem, such as a blockage, and that's a definite reason to see your doctor.

Research suggests that a low-FODMAP diet can be helpful for dissipating or preventing gas. And there are a few other things you can do: quit smoking, avoid gum chewing and sugar alcohols (including sorbitol, maltitol, and mannitol, which are actually the *P* in FODMAP), chew your food well and eat slowly, don't eat past being comfortably full, avoid carbonated beverages, and go easy on gas-causing foods (including beans; fried, fatty fare; and cruciferous veggies). Some people are sensitive to high-fiber foods. Others find cooked veggies easier on the gut than raw.

To start feeling better—and to clear the air—add the following gas-busting foods and seasonings to your menu.

1. Probiotics

(Yogurt and Kefir)

Probiotics have been shown to be beneficial for a number of belly-related issues, including constipation and diarrhea. These good bacteria are live microorganisms that, when eaten, help prevent gas attacks by breaking down difficult-to-digest components in certain foods. Yogurt and kefir are the two richest food sources of probiotics. However, these foods are not appropriate for people with lactose intolerance, unless you can find a lactose-free version. And while not considered low-FODMAP, they still offer some serious gas-reducing power.

Although studies on probiotics and gas are somewhat limited, one meta-analysis looking at 10 randomized controlled trials (the gold standard of all studies) showed some encouraging results: All eight probiotics tested for flatulence significantly improved symptoms. Some of these probiotics are found only in supplement form, but some, including *B. breve*, *L. acidophilus*, *L. casei*, *Streptococcus salivarius* ssp, thermophiles, *Lactobacillus bulgaricus*, *B. longum* and *L. plantarum*, are in foods like yogurt and kefir. The probiotic that shows the most promise for helping IBS symptoms is *B. infantis 35624*, but unfortunately, at this point, you cannot find it in any foods—it's available only in pill form. If you don't get immediate results, be patient. One study suggests that it can take about a month to start to see the benefits.[1]

In another study, kefir, which comes from a Turkish word that means "feeling good," proved to be as beneficial as yogurt at reducing flatulence.[2] That's because it has a higher beta-galactosidase activity, meaning the enzyme in kefir was more active at breaking down the lactose in dairy that can cause gas.

Greek yogurt (with "live and active cultures") is delicious as a stand-alone, mixed with fruit or granola, or as a replacement for sour cream. Kefir can be used as a swap for milk or yogurt—I use it for overnight oats and in smoothies. Finally, some cheeses—like aged and soft cheeses (Gouda and Camembert)—may contain probiotics, but it can be tough to tell because the heating process kills the beneficial bacteria, and of those that survive, many will die off during storage. That being said, "probiotic cheese" may eventually be something to look out for.

2. Dill

When it comes to gas prevention, this herb is a pretty big dill.

Dill, also called dill weed, has long been used for digestive issues—it's an ingredient in gripe water, a remedy for colic in infants and gas in children. The whole plant—both the seeds and the leaves—seems to be helpful with flatulence.[3] One study showed that an essential oil made from the herb helped cut gas by 33 percent compared to just 12 percent in the placebo group in women who'd just had a C-section. It also relieved intestinal pain three times more than placebo,[4] as gas can be a side effect of the procedure.

With its distinct fragrance, the feathery herb provides a tangy addition to your favorite recipes. I love to combine ½ cup of plain nonfat Greek yogurt (another gas-busting food as long as you're not lactose intolerant) with 1 tablespoon of lemon juice and ½ teaspoon of chopped dill in a bowl and serve it as a delish dip with easy-to-digest veggies like carrots and celery. It's also wonderful mixed into egg, tuna, or potato salad, and it's a fabulous flavoring for homemade vinaigrette.

Note that dill, a member of the parsley family, is best used fresh because the aromatic herb quickly loses flavor when it's dried. It pairs perfectly with salmon, but it's also great for seasoning chicken, soups, and sauces, too. It is tasty in fresh summer salads along with crisp cucumbers and sweet tomatoes with a splash of olive oil, lemon juice, salt, and pepper. You may know it best as a flavoring for pickles, but you can also use the leaves to prepare a cup of tea— just remember to sip slowly.

Have a lot of leftover fresh dill? Try this quick trick so you don't have to toss wilted herbs: Chop and divide the dill among the sections in an ice cube tray. Pour in broth or water or drizzle on some olive oil and freeze. Once frozen, pop the cubes out into a resealable bag and store them in the freezer for future use. You can melt them in a pan for sauces, soups, and casseroles, or add into dips for a delicious flavor infusion.

3. Cumin

Cumin, another member of the parsley family, secures its spot in this chapter. The herb, which can be found in whole form as a seed or ground, has been used since ancient times as a digestive aid and has been suggested to help decrease gas and relieve other symptoms of IBS.[5] It is a common ingredient in Mexican and Indian cuisines, often used in chili and featured in curry powder.

With its dash of heat and strong, warm aroma, it adds an earthy flavor to dishes. I often make roasted cumin carrots by coating carrots with olive oil (or misting with oil spray), seasoning them with cumin, thyme, turmeric, paprika, salt, and pepper and baking them at 425°F for about 20 to 30 minutes (or until soft). It's a side dish that disappears in a flash shortly after I place it on the table in my house.

You can also whip up my easy, incredibly tasty DIY taco seasoning blend. Mix together 1 tablespoon chili powder; ¼ teaspoon each garlic powder, dehydrated onion flakes, red pepper flakes, and dried oregano; ½ teaspoon paprika; 1 ½ teaspoons ground cumin; 1 teaspoon kosher salt; and 1 teaspoon ground black pepper. This simple recipe makes plenty, so you'll be ready to flavor up countless meals.

You can also create deliciously seasoned nuts using ground cumin. Here's one of my favorite creations: Combine 1 egg white, 2 teaspoons Old Bay seasoning, 2 teaspoons sweet or hot paprika, ½ teaspoon cayenne pepper (I tend to like things spicy-hot, so this is optional), 2 teaspoons ground cumin, 1 teaspoon salt, and 1 tablespoon sugar in a large bowl. Add nuts (low-FODMAP varieties, like walnuts and peanuts) and mix to coat. Place on a baking sheet misted with oil spray and bake for about 15 minutes at 375°F, stirring occasionally, until fragrant. Allow the nuts to cool and enjoy. Or if you're looking to whip up something easier, you can mist nuts with oil spray, sprinkle on cumin and other seasonings of your choice (salt, pepper, chili powder, and more), and bake in the oven at 375°F until they're warm and toasty. Feel free to experiment and adjust seasonings to your liking. You can't go wrong; they're finger-licking good.

4. Peppermint Oil

Peppermint is a powerhouse plant. It makes another appearance here for its ability to tame gas, making it a three-time winner (read how it can help you beat the bloat, page 42; and more generally, how "mint" can freshen breath, page 200).

It has been used for centuries as a digestive aid, and peppermint oil, specifically, has been particularly beneficial for belly issues. Peppermint is classified as an antispasmodic, which means it prevents the gastrointestinal tract from involuntarily contracting. Peppermint may help with IBS symptoms (one of which is gas).[6] Enteric-coated peppermint oil is the most studied and recommended (note that simply swallowing peppermint oil can be dangerous). The active ingredient, menthol, has been shown to have carminative, or antiflatulent, effects.

One of the best ways to get your fix is with a nice, soothing cup of warm peppermint tea. You can also whip up a flavorful peppermint hot cocoa (use a dairy-free milk alternative if you react negatively to milk). A refreshing glass of peppermint water can help tame tummy troubles and decrease gas too; simply add a few mint leaves in a pitcher filled with water and chill in the fridge. You can make a refreshing sip by combining flat water with mint leaves, along with other fruits, such as strawberries or cucumbers, or even a handful of blueberries or raspberries. You can also add peppermint leaves or a few drops of peppermint extract or oil to foods (be conservative; a little goes a long way).

Pass on the peppermint gum, though, as swallowing excess air can contribute to gas. Plus, many brands contain sugar alcohols, which can worsen gas. Peppermint candies are not an effective fix either as they're typically mostly sugar with very little actual peppermint.

5. Coriander

You may know this one better as cilantro, the herb you love to hate . . . or love, depending on whether or not you have the gene that makes you register the taste as soapy. I'm actually going to focus on the seeds of the plant—coriander seeds—which should not be used interchangeably with the leaves because the flavor is quite different. The dried seeds of the cilantro plant (also called Chinese parsley) come whole or ground and have a warmer, subtler citrusy flavor.

Coriander has been used in Indian traditional medicine as a digestive aid for centuries because of its carminative properties. A recent study even tested a natural treatment for gas, which incorporated an extract from the herb (in addition to mint and lemon balm extracts), and found it helped to relieve gastrointestinal symptoms in people with IBS better than a placebo.[7]

Because of its mild flavor, coriander is often combined with other spices. (An easy trick: It typically works well with other seasonings that start with the letter c.) Coriander is usually paired with its partner in crime, cumin, another gas-preventing spice. It tastes delish with cinnamon, chili powder, and curry, too. In fact, it's a standard ingredient in most curry dishes and curry seasoning blends.

You can add coriander to a spice rub to season chicken or fish. Or you can add it to stir-fries, throw some into a smoothie, or mix it into guacamole. Another interesting idea: Liberally coat a skillet with oil spray and toast a handful of the whole seeds over medium heat. Season with salt and pepper (and cumin, if desired), mixing every few seconds, until fragrant. Sprinkle on top of cottage cheese (if you don't have issues with dairy) for a quick and satisfying snack or mix into salsa or even smoothies . . . without the side of gas!

Note that ground coriander seeds tend to lose their freshness quickly, while whole seeds maintain their flavor for much longer (about a year) when they're stored properly in a cool, dry place. I suggest buying them whole, and you can always grind your own seeds as needed to make sure you're getting the tastiest and most potent spice.

Dill French Fries with Lemony Dip

MAKES 4 SERVINGS AND ½ CUP DIP

For the fries

2 large russet potatoes, cut into thin french-fry-like strips

2 tablespoons olive or canola oil

2 tablespoons chopped fresh dill

½ teaspoon kosher salt

¼ teaspoon ground black pepper

For the Lemony Dip

½ cup nonfat or low-fat plain Greek yogurt*

1 tablespoon fresh lemon juice

1 to 2 tablespoons chopped fresh dill

2 teaspoons ground coriander

¼ teaspoon kosher salt

Preheat the oven to 425°F and mist a baking sheet with oil spray. Set aside.

Toss the cut potatoes with the oil, dill, salt, and pepper in a large bowl and mix until the fries are evenly coated. Spread the fries out in a single layer on the prepared baking sheet and roast in the oven for 20 minutes. Remove from the oven and flip the fries as best you can (tongs make it easier). Then place the fries back in the oven and roast for 5 more minutes. Season with additional salt, pepper, and dill to taste.

While the potatoes are roasting, prepare the lemon-dill yogurt dipping sauce. Combine all the dip ingredients in a small bowl and serve alongside the oven-roasted dill french fries.

* If you're lactose-intolerant, skip the dip or swap in lactose-free yogurt.

NUTRITIONAL INFORMATION

Per serving of fries: 120 calories • 2 g protein • 7 g total fat (1 g saturated fat, 6 g unsaturated fat) • 0 mg cholesterol • 13 g carbs • 1 g fiber • 1 g total sugar (1 g natural sugar, 0 g added sugar) • 240 mg sodium

Per 1 tablespoon dip: 10 calories • 1 g protein • 0 g fat • 0 mg cholesterol • 1 g carbs • 0 g fiber • 0 g total sugar • 65 mg sodium

Greek Chicken Kebabs

MAKES 4 SERVINGS

For the kebabs

½ cup roughly chopped fresh parsley
½ cup roughly chopped fresh cilantro
1 tablespoon fresh dill
1 tablespoon ground cumin
1 tablespoon ground coriander seeds
3 to 4 tablespoons extra-virgin olive oil

1 ¼ teaspoons kosher salt, divided
¼ teaspoon ground black pepper
1 ½ pounds boneless, skinless chicken
   breasts, cut into bite-size pieces
Metal or wooden skewers

For the Creamy Herb Sauce

1 cup nonfat plain Greek yogurt
   (for a thicker sauce) or low-fat kefir
   (for a thinner sauce)
½ cup fresh parsley leaves
1 tablespoon fresh dill

1 teaspoon ground coriander
2 teaspoons ground cumin
¼ teaspoon kosher salt
¼ teaspoon ground black pepper

If you're lactose intolerant, swap in a lactose-free kefir or yogurt.

Combine the parsley, cilantro, dill, cumin, coriander, oil, salt, and pepper in a food processor. Add the mixture to a ziptop bag or bowl with the chicken and mix thoroughly. Allow to marinate in the refrigerator for at least 1 hour. If using wooden skewers, make sure to soak in water for at least 30 minutes prior to using.

When ready to cook, preheat the oven to 400°F and line a rimmed baking sheet with parchment paper. Place the chicken pieces on the skewers and discard any leftover marinade. Roast the chicken skewers for 20 minutes, turning halfway through at the 10-minute mark. Remove from the oven and sprinkle the remaining ¾ teaspoon salt over the tops, flipping the kebabs to season both sides.

To make the Creamy Herb Sauce, place all the ingredients in a food processor or blender and puree until smooth and creamy. Season with additional herbs to taste and serve alongside kebabs for delicious dipping.

NUTRITIONAL INFORMATION

Per serving: 320 calories • 39 g protein • 16 g total fat (2 g saturated fat, 14 g unsaturated fat) • 125 mg cholesterol • 2 g carbs • 1 g fiber • 0 g total sugar • 680 mg sodium

Per 2 tablespoons sauce: 20 calories • 3 g protein • 0 g total fat • 0 mg cholesterol • 2 g carbs • 0 g fiber • 1 g total sugar (1 g natural sugar, 0 g added sugar) • 75 mg sodium

Comfort Tea

MAKES 1 CUP

1 peppermint tea bag
¹⁄₂ teaspoon whole coriander seeds
¹⁄₂ teaspoon whole cumin seeds

Boil 1 to 1 ¹⁄₂ cups water in a small pot.

Add the peppermint tea bag, coriander, and cumin. Steep for about 5 minutes in the boiling water.

Remove the tea bag and strain the coriander and cumin seeds from the pan. Pour this soothing comfort tea into a mug and enjoy.

NUTRITIONAL INFORMATION
0 calories • 0 g protein • 0 g fat • 0 mg cholesterol • 0 g carbs • 0 g fiber • 0 g total sugar • 10 mg sodium

5 FOODS TO ENHANCE DULL, DRY HAIR

Salon-perfect hair: luxuriously shiny and full of body. If only we could all have locks like that. In real life, most of us suffer with hair that's thinning, limp, or brittle.

Fortunately, hair is one of the fastest-growing tissues in the body—it grows about six inches per year (about a half inch per month). It's completely natural to lose about 100 hairs per day. But losing more than that for longer than a few weeks could be an indication that something is wrong.

Thyroid problems, stress, hormonal shifts, heredity, certain medications (including blood thinners and antidepressants), and menopause can all cause hair loss. So can nutritional deficiencies. In fact, when you're missing the mark on a particular nutrient, early signs will often appear on your scalp. Crash diets can lead to hair loss because you're not getting enough calories or nutrients.

Treat your tresses right. For instance, semipermanent dye is less damaging than permanent. Avoid heat as much as possible—air dry or blot dry when you can. Don't keep your hair in tight ponytails or buns, and don't wash your hair every day. Also, feed your hair from the inside out, particularly with nutrient-rich foods containing protein and iron. Protein gets broken down by the body into amino acids, which are then used to make keratin, the compound hair shafts are made of. It's your number-one nutrient when it comes to lustrous hair, and each day you should aim to eat at least half your body weight in grams.

Iron is key for producing hemoglobin, a protein in red blood cells that gives them their color and carries oxygen. Anemia (a blood disorder in which there are too few red blood cells, often caused by iron deficiency) can lead to hair loss.

There are so many great iron-rich protein sources—including lean beef, pork, poultry, fish, seafood, and eggs. Try to prioritize plant-based, iron-rich protein picks—lentils, beans, and soy (like tofu and soybeans)—which offer additional health perks to both you and the environment. The good news: The following star foods can make the difference between a dull, drab 'do and a vibrant one.

1. Mollusks/Shellfish

(Clams, Mussels, and Oysters)

Mollusks are easy to enjoy and are rich in iron and protein, two nutrients essential for hair health. Depending on the type of oysters cooked, you'll score between 6 and 8 mg of iron per 3 ounces (without the shell) and anywhere from 6 to 16 grams of protein. The same amount of mussels (again, no shell) delivers nearly 6 mg of iron and more than 20 grams of protein. Clams offer a range of 3 to 12 mg iron and anywhere from 12 to 22 g of protein per 3 ounces without the shell.

Prep is easy with a few simple rules. Store shellfish covered with a damp cloth in the fridge for a day or two—no more—and not in plastic, where they won't be able to breathe. When ready to cook, toss any with broken, damaged shells. Clam and mussel shells should be slightly open and close when you tap them. If they're closed, fail to shut when tapped, or float in the water, they're dead—get rid of these. Oysters should be closed firmly and smell fresh, without a fishy odor.

Clean using a stiff brush or scrubber and cool, running water. Remove any beards (the tough strings or bristles used to attach to rocks or other places) or barnacles (the small shellfish that attach themselves to other surfaces or creatures). For stubborn grit, soak in saltwater for at least an hour and up to overnight in the fridge. If you buy them pre-cleaned, rinse them well with cold water in a colander.

You can steam mussels and clams, using just enough liquid to fill the bottom of the pot. When the liquid boils, add the shellfish and cover. Cook until the shells just pop open—anywhere from 3 to 10 minutes. Spoon the cooking liquid over the shellfish, and get rid of any that don't open. You can also bake or grill shellfish—it's just as delish.

Most recipes call for oysters to be shucked. Insert a special shucking knife at the hinge, with the round side of the oyster down on the counter or table, holding the other end with a towel. Gently and slowly rock the knife back and forth to wedge it in, until you can pop open the oyster. Once the knife is in, you can circle it around the entire shell and pop off the top, preserving all the liquid inside. Then serve the oyster raw, with lemon and some Tabasco sauce.

2. Beans and Lentils

All beans are a good source of protein with anywhere from 10 to 17 grams per cooked cup; they're also a terrific source of iron (providing around 10 percent of the recommended daily allowance per cup). But cannellini (white kidney) beans are particularly rich in iron—delivering almost 6 mg of plant-based iron, about 15 percent. And don't forget about lentils! They offer similar amounts of iron and about 18 grams of protein per cooked cup on average.

Beans are a stellar budget-friendly pick. When buying canned, I look for low-sodium varieties, but when I'm unable to find them, I rinse them well in a colander under cool, running water. This helps get rid of a surprisingly large amount of salt. Dried beans need to soak in cold water to cut cooking time and make them easier to eat. You can skip this soaking step with dried lentils and head straight to boiling: Use about 3 cups of water or broth for every cup of dry lentils. It takes about 15 to 20 minutes to cook whole lentils, and all colored varieties offer similar perks.

White beans and lentils both work well as a replacement for chickpeas in hummus (check out my lentil hummus on page 84). You can also use white beans as a secret ingredient in baked goods like cake mixes or blondies (puree a drained can in a blender with 1 cup of water and add it into your batter). And you can use black beans in the same way for chocolate cakes and brownies. I like to add a couple cups of cooked beans to simmering soups, using an immersion blender to puree the soup for a creamy, indulgent (and vegan) feel. Lentils work great as a replacement for ground meat. Or you may decide to go 50-50 with ground meat and lentils.

You can also keep it simple by adding beans or lentils to stews, salads, or even scrambled eggs and frittatas. Beans are great to add to dips, either whole or mashed up, as they make a tasty base with flavorful seasonings.

And here's one of my quick vegan entrées: In a large skillet heated with olive oil, sauté a diced yellow onion, diced carrot, and diced red bell pepper for about 6 minutes until they're soft and lightly brown. Add 1 can of drained beans or a couple cups of cooked lentils, stir, and continue cooking for 1 to 2 minutes, until everything is warmed. Season with salt, ground black pepper, a few teaspoons of fresh lemon juice, and anything else you'd like to flavor it up with (Italian seasoning, garlic, thyme, sage, rosemary, taco seasoning blend).

3. Bell Peppers

Saved by the bell . . . pepper, that is. The versatile veggie is a super source of vitamin C, which research suggests is needed to form a healthy hair shaft.[1] Vitamin C is used to create collagen, a structural fiber that helps our bodies— literally!—hold everything together. Hair follicles, blood vessels, and skin all require collagen to stay healthy for optimal growth. Even minor vitamin C deficiencies can lead to dry, splitting hair that breaks easily. Vitamin C also helps to increase the absorption of plant-based iron found in leafy greens, beans, and nuts, and I've already mentioned that not getting enough iron has been associated with hair loss.

Here's a little-known fact: While oranges are a terrific source of vitamin C, one bell pepper has twice as much vitamin C. A large green pepper delivers 130 mg. A large red pepper packs more than 200 mg. And yellow offers up the most at about 300 mg. It's like a traffic light of vitamin C. The multicolored peppers all come from the same plant: Red, yellow, and orange peppers are simply green peppers that have been allowed to ripen longer. Red have fully matured whereas green have been picked earliest. Yellow and orange are smack-dab in the middle.

Men need 90 mg of vitamin C each day; women need 75 mg (pregnant and nursing moms need a little more). Eat a pepper a day, and you've more than covered your daily requirement.

In my house, we love munching on crunchy, raw bell pepper strips (red, yellow, and orange are sweet like candy—green tends to be a little less so). They're a regular addition to salads, pasta dishes, frittatas, and stir-fries at dinnertime. For a quick snack, try wrapping turkey breast slices around pepper sticks. Dip them in mustard or hot sauce, and you've got a triple dose of hair help—iron, protein, and vitamin C.

4. Guava

Guava is one the richest fruit sources of vitamin C; one guava packs 125 mg of the immune-boosting vitamin (which earned it a spot in the colds and flu chapter; page 66). As I mentioned earlier, vitamin C helps produce collagen and increases the body's absorption of plant-based iron, a mineral that's needed to produce hemoglobin, which carries oxygen throughout the body and helps promote growth of cells and tissues, including hair.

Look for guavas that are a yellowish-green color; that's an indication that the fruit is ripe—it may even have a hint of pink. Avoid any fruit with blemishes, bruises, or brown spots. It should be soft to the touch and have a sweet fragrance without having to put it too close to your nose. You can look for regular or mini-size fruit—both are scrumptious.

You can eat the entire guava as is—the rind is edible as are the hard seeds in the center, although some people like to scoop out and discard the center. You can also slice it like you would an apple. It has a similar consistency to a pear with an almost citrus-like taste. You can add chunks to a smoothie or use it to make ice pops, mixed with other refreshing tropical fruit. Toss it with other fruit options to make a tasty fruit salad or use it to make a yummy jam, chutney, marmalade, or sauce. You can also use the pureed flesh for sweet dessert dishes. Another option: guava juice or nectar, but use these beverages sparingly. I'd recommend mixing them with water or seltzer to keep calories and sugar in check. And as always, check labels to make sure you choose a product that is free of suspect ingredients like artificial dyes and sweeteners.

5. Dates

Silicon, a trace element that can be found in a variety of foods, doesn't have a daily requirement. Yet research suggests it plays a role in healthy connective tissue, including hair and nails (see page 237).[2] In fact, quite a few animal studies have shown that the highest levels of silicon are found in bone and connective tissue, such as hair, and it's thought to be similar in humans, too.[3]

Dates are a good source of this mineral. Three pitted dried dates contain about 7.5 mg. (Interestingly, beer also delivers a good amount.)

Another score for dates: These sweet and satisfying gems provide a bit of iron. One pitted medjool date contains about .25 mg. Enjoy four and you'd get just about 1 mg—a decent amount for a plant-based source. Iron, as I've mentioned, is another important nutrient for hair health.

You can enjoy dates plain or get a little more creative. You can easily remove the pit and stuff it with a nut (try an almond, walnut, or cashew) or peanut butter or almond butter for a tasty snack. Or try tossing pitted dates into smoothies, parfaits, salads, oatmeal, and sandwiches to sweeten them up naturally. Pureed dates can also be made into a paste or syrup and used as a substitute for sugar in baking recipes, like brownies and cookies. You can also incorporate dates into entrées that feature chicken or pork, or side dishes with veggies such as brussels sprouts, squash, or lentils.

Like any date—it's good to keep your options open. Deglet Noor dates tend to keep a little longer than other kinds and are great for a variety of uses. They're the most common in the United States and the ones I use most often for baking. Halawi are smaller and may appear on cheese platters. They are thick with a sweet, caramel flavor. The larger medjool dates are semisoft and sweet and work really well in just about any dish, including smoothies. Thoory are harder (they have firm, dry skin and chewy flesh) and are good for snacking.

Blender Cupcakes with Date-Guava Frosting

MAKES 18 TO 20 CUPCAKES AND 1 CUP FROSTING

Blender Cupcakes

One 15-ounce can cannellini beans, drained and rinsed

One 16-ounce box angel-food cake mix

1 cup pitted dates, chopped (about 20 small or 10 large)

1 cup chopped nuts (optional)

Date-Guava Frosting

½ cup pitted dates (about 10 small or 5 large)

½ cup canned cannellini beans, drained and rinsed

¼ cup guava nectar or juice*

5 medium strawberries

2 tablespoons chia seeds

*If you can't find guava nectar or juice, 100 percent orange and pineapple juices can be used as a substitute.

For the cupcakes: Preheat the oven to 350°F. Prep a standard muffin tin with paper liners or mist with oil spray. Set aside. Puree the beans and 1 cup of water in a blender. Add the cake mix and dates to the blender and combine until smooth. Stir in the nuts by hand, if using. Pour the batter into the prepared muffin tins about three-quarters of the way high and bake for about 18 to 24 minutes or until an inserted toothpick comes out clean. *Note: Cook immediately or the angel food cake will deflate, and you'll wind up with flattened (albeit delicious!) cupcakes.*

For the frosting: Add the dates, beans, nectar, berries, and ¼ cup water to a blender and puree until smooth. Stir in the chia seeds and refrigerate for at least 30 minutes. (Chia seeds act as a gel to firm mixture into a frosting-like spread.) Top each cupcake with 1 tablespoon frosting.

NUTRITIONAL INFORMATION

Per standard plain cupcake: 120 calories • 3 g protein • 0 g total fat • 0 mg cholesterol • 28 g carbs • 2 g fiber • 17 g sugar (5 g natural sugar, 12 g added sugar) • 160 mg sodium

Per 1 tablespoon spread: 25 calories • 1 g protein • 0.5 g total fat (0 g saturated fat, 0.5 g unsaturated fat) • 0 mg cholesterol • 5 g carbs • 1 g fiber • 3 g total sugar (3 g natural sugar, 0 g added sugar) • 5 mg sodium

HAIR'S A SWEET TIP Enjoy the Guava-Date Frosting on whole-grain toast as a spread, or mix it into plain yogurt, oatmeal, or ricotta or cottage cheese to add delicious flavor and a dose of hair-helping nutrients.

Mussel Stew

MAKES 4 SERVINGS

2 pounds mussels, scrubbed
½ cup dry white wine (such as chardonnay, pinot grigio, or sauvignon blanc)
2 tablespoons extra-virgin olive oil
2 garlic cloves, minced
1 bell pepper (red, yellow, or orange), diced

One 15-ounce can diced tomatoes
Two 15-ounce cans cannellini beans, drained and rinsed
¼ teaspoon crushed red pepper
½ teaspoon kosher salt
¼ teaspoon ground black pepper
¼ cup fresh chopped parsley
¼ cup fresh chopped basil

Place the mussels and white wine in a large pan over high heat. Cook, stirring frequently, until all the mussels have opened. (The mussels will start to open around 1 minute; all should be open at about 3 minutes.) Remove from heat and set aside.

When the mussels are cool enough to handle, remove and discard the shells while preserving the flesh and the liquid they were cooked in.

Warm the oil in a large sauté pan or saucepan over medium heat and add the garlic. Cook until fragrant, about 1 to 2 minutes.

Add the bell pepper and cook for about 5 minutes, or until soft. Add the tomatoes and cook on low for about 10 minutes.

Finally, stir in the beans and simmer for about 10 more minutes.

Add the cooked mussels, mussel liquid, crushed red pepper, and salt and pepper. Stir to combine.

Add the fresh parsley and basil and serve immediately.

NUTRITIONAL INFORMATION *Per serving*
480 calories • 38 g protein • 14 g total fat (2 g saturated fat, 12 g unsaturated fat) • 65 mg cholesterol • 44 g carbs • 10 g fiber • 6 g total sugar (6 g natural sugar, 0 g added sugar) • 900 mg sodium

Pizza Peppers

MAKES 4 SERVINGS

1 pound ground turkey
  (93 percent lean)
1 tablespoon Italian seasoning
1 teaspoon crushed red pepper
  (optional)
1 ½ cups marinara sauce, divided
One 15-ounce can black beans, drained
  and rinsed
4 bell peppers, sliced in half from top
  to bottom, and deseeded

½ cup shredded part-skim
  mozzarella cheese
¼ cup grated fresh Parmesan cheese
¼ cup cherry tomatoes, sliced in rings
  like mini pepperonis
½ cup red onion, diced
Preferred seasonings (garlic, oregano,
  red pepper flakes, etc.)
Chopped fresh basil for garnish

Preheat the oven to 350°F. Line a baking sheet with parchment paper.

Liberally coat a large skillet with oil spray and warm over medium heat. Cook the turkey with the Italian seasoning and crushed red pepper, if using, in the skillet for about 4 minutes, or until the turkey is no longer pink, breaking it up into small pieces with a wooden spoon or spatula. Drain off the fat; then add 1 cup marinara and cook for an additional minute. Add the beans and cook until everything is warm, about 1 to 2 more minutes.

Place the bell peppers on the prepared baking sheet and fill each with an equal amount of the meat-sauce mixture. Place the stuffed peppers in the oven and cook for 25 minutes.

Remove the peppers from the oven and top each with 1 tablespoon of the remaining sauce. Sprinkle the mozzarella, Parmesan, sliced tomatoes, and onions evenly over the tops of each pepper.

Place the pepper pizzas in the oven for an additional 10 minutes or until the cheese is melty and bubbly. Garnish with the preferred optional seasonings and fresh basil. Allow to set 5 minutes before serving. Enjoy.

NUTRITIONAL INFORMATION *Per 2 pizza peppers*
370 calories • 37 g protein • 13 g total fat (3.5 g saturated fat, 9.5 g unsaturated fat) •
80 mg cholesterol • 29 g carbs • 8 g fiber • 9 g total sugar (9 g natural sugar, 0 g added sugar) •
340 mg sodium

5 FOODS TO
FIGHT PMS

PMS—three little letters that combine to form what most women consider to be a four-letter word. For a few days every month, countless women are forced to deal with tender, swollen breasts; acne (well beyond those awkward puberty years); bloating; powerful food cravings; mood swings; cramps; diarrhea; fatigue; headaches; back pain; and more. And that's all before the menstrual cycle even begins.

It's hard to quantify exactly how many menstruating women suffer from premenstrual syndrome—the numbers are as high as 90 percent by some estimates.[1] And for many women (up to 8 percent, according to some reports), the symptoms are so bad, it affects their daily life.

PMS is more than a cliché—it's a diagnosable disorder. To qualify as a medical issue, a woman must suffer symptoms five days before her period for at least three menstrual cycles in a row; they must end within four days after her period starts; and the symptoms must interfere with normal activities. There's an even more severe form, called premenstrual dysphoric disorder, or PMDD, which affects a much smaller number of women.

No one knows the exact cause(s) of PMS, but experts suspect hormonal changes can trigger symptoms. Stress can also make symptoms worse. Over-the-counter medications like ibuprofen or acetaminophen can help, as can logging enough shut-eye, staying properly hydrated, practicing stress-relieving techniques like deep breathing, meditation, and yoga, and getting plenty of exercise. Dietary fixes have been shown to help ease symptoms as well. This includes limiting salt and avoiding alcohol.[2] Research also suggests certain key nutrients may be helpful: magnesium, calcium, vitamin E, and vitamin D. With that in mind, I've chosen five foods that are super sources of one or more of these nutrients, in addition to being versatile, accessible, and having mass appeal. Study them and stock them for some tasty relief.

1. Salmon

No surprise here, but salmon have swum their way onto another list in this book (see the minimize belly fat chapter, page 5, and the ease anxiety and stress chapter, page 29). Normally known for their omega-3s, these fish are also among the top sources of vitamin D, which is what makes them a winning pick for PMS.

Research suggests that vitamin D may decrease PMS symptoms. For instance, one study of more than 1,000 women found that those who had the highest intake of vitamin D (through either diet or supplements) had a 40 percent lower chance of experiencing PMS.[3]

In another study, girls and young women who were short on D and took a supplement for four months to increase their levels suffered fewer mood issues (including anxiety, irritability, crying easily, and sadness) compared to those who took a placebo. As a result, they saw an improvement in relationships and quality of life.[4]

Not to mention, people who suffer from depression and other mood disorders get a boost when they pump up their intake of omega-3s. Reeling in more of these healthy fats certainly can't hurt, considering that moodiness is a typical part of the syndrome.

Wild Alaskan salmon is your best (and safest) bet to avoid contaminants. Canned wild salmon is another affordable and convenient option. I love grilled, baked, or broiled salmon fillets. I also use canned to make tasty salmon cakes or a simple salmon salad (with extra-virgin olive oil, red vinegar, chopped onion, and seasonings). Either way, it's easy to get hooked on this fantastic fish.

2. Yogurt

Want to balance out mood swings? Say yes to yogurt. This rich, creamy treat is packed with calcium, the mineral known for building strong bones and helping to ease anxiety, reduce depression, and calm other emotional changes associated with PMS. In a recent study, a small group of women who took an extra daily dose of 500 mg of calcium for two months were less likely to suffer mood issues and water retention during that time of the month compared to those who took a placebo.[5]

Researchers have known that some PMS sufferers have low levels of calcium in their blood, and this study offers further proof that people who get extra calcium are able to find relief from some of their symptoms. Milk may be the obvious choice, but yogurt has a real comfort-food feel because it's so creamy and can easily be used to lighten up many of our indulgent favorites. Bonus points for choosing a yogurt that's also enriched with vitamin D, as D helps the calcium become bioavailable and better absorbed. Plus, as I mentioned earlier, D can also help relieve some PMS symptoms.

Opt for low-fat or nonfat yogurt if you're looking to curb your saturated fat intake. Go for plain varieties to keep a lid on sugar, or pick flavored varieties that have no more than 14 grams of sugar per single container (about 6 ounces). You can always flavor it up with fresh fruit and/or a little bit of honey, maple syrup, or other sweetener of choice.

Make a breakfast parfait by layering yogurt with fruit like chopped strawberries or blueberries and nuts or seeds. You can also enjoy it as a stand-alone snack or use it as a substitute for sour cream or mayonnaise. Or try using it in cakes and brownies, chocolate mousse, mac and cheese, or on top of creamy soup.

I use Greek yogurt as the base in my Bleu Cheese Dip, which I serve alongside my healthified Buffalo Wings and Buffalo Cauliflower "Wings." To make the dip, combine a single container (about 6 ounces) of nonfat plain Greek yogurt, ¼ cup blue cheese crumbles, ¼ teaspoon each garlic powder and onion powder, and some ground black pepper.

Traditional yogurt tends to have a little more calcium (because the calcium-rich liquid is not strained off), while tangy Greek offers twice the protein (which can help keep you feel full longer). Both are winners in my book.

3. Sunflower Seeds

Two more essential nutrients for fighting PMS are magnesium and vitamin E. Magnesium is a mineral that has been shown to help with anxiety, depression, diarrhea, constipation, breast pain, weight gain, and headaches.[6] According to one study, more than 33 percent of PMS sufferers were deficient in magnesium.[7] Adult women need 310 mg daily until age 30 and then 320 mg from age 31 on. Adult men need 400 mg daily until age 30; from 31 on, they need 420 mg. Vitamin E is shown to be equally impressive when it comes to easing breast pain. Adult men and women need 15 mg daily (breastfeeding women need 19 mg).

One little food that packs both vitamin E and magnesium is sunflower seeds. One-quarter cup of sunflower seeds out of the shell contains 8 mg vitamin E (that's more than 50 percent) and a little over 40 mg magnesium. FYI: They're also rich in protein and fiber, a winning combo for steadying blood sugars and keeping your mood even-keeled. Also, the protein and fiber may help curb your appetite and sugar cravings.

You can enjoy the seeds as a quick and easy snack in the shell or out—either way they're delicious. However, in the shell takes more time to savor and slows down your pace, which is great for those who are watching their weight or need a distraction or a de-stressing activity. If bloating is an issue for you, you might want to opt for unsalted (sodium causes women to hold on to water and makes bloating worse). But if you need a salty fix, it's actually okay to enjoy salted, since they're typically not seasoned with as much sodium as people assume. Or you can try mixing half unsalted with half salted.

The seeds can also be worked into meals. They're delicious sprinkled on top of salads or oatmeal, added to a homemade trail mix, or stirred into yogurt (another PMS-fighting food). I like to top 1 cup cooked quinoa (more on this helpful food soon) with a big dollop of Greek yogurt, and then sprinkle on some roasted sunflower seeds and sliced grapes. You can also enjoy sunflower-seed butters, which are a good option for people with nut allergies.

4. Quinoa

Quinoa (pronounced *keen*-wah) has solidified its spot as a true superfood, and as a result has become much more mainstream—you can find it in most supermarkets. It cooks up just like brown rice in about 15 minutes and makes an excellent and easy side dish. It's a super source of magnesium, which, as I've mentioned, is a key nutrient that can help soothe PMS symptoms, particularly mood swings.

The whole grain, which is actually a seed, contains about 120 mg of magnesium per 1 cup cooked. (Amaranth, which also makes an appearance in this book, is another top-notch whole-grain choice for PMS, as it's also extremely rich in magnesium.) Another perk: Quinoa is rich in protein—8 grams per 1 cup cooked. This can help stabilize appetite and potentially ward off cravings. It also is a source of iron. You'll get about 3 grams of iron per 1 cup cooked. This can help boost energy and fight fatigue, and also restore iron levels, which may become depleted after your period. And side benefit: It chips in a little bit of calcium, too.

Quinoa is a versatile side dish that works well with virtually any main meal, from pork to chicken to fish to vegetarian entrées. I often use quinoa instead of rice in classic dinner dishes and casseroles, and as a base for stir-fries. You can also add veggies, black beans (more magnesium!), chopped nuts, and plenty of flavorful seasonings to make a delicious vegetarian feast. Or think out of the box and use it to make a parfait, layering it with yogurt, fruit, and sunflower seeds.

The easiest way to incorporate this great grain into your diet? Cook up a big batch and add a scoop to your salads and soups, or mix some cooked quinoa into your burger and meatball batter. You'll get a dose of filling protein and PMS-blasting magnesium.

5. Wheat Germ

Are you wondering what, exactly, wheat germ is? You're not alone. It's not terribly surprising if you haven't heard of the ingredient or used it much in your own kitchen, because it's the part of wheat that's removed when the plant is processed into white flour. And that's a real shame, because wheat germ, or the embryo of the seed, is the most nutritious part of the wheat kernel.

It contains magnesium, vitamin E, and calcium, making it a true triple threat against PMS. A study done specifically on wheat germ suggests it helped improve physical symptoms, including fatigue and breast tenderness, as well as psychological symptoms such as irritability and mood swings.[8]

Sprinkle 2 tablespoons of wheat germ into yogurt, your favorite cereal, or a bowl of oatmeal. Because it's relatively flavor-neutral, you can also add it to any fruit smoothie (along with calcium- and vitamin-D-rich yogurt or milk for a double dose of PMS-busting power). Or use it as a replacement for up to ½ cup of flour in recipes for baked goods like cookies, cakes, and muffins. Another healthy hack: Use it in place of bread crumbs as a binder in meatloaf and meatballs. You can even use it as a dessert topper for pies, crumbles, and ice cream.

For a richer, nuttier flavor, try toasted wheat germ. You can buy it already toasted or toast it yourself: Heat the oven to 350°F. Spread the wheat germ out on a cookie sheet and bake for 5 to 10 minutes, stirring constantly, until lightly browned and toasted. And be sure to always keep wheat germ (raw and toasted) in a sealed container in the refrigerator or freezer if you won't use it up in time, as it can easily go bad (refer to the "best by" date on the package).

Greek Salmon with Tzatziki and Tabbouleh-Style Quinoa

MAKES 4 SERVINGS AND 1 CUP SAUCE

Greek Salmon

4 salmon fillets (about 5 ounces each)
¼ teaspoon kosher salt

¼ teaspoon ground black pepper
2 tablespoons lemon juice

Tzatziki Sauce

1 cucumber (preferably European seedless), skin intact
2 cups plain Greek yogurt
¼ teaspoon garlic powder

2 tablespoons fresh lemon juice
3 to 4 tablespoons chopped fresh dill
½ teaspoon kosher salt
Ground black pepper to taste

Tabbouleh-Style Quinoa

1 cup uncooked or 3 cups cooked quinoa
4 tablespoons fresh lemon juice
1 teaspoon lemon zest
1 garlic clove, crushed and diced (or ¼ teaspoon garlic powder)
1 tablespoon extra-virgin olive oil

½ cup finely chopped fresh flat-leaf parsley
1 cup cherry (or grape) tomatoes, halved
1 cucumber, diced (skin on or off)
Half a red onion, diced
1/2 teaspoon kosher salt
Ground black pepper to taste

For the Greek Salmon: Preheat the oven to 420°F. Mist the salmon fillets with oil spray and season with salt and pepper. Drizzle the lemon juice over the tops. Place salmon on a baking sheet lined with parchment paper, skin side down, and bake for 12 to 15 minutes, or until desired doneness. (The general rule of thumb is 5 to 7 minutes per ½-inch thickness.) To get the top of the fish brown and crispy, finish under the broiler for 2 to 3 minutes. Remove from the oven and cover to keep warm.

For the Tzatziki Sauce: Grate the cucumber into a bowl lined with two layers of paper towels. When finished, squeeze the towels, expelling as much excess water as possible (you may need extra paper towels). Whisk together the cucumber, yogurt, garlic powder, lemon juice, and dill in a medium bowl. Season with salt and pepper. Refrigerate until ready to serve.

For the Tabbouleh-Style Quinoa: If using uncooked quinoa, place dry quinoa and 2 cups water in a medium saucepan. Bring to a boil over medium-high heat. Reduce the heat, cover, and simmer over low heat until the quinoa is tender and the water is absorbed, about 15 to 20 minutes. Remove from the heat and let sit, covered, for about 5 minutes. Remove the lid, fluff with a fork, and set aside. Meanwhile, whisk the lemon juice, lemon zest, and garlic in a medium bowl. Gradually whisk in the oil. Mix in the cooked quinoa and toss to coat thoroughly. Add the remaining ingredients and toss until well combined. Season with pepper to taste.

To assemble: Place 1 piece of salmon on each plate, top each with about ¼ cup tzatziki sauce, and serve with 1 cup of Tabbouleh-Style Quinoa on the side.

NUTRITIONAL INFORMATION *Per 1 fillet, ¼ cup sauce, and 1 cup Tabbouleh-Style Quinoa*
330 calories • 38 g protein • 10 g total fat (1 g saturated fat, 9 g unsaturated fat) • 75 mg cholesterol • 21 g carbs • 3 g fiber • 4 g total sugar (4 g natural sugar, 0 g added sugar) • 410 mg sodium

Quinoa Yogurt Parfait

MAKES 1 SERVING

1 teaspoon honey

1 single container (about 5 ounces) nonfat or low-fat plain Greek yogurt

1 ½ teaspoons lemon zest

½ cup cooked quinoa

½ cup mixed berries

1 tablespoon sunflower seeds

1 teaspoon toasted wheat germ

Combine the honey, yogurt, and lemon zest in a small bowl.

Layer the yogurt mixture, quinoa, and berries in a pretty glass and top with the sunflower seeds and wheat germ. Garnish with optional mint.

NUTRITIONAL INFORMATION *Per serving*
310 calories • 21 g protein • 7 g total fat (0 g saturated fat, 7 g unsaturated fat) • 5 mg cholesterol • 41 g carbs • 6 g fiber • 16 g total sugar (11 g natural sugar, 5 g added sugar) • 60 mg sodium

Salmon Quinoa Patties

MAKES 7 PATTIES

Salmon Quinoa Patties

15 ounces canned boneless, skinless salmon, drained
¼ cup chopped fresh chives
¼ cup chopped fresh parsley
2 tablespoons lemon juice
2 eggs

¼ cup sunflower seeds
¼ cup toasted wheat germ
1 cup cooked quinoa, cooled
1 teaspoon kosher salt
¼ teaspoon ground black pepper

Lemon-Dill Yogurt Topping

1 cup nonfat or low-fat plain Greek yogurt
2 tablespoons lemon juice

1 to 2 tablepoons fresh chopped dill (or 1 to 2 teaspoons dried dill)

For the patties: Mash up the salmon in a large bowl. Mix in the chives, parsley, lemon juice, eggs, sunflower seeds, and wheat germ until thoroughly combined. Stir the quinoa, salt, and pepper into the salmon mixture until well combined. Press down with a fork or spoon to condense the mixture in the bowl. Cover and refrigerate for at least 30 minutes to overnight (this will help firm up the patties so they don't break apart when cooking).

After the mixture has chilled, use your hands to form 7 equal-size balls, squeezing each and then flattening them out to form the patties. Liberally coat a large skillet with oil spray and warm over medium-high heat. Add patties to the skillet and cook for about 5 to 6 minutes per side. Before carefully flipping each patty, mist the tops with more oil spray to prevent sticking.

For the sauce: Thoroughly combine all the sauce ingredients in a small bowl.

To assemble: Serve each Salmon Quinoa Patty with a dollop of Lemon-Dill Yogurt Sauce.

NUTRITIONAL INFORMATION *Per serving*
200 calories • 23 g protein • 7 g total fat (1 g saturated fat, 6 g unsaturated fat) • 100 mg cholesterol • 11 g carbs • 1 g fiber • 2 g total sugar (2 g natural sugar, 0g added sugar) • 540 mg sodium

5 FOODS TO
LOWER HIGH
BLOOD PRESSURE

When the heart beats, blood is pushed through your circulatory system, creating a pressure within your arteries. This is blood pressure. About 75 million Americans over the age of 18 (about 30 percent of us) have high blood pressure. If left untreated, it can damage the circulatory system and increase the risk for heart attack, stroke, heart failure, kidney failure, and peripheral artery disease. High blood pressure means your heart is working harder, though less efficiently, to get oxygenated blood to the rest of your body. As time goes on, the pressure and friction damage tissues inside arteries, allowing LDL ("bad") cholesterol to form plaque along artery walls; this is called atherosclerosis. The more plaque, the narrower and harder the arteries become and the higher blood pressure goes.

A blood pressure reading is given in two numbers: systolic (top number) over diastolic (bottom number). Systolic is the pressure your blood exerts against artery walls when the *heart beats*. Diastolic is the pressure your blood exerts against artery walls in between heartbeats, when your *heart relaxes*.

BLOOD PRESSURE CATEGORY	SYSTOLIC MM HG (UPPER #)		DIASTOLIC MM HG (LOWER #)
Normal	less than 120	and	less than 80
Prehypertension	120–139	or	80–89
High Blood Pressure (Hypertension) Stage 1	140–159	or	90–99
High Blood Pressure (Hypertension) Stage 2	160 or higher	or	100 or higher
Hypertensive Crisis (Emergency care needed)	Higher than 180	or	Higher than 110

While high blood pressure can't be *cured*, it can be *managed*. A review of 98 studies and nearly 8,000 people found that you can significantly drive down blood pressure numbers by exercising, and eating well, including these five tasty foods.[1]

1. Cocoa Powder

Everyone is sweet on dark chocolate, and it's not just the luxurious flavor that makes it the most widely craved food. The treat is also loaded with health perks, thanks to its high level of flavanols, plant-based nutrients that help reduce blood pressure. (Keep in mind, the darker the chocolate, the more flavanols it contains, and the more health perks you'll enjoy.)

According to numerous studies, these flavanols help to lower blood pressure by promoting *vasodilation* (a fancy word that basically means they help dilate, or "open up," blood vessels). This helps increase the elasticity of blood vessels so blood flows more easily.[2]

But cocoa powder is the real hero—it's 100 percent cocoa and contains a hearty dose of these flavanols without the sugar and calories found in chocolate. In fact, 1 tablespoon of cocoa is a mere 12 calories compared to 150 to 170 calories in an ounce of chocolate, *and* 1 tablespoon of cocoa contains 2 grams of fiber (huge bonus).

When buying cocoa powder, go for unsweetened varieties, avoid brands that have been "dutched" or processed with alkali (this is done to remove bitterness, but it destroys some of the flavanols), and look for varieties with at least 200 mg flavanols.

Granted, cocoa powder on its own is not indulgent or delicious like chocolate, but there are so many creative ways to use it and reap the medicinal benefits. Try adding 1 to 2 teaspoons of cocoa powder to oatmeal with a dash of sweetener and some nuts and berries. Stir 1 teaspoon into a cup of warm milk or coffee. Mix 1 tablespoon into smoothies or chili sauce. You can also toss some into muffin and pancake batters, or create a savory mole sauce by mixing tomatoes, chopped onion, broth, olive oil, and cocoa powder with seasonings of your choice, like cinnamon, cumin, cilantro, garlic, and chili powder.

An out-of-the-box breakfast idea worth waking up for: Chocolate-Ricotta Toast. To make, mix 1 tablespoon part-skim ricotta with ½ teaspoon cocoa powder until well combined. Spread the ricotta mixture on a slice of whole-grain toast, top with a sprinkling of chopped peanuts or toasted pecans, and drizzle on ½ teaspoon honey. Enjoy warm or at room temperature.

2. Pumpkin

For many of us, the most exciting part of the fall season is the arrival of pumpkin—even more so than the changing leaves, cooler weather, and warm, cozy sweaters. And you'll find this superfood in everything from coffee and pie to cookies and snack foods. But year-round, you can get great deals on canned pumpkin, and it lasts a year or two in the cupboard (though hopefully it doesn't sit that long in *your* kitchen).

Pumpkin contains 40 calories per ½ cup and provides more than 3 g of fiber. But what makes it such a great pick for blood pressure? It's slimming, sodium-free, and loaded with potassium—250 mg per ½-cup scoop; that's about 10 percent of your daily requirement.

Potassium is like the anti-sodium. When potassium is low, the body retains extra sodium, and sodium draws water into the blood, raising the pressure on the arterial walls. On the other hand, when you eat a potassium-rich diet, the body becomes more efficient at getting rid of excess sodium (and the extra water, too, which in turn lowers your pressure).

I love pumpkin not only because of its delicious flavor, but also because of its versatility. You can just as easily add a dollop of pumpkin puree into oatmeal, yogurt, and smoothies as you can into cooked ground meat to make a pumpkin chili. I also often add some into seasoned taco meat before serving up a Tex-Mex spread, and I've been known to pumpkin up my marinara sauce with a bit of orange goodness. And here's a clever baking tip: Canned pumpkin puree works as a fat substitute in baked goods—use a 1-to-1 ratio in muffins, cakes, and brownies when they call for oil or butter (your finicky friends won't ever be able to tell . . . I promise).

3. Spinach

This super green is loaded with not one, not two, but three blood-pressure-lowering ingredients, making it a true triple threat. Those three power nutrients are potassium, folate, and magnesium.

Potassium helps to release sodium from the body and lower blood pressure. The higher your potassium intake, the more sodium will be flushed out of the body through urine. Therefore, potassium helps ease tension in blood vessel walls.

Magnesium enables our tiny blood vessels to relax, helping to maintain elasticity and normal blood flow.

Folate, a B vitamin (B$_9$), acts like a "heart-healthy soldier" by helping to break down homocysteine, an amino acid that has the potential to damage inner artery walls.

Not to mention, spinach is low-calorie and brimming with fiber, which is a win-win for your health and waistline.

You can toss fresh baby spinach leaves in salads or layer spinach leaves on sandwiches instead of romaine or iceberg. I love wilting spinach leaves into a pot of simmering soup right before serving. Extra credit for adding a handful of baby leaves into smoothies to amp up the nutrition without affecting the taste (I swear). I also add chopped spinach leaves (fresh or frozen, thawed and drained) into lean ground turkey meat (with a variety of seasonings) to make a healthier, more flavorful burger.

4. Garlic

This kitchen staple does more than add flavor to dishes. It can also help manage blood pressure, thanks to its high content of allicin, an active compound that protects against endothelial dysfunction, a condition that affects the lining of the blood vessels and can lead to hypertension, among other diseases.

Garlic also contains glutamylcysteine, a compound that is said to be a natural ACE inhibitor, an enzyme that helps blood vessels relax.

Fresh garlic cloves (chopped or minced), as well as garlic powder, both offer benefits.

And check this out: According to studies, unlike medications and supplements, which can cause side effects, garlic offers these blood-pressure-lowering benefits without any drawbacks, except a potential potent garlic odor—nothing a good strong breath mint can't mask.

You can add chopped or minced garlic to any sautéed vegetable, or just about any soup, casserole, or stir-fry. You can also try making your own homemade garlic bread by creating "spreadable" garlic paste. Simply trim the head off a clove of garlic to expose the top of the cloves, drizzle olive oil over them, sprinkle with ground black pepper and some optional herbs, and wrap the whole thing with foil. Roast the bundle in a 450°F oven for about 30 minutes until the cloves are nice and soft. Then remove the garlic from the oven and gently squeeze the cloves from the papery skin. Spread the flavorful, softened cloves onto whole-grain toast or crackers or pita—or dip away with crunchy vegetables.

5. White Beans

(Great Northern, Navy)

We all know why beans are good for your heart (haha)—but they're also beneficial for blood pressure.

All beans contain fiber (cooked beans contain anywhere from 10 to 20 g per cup cooked—very impressive), protein (between 10 and 17 g per cup), and iron (about 10 percent the required daily allowance per cup). All of these nutrients work to keep your heart healthy because they help control weight, reduce cholesterol, and provide magnesium and potassium, which, as I've mentioned earlier, help with blood pressure.

But white beans are the better bean in this case, because they also chip in calcium (about 160 mg of calcium per cup, cooked). Calcium plays an important role in managing blood pressure because it helps blood vessels tighten and relax when necessary.

Both dried and canned beans offer the same nutrition perks, so feel free to enjoy whichever you prefer. Sometimes you can get the better deal on bagged (which are dried), so those certainly are a good option. It really comes down to how much work you want to put in, because you have to soak dried beans in cold water for at least eight hours or overnight to reduce cooking time and make them easier to eat. Canned beans, on the other hand, are pre-cooked and ready to add into just about any recipe creation.

If you're choosing canned, look for low-sodium varieties, or you can simply rinse beans off in a colander under cold water. Doing so removes a great amount of the sodium.

You can add white beans to salads, soups, or mix into meatballs, meatloaf, and burger patties. I like to create a smashed white bean dip by mashing a drained, rinsed can of beans with extra-virgin olive oil, lemon juice, garlic, ground black pepper, and preferred seasonings, like thyme or cayenne pepper. I sometimes use white beans instead of chickpeas to whip up hummus. You can even use white beans to create nondairy vegan "cream" soups by pureeing them along with some low-sodium broth and other flavorful ingredients into a deliciously rich and smooth mixture.

Pumpkin and Spinach Meatballs

MAKES ABOUT 36 MEATBALLS

1 ⅓ pounds ground turkey (at least 90 percent lean)

2 cups loosely packed spinach, finely chopped (yields about 1 cup)

One 15-ounce can white beans, drained, rinsed, and partially mashed by hand (about half)

¾ cup canned pumpkin puree

1 egg, slightly beaten

2 tablespoons packed brown sugar

¼ teaspoon ground nutmeg

2 teaspoons ground cinnamon

¼ teaspoon ground ginger

½ teaspoon garlic powder

¼ teaspoon kosher salt

¼ teaspoon ground black pepper

Low-sodium marinara sauce (optional)

Preheat the oven to 350°F. Line a baking sheet with parchment paper.

Mix together all the ingredients in a large bowl until well combined and sticky, about 30 seconds. Do not overmix.

Using the palms of your hands, form the turkey mixture into light and fluffy golf-ball-size meatballs. You should end up with about 36 in total. Batter will be sticky. If you have difficulty, refrigerate the mixture for about 30 minutes to firm it up.

Bake the meatballs for 45 minutes on the middle rack. Remove from the oven and enjoy on a bed of fresh spinach leaves topped with some warm, low-sodium marinara sauce.

NUTRITIONAL INFORMATION *Per 4 meatballs*
140 calories • 19 g protein • 1.5 g total fat (0 g saturated fat, 1.5 g unsaturated fat) •
50 mg cholesterol • 12 g carbs • 2 g fiber • 4 g total sugar (2 g natural sugar, 2 g added sugar) •
140 mg sodium

Cocoa Smoothie

MAKES 1 SERVING (2 ¼ cups)

1 cup unsweetened vanilla almond milk
   (or skim or soy milk)
1 ripe banana, sliced
   (fresh or frozen)

2 tablespoons cocoa powder
1 cup baby spinach leaves,
   loosely packed
3 to 5 ice cubes (optional)

Combine all the ingredients in a blender until creamy and smooth. For an icier consistency, add a few cubes.

NUTRITIONAL INFORMATION *Per serving*
170 calories • 6 g protein • 4 g total fat (0 g saturated fat, 4 g unsaturated fat) • 0 mg cholesterol
36 g carbs • 8 g fiber • 14 g total sugar (14 g natural sugar, 0 g added sugar) • 120 mg sodium

Pumpkin Turkey Chili

MAKES 6 SERVINGS

1 large yellow onion, diced
   (about 2 cups)

1 medium bell pepper (red, yellow,
   or orange), diced

6 garlic cloves, minced
   (or ¾ teaspoon garlic powder)

1 ⅓ pounds ground turkey or chicken
   (at least 90 percent lean)

One 15-ounce can white beans,
   drained and rinsed

One 28-ounce can diced tomatoes
   with liquid, preferably reduced-
   sodium

¼ cup tomato paste, no salt added

One 14-ounce can pumpkin puree

1 cup reduced-sodium chicken or
   vegetable broth

2 tablespoons chili powder

1 tablespoon cocoa powder

1 ½ teaspoons ground cinnamon
   (or 1 tablespoon pumpkin pie spice)

2 ½ teaspoons ground cumin

½ teaspoon ground black pepper

½ teaspoon cayenne pepper
   (optional)

4 cups spinach leaves

Avocado (optional)

Nonfat plain Greek yogurt (optional)

Cilantro (optional)

Salsa (optional)

Liberally coat a large pot or Dutch oven with oil spray and warm over medium-high heat. Add the onion and bell pepper and sauté, stirring occasionally, for about 7 minutes, or until the onion softens. Add the garlic, stir everything together, and cook until fragrant, about 30 seconds.

Add the ground turkey or chicken. Use a spatula or large spoon to break up the meat as it cooks. Continue to cook about 6 to 7 minutes, until fully cooked.

Add the beans, diced tomatoes, tomato paste, pumpkin puree, broth, chili powder, cocoa powder, cinnamon (or pumpkin pie spice), cumin, black pepper, and optional cayenne pepper, and stir. Reduce heat and simmer for 20 to 30 minutes, stirring occasionally.

Right before serving, add the spinach and mix throughout. Enjoy the chili with desired toppings, such as avocado, nonfat plain Greek yogurt, cilantro, and salsa.

NUTRITIONAL INFORMATION *Per serving (about 1 ½ cups)*
300 calories • 27 g protein • 8 g total fat (0 g saturated fat, 8 g unsaturated fat) •
55 mg cholesterol • 31 g carbs • 8 g fiber • 10 g total sugar (10 g natural sugar, 0 g added sugar) • 250 mg sodium

5 FOODS TO **BATTLE BAD BREATH**

It's estimated that 25 percent of people suffer from halitosis, the official name for bad breath, on a regular basis. Unfortunately, you may not even know you are one of them because we tend to adapt to the odor. And no, a quick sniff test—exhaling and inhaling in your hand—is not super reliable. A better gauge: Lick your skin, let it dry, and take a whiff. Or you can simply ask a close friend or partner.

While there are many causes, 90 percent of bad breath stems from the oral cavity.[1] Bacteria in the mouth break down food particles and other debris, leading to the production of volatile sulfur compounds (VSCs) that are responsible for the funky odors. Most of the VSCs form on the back of the tongue, but they can also be in the spaces between teeth and the areas between the gum and teeth.

The other 10 percent of bad breath cases are caused by poor diet or certain foods (like garlic, onions, and dairy) and alcohol, some of which get broken down by the body and cause a stinky odor from the lungs and even the pores. Following a very low-carb diet can also cause bad breath; when you restrict carbs and the body begins to burn fat, chemicals called ketones are released, which can lead to a stinky mouth. Being dehydrated or anything causing a dry mouth is problematic. Certain medications, smoking, and respiratory conditions like sinusitis or tonsillitis may also contribute. And, of course, we can't forget that bacteria having an entire night to sit and stew without any saliva to rinse them away results in morning breath.

It goes without saying that proper hygiene is absolutely essential. This means brushing and flossing regularly—in the morning, before bed, and after meals—to prevent bacteria from getting stuck between the teeth and the gums. Brushing your tongue, or better yet, using a tongue scraper in addition to rinsing with a mouthwash, may also be a good idea, as that's where bacteria often linger.[2]

Keeping the mouth moist is another way to stifle the stench, so make sure to drink plenty of water throughout the day. Chewing sugarless gum (mint and cinnamon flavors are a plus) can also help promote saliva production. Eating anything can temporarily help freshen breath because it, too, stimulates the production of saliva,[3] but there are certain foods and herbs that seem to be more effective than others at taming bad breath.

1. Green Tea

Instead of taking a swig of mouthwash, try taking a sip of green tea—it's both soothing and scent-eliminating. Green tea (both regular and decaf) is rich in polyphenols, which can help undo the unpleasant odor because they help prevent the growth of bacteria in the mouth.

Want an extra perk? Add a squirt of lemon to your mug. One study found that drinking a cup of green tea with some added lemon juice helped to stamp out the stink of four particularly smelly VSCs for a full hour after sipping.[4] Without the lemon, the brew eliminated one of these VSCs for only about half the time.

In another study, the polyphenols in green tea were shown to have greater antimicrobial activity against the bacteria in the mouth—which helped fight bad breath—than other substances, including chewing gum and mints.[5] Green tea both disinfects and deodorizes, giving bad breath a one-two punch.

Enjoy a cup of hot or iced green tea with breakfast, lunch, and dinner, or even before bed as a way to relax and unwind. If you're having a cup close to bedtime, opt for decaf so it doesn't interfere with sleep. And feel free to brew a cup using a tea bag, powder, or leaf—all should offer similar breath-freshening benefits. Matcha powder is another solid option. The finely ground tea can offer a more potent punch of antioxidants because you end up consuming the whole leaf. Sip a cup of regular or decaf matcha tea for some sweet-smelling breath.

2. Apple

Apples are Mother Nature's breath mint. They contain two different types of beneficial compounds to keep your breath smelling sweet: polyphenols, which keep odor-causing bacteria at bay, and enzymes that work against a number of particularly stinky VSCs found in garlic and other foods.

Raw apples have a slight edge over cooked because they contain both polyphenols and enzymes. Cooked apples contain only polyphenols (heat destroys the enzymes). In one study, researchers tested both raw and microwaved Pink Lady apples. Both types were effective in reducing garlicky breath, but raw apples packed a more potent punch because they have enzymatic activity, and therefore provide a double dose of breath-freshening ingredients.[6]

Not a fan of Pink Ladies? No worries. Another study showed that a number of different apple varieties have the same benefits.[7] So choose your favorite and enjoy.

There's another perk to apples. They're high in fiber and require a lot of chewing—this combo creates a gentle "sandpaper effect," during which VSCs are brushed off the teeth and tongue.[8] Perhaps another reason raw apples have a slight edge over cooked is their extra chewing requirement.

Apples are one of my favorite go-to snacks—they're portable and perfectly portioned. Have one whole or cut into slices and use them as dippers for nut butter. Another creative spin: Use raw apples to make delicious healthy "doughnuts." Remove the center of the apple with an apple corer. (If you don't have an apple corer, you can slice the apple and use a pastry tip to make a hole in the center of each slice.) Slice the apple sideways into about ¾-inch-thick slices. Top each "doughnut" slice with vanilla yogurt and sprinkle on a dash of optional spices, such as cinnamon, nutmeg, or apple pie seasoning. Add your preferred toppings evenly among all the slices, such as chopped nuts and seeds, berries, shredded coconut flakes, or granola cereal.

I've even used apples to make nachos. Thinly slice a few apples, spread on some nut butter, and layer on a plate. Sprinkle with chopped, toasted nuts and seeds, and raisins. It's a delicious way to take your nachos up a nutritional notch.

3. Whole-Grain Rolls

So many of us bypass the bread basket before dinner to curb carbs and calories. But if you suffer bad breath, the bread basket can be your BFF.

Eating causes what researchers describe as a "self-cleaning" effect. The chewing and the increased production of saliva can help remove bacteria from the teeth and tongue, and this effect tends to last for a few hours after eating. But the effect seems to be even greater when you choose high-fiber, chewy foods, like whole-grain rolls or baguettes. In one study, people who ate a high-fiber, chewing-intensive breakfast that consisted of a fibrous whole-grain roll with jelly and fruit were rated to have better breath than those who ate a lower-fiber, less chewy breakfast of a soft white roll with jelly and fruit.[9]

When dining out, choose the grainiest bun in the basket (a hard, thick outer crust is a big bonus). Even whole-grain crackers, bagels, or dry cereal can offer a similar benefit—anything that requires you to work those chompers. Typical store-bought whole-grain bread tends to be a bit softer, which is why I'm not including it in this roundup. If you're buying rolls and have the luxury of a label, aim for one that offers at least 5 grams of fiber per serving with a grainy texture (the chewier the texture, the better). Check the ingredients list on the label and ensure the first ingredient is indeed a whole grain (whole wheat, oats, quinoa, sorghum, brown rice, and millet are the most common types used).

Enjoy your whole-grain roll plain or with a healthy spread like hummus, avocado, or nut butter. You can also serve it on the side with an egg omelet or use it to make a delicious egg sandwich. Of course, there are hundreds and hundreds of tasty sandwich combinations to be made. To score double the bites—and double the chewing—eat your roll open-faced.

4. Mint

There's a reason mint is one of the most popular flavors of various brands of toothpastes, mouthwashes, and chewing gums . . . it works.

Peppermint and spearmint are two herbs that have a fresh aroma and taste, which studies show work against those malodorous VSCs to keep your breath smelling . . . well, minty fresh. In one study, a peppermint essential oil was one ingredient in a mixture that helped cut back on VSCs and reduce bad breath better than an over-the-counter oral mouth rinse.[10] Mint leaves are rich in polyphenols and have enzymatic properties to help deodorize your mouth. Another study suggests mint was even effective against pungent garlic VSCs.[11]

Whatever leaf you love is fine—both work in a wide variety of dishes. Spearmint tends to be a little sweeter than peppermint, which has a cooling, menthol flavor. If you simply see "mint" listed in a recipe, it's usually "spearmint."

You can add mint to dishes like roasted chicken or baked fish, to sides like grilled vegetables, and to toppings like sauces and dressings. I love chopping mint into diced pineapple for a simple dessert or sprinkling it onto shredded grapefruit (see the cold and flu chapter, Grapefruit Relish recipe on page 72). It's also delicious mixed into cool desserts, such as my Mango-Strawberry Sorbet. To make, combine 1 ½ cups frozen mango, 3 to 5 large strawberries, ¾ cup light coconut milk, and 5 to 6 mint leaves in a blender until smooth. Divide the mixture evenly among a few small bowls and freeze until firm, about 3 hours. Then grab a spoon and enjoy.

Mint is also delicious added to beverages. Brew up a big pitcher of iced mint or peppermint tea. Or try a warm mug of green-mint tea for double the power. Or, simply add a few crushed or torn mint leaves to your water bottle for a refreshing break any time of day.[12]

Mint extract is another option, but it's pretty potent, so go easy. Remember, you can always add more to intensify the flavor, but you can't subtract once it's added. Add a small dash to hot cocoa or vanilla or chocolate ice cream and smoothies for a cool, crisp flavor that freshens breath.

5. Parsley

Parsley is often used as a garnish in restaurants, but it's so much more than mere plate decoration. In fact, adding the herb to your cooking—or even better, chewing on a few sprigs post-meal—can help make offensive breath less offensive.

Just like apples help freshen breath after eating garlic, so does parsley.[13] People often suspect this breath-bettering benefit is the work of chlorophyll, the compound that gives the herb its green color. However, researchers theorize it could be another unknown substance at work.

Whatever the reason, load up on the herb and start sprinkling. Parsley pairs well with fish and chicken, but also works in salads, dips, stews, and meatballs. I love to whip up a whole-grain pasta with roasted tomatoes, green peas, scallops, or sea bass and finish it off with parsley—it's a huge hit in my house. Because it's so versatile, there's really no wrong way to use it. And the whole-grain penne cooked to al dente can help promote fresh breath too, thanks to the fiber and chew factor. Just be sure to skip the garlic (apologies!).

Another fun flavor trick: Freeze leftover broth in ice cube trays and toss in some chopped fresh parsley. Simply defrost the herb-infused broth cubes whenever you need to add extra flavor (and breath-freshening power) to sauces, soups, or stews.

There are two main types of parsley—curly leaf and Italian (or flat leaf). Curly leaf tends to have a milder flavor and is often used as garnish, while Italian has a stronger flavor (though some people disagree with this taste description). Both types can be used in recipes. Feel free to incorporate the leaves and the stems; the stems can be more potent than the leaves.

Helpful tip: You can store fresh parsley in the freezer. Gently rinse the parsley, wrap it in a paper towel, and then put it in a baggie in the freezer. It will keep for about a week. You can also swap 1 teaspoon dried for 1 tablespoon fresh in recipes, although I'd recommend fresh for the chewing, which truly does offer breath-freshening benefits. Not to mention, dried parsley is much less flavorful.

Turkey-Apple Sandwich

MAKES 1 SANDWICH

**4 to 5 slices roasted turkey
(about 3 ounces)**
¼ apple, thinly sliced
Lettuce leaves
6 mint leaves

1 whole-grain roll, sliced in half
**1 to 2 tablespoons reduced-fat
mayonnaise**
**1 to 1 ½ tablespoons finely chopped
fresh parsley**

Layer the turkey, apple, lettuce, and mint on one half of the roll.

Mix the mayo and parsley together in a small bowl. Spread the parsley-mayo on the other half of the roll, top the sandwich, and enjoy!

NUTRITIONAL INFORMATION *Per sandwich (using a 150-calorie roll)*
320 calories • 25 g protein • 8 g total fat (0.5 g saturated fat, 7.5 g unsaturated fat) • 60 mg cholesterol • 39 g carbs • 3 g fiber • 14 g total sugar (14 g natural sugar, 0 g added sugar) • 650 mg sodium

Iced Mint Green Tea

MAKES 4 CUPS

1 tablespoon honey (optional)
4 to 5 green tea bags

1 lemon, sliced (optional)
1 cup fresh mint leaves

Bring 4 cups of water to a boil. Add the honey to the boiling water, if using. Stir to dissolve and remove from heat.

Add the tea bags to the water along with the lemon slices, if using. Steep for 1 to 3 minutes. Let the tea cool to room temperature.

Remove the tea bags and pour the tea into a pitcher or large mason jar. Add the fresh mint leaves and store in the refrigerator until ready to serve. Enjoy chilled over ice.

NUTRITIONAL INFORMATION *Per 1 cup**
5 calories • 0 g protein • 0 g fat • 0 mg cholesterol • 1 g carbs • 0 g fiber • 0 g sugar • 10 mg sodium

Note: If using honey, add 15 calories per cup.

SIMPLE SIP This recipe features only two bad-breath-fighting foods, but it's so simple to make and it also contains water, which helps temporarily wash VSCs from the tongue and mouth. Feel free to add cucumber slices, grapefruit, and other citrus fruits to flavor your cup.

Parsley Hummus

MAKES 1 ¹/₂ CUPS

**One 15-ounce can chickpeas, drained
  and rinsed**
**3 tablespoons tahini (sesame seed
  paste)**
3 tablespoons lemon juice
3 tablespoons water

1 teaspoon kosher salt
**1 teaspoon extra-virgin olive oil
  plus more for optional garnish**
**¼ cup finely chopped fresh parsley,
  plus more for optional garnish**

Place all the ingredients in the bowl of a food processor. (For a prettier presentation, do not add parsley into food processor and instead mix in at the end by hand for a splash of green color throughout.) Pulse to blend all the ingredients, scraping down the sides of the bowl as necessary.

Season with additional salt and ground black pepper to taste. Garnish with an optional drizzle of extra-virgin olive oil and a sprinkle of parsley leaves.

Enjoy the hummus on apple slices or with your favorite whole-grain bread. It makes a delicious sandwich spread too.

NUTRITIONAL INFORMATION *Per 2 tablespoons*
60 calories • 2 g protein • 3 g total fat (0 g saturated fat, 3 g unsaturated fat) •
0 mg cholesterol • 6 g carbs • 2 g fiber • 1 g total sugar (1 g natural sugar, 0 g added sugar) •
200 mg sodium

5 FOODS TO
BOOST LIBIDO

How often are you getting busy? Getting it on? Getting some action? There are quite literally hundreds of ways to refer to the act of sex.

But no matter how perfect the mood—candles, flowers, silk sheets, John Legend tunes—you have to be in the mood. And the truth is, many of us struggle with a low libido, which is defined as having little or no interest in sex (with a partner or alone) as well as a lack of sexual thoughts or fantasies. In one report that surveyed more than 30,000 women, 33 percent said they had low sexual desire.[1]

Libido naturally fluctuates, taking a dip during major life changes, like pregnancy and menopause. And libido lessens as you age: The sex drive of a 60-year-old is nowhere near as buoyant as that of a 16-year-old.

Not surprisingly, if you're feeling stressed or tired or upset, your libido will most likely be negatively affected. The same goes for relationship problems with your significant other—if you're not connecting with your partner on an emotional level, you're less likely to want to connect on a physical level. So resolving any issues you may be having can help set the stage for sexy time. Having low self-esteem is also likely to interfere with your ability to perform.

Other lifestyle habits can wreck the romance. Smoking affects blood flow, which can interfere with arousal, and too much alcohol can decrease sexual desire. If you want to get lucky, scientific evidence strongly suggests steering clear of cigarettes, excessive booze, and recreational drugs. The research on marijuana is mixed; some say it boosts libido while others say it interferes with sex drive.

Changes in hormones, illnesses, or conditions like high blood pressure, diabetes, and arthritis, as well as medications like antidepressants can all affect your sex drive. And if you suffer from sexual problems like pain during sex or difficulty having an orgasm, you're less likely to want to be intimate.

If you notice that you consistently have no interest in sex and/or you have issues performing, check with your doctor to rule out a more serious problem and to discuss treatment options. Otherwise, for the occasional dip in desire, try these delicious libido-boosting bites.

1. Ginger

Ginger may help spice things up a bit between the sheets. It has been a known natural aphrodisiac for centuries because it improves blood flow throughout the whole body, including south of the border. In studies on animals and in humans, the spice has been shown to help increase levels of testosterone, the hormone that regulates sex drive in men.[2]

It's not just an edible remedy. Ginger has a strong, unique aroma, and the scent alone can be arousing. Ginger also has a bit of a kick to it, which causes you to perspire and can slightly increase your heart rate (similar to sex). As an extra perk, ginger helps to alleviate aches and pains (see page 89 in the aches and pains chapter), so it may leave you feeling a bit more comfortable in your skin, or flexible, which may lead you to be a little more adventurous with your partner.

Ginger is delicious added to hot or cold beverages. Try adding 1 teaspoon minced fresh ginger into a fruit smoothie. (I make one with mango, peach, and milk that's incredibly tasty.) You can also steep a few slices of fresh gingerroot in a mug of hot green tea for about 5 minutes for a soothing and sensual sip.

Ginger can also be incorporated into homemade muffins (try it with pumpkin, another libido-booster, to pump up the passion), pies, or cookies. I like to sprinkle it on top of roasted carrots with a dash of salt and pepper. Fresh grated or minced ginger is also a wonderful addition to soups, stir-fries, and salad dressings.

You can use fresh gingerroot (store it in the freezer tightly wrapped in a plastic bag and use as needed for up to two months) or opt for ground ginger, which is super convenient and just as healthful as fresh.

2. Watermelon

If seed-spitting contests aren't enough to get you all hot and bothered, maybe this study will: Watermelon can have a Viagra-like effect. The perky pick contains a phytonutrient called citrulline, which is converted by the body to arginine, an amino acid that in turn increases levels of nitric oxide. Nitric oxide helps to relax blood vessels in the same way the little blue pill is known to do.[3]

In some cases, citrulline may be found at higher levels in the rind, which is edible. (You can pickle the rind, blend it into a smoothie, or thinly slice the white part and toss it into a stir-fry.) But this can vary by the type of watermelon and where it's grown, so feel free to just enjoy the juicy pink part knowing it may very well help to boost your sex drive. Another tasty option is watermelon juice, which also contains the libido-boosting compound. When choosing juice, I recommend mixing it with water or seltzer to dilute the calories and sugar.

Watermelon is the ultimate summer fruit, so slice one up and enjoy a wedge to refresh and beat the heat. Or get a little fancier and serve it up as a delicious appetizer or dessert for guests. Try my Watermelon-Feta Bites: Use a toothpick to skewer a 1-inch watermelon cube, a small cube of feta cheese, and a mint leaf. Drizzle on some balsamic vinegar and dig in. I also like to make Mini Watermelon Cakes: Cut watermelon into rounds using a cookie cutter and garnish each one with a generous squirt of aerated whipped cream, chopped mint leaves, and slivered almonds. (The whipped cream will melt quickly, so make sure to serve immediately after adding it.)

3. Pumpkin

Pumpkin was part of Cinderella's happily ever after, so why not yours? Pumpkin is rich in potassium, which helps increase blood flow to *all* extremities. Better blood flow isn't the only benefit of the orange orb—it can also lead to increased energy and improved mood,[4] which in turn can enhance our lustful desires.

Similar to ginger, the scent of pumpkin is sensual. A study from the Smell & Taste Treatment and Research Foundation in Chicago found that the aroma of pumpkin pie increased blood flow below the belt in men.[5] When it comes to libido, scent can actually offer a greater boost than consuming food. This makes sense because most of what we perceive as taste is really smell. Plus, the aroma of certain foods (pumpkin included) can calm anxiety, which helps remove inhibitions and get you in the mood.

I like to add a dollop of pumpkin to my oatmeal and mix with some vanilla extract, cinnamon (or pumpkin pie spice), maple syrup, and toasted pecans. For a romantic dinner-dessert combo, try this pairing: Add a scoop of pumpkin puree into simmering turkey meat sauce and toss with whole-grain pasta. Then complete your feast with creamy and indulgent pumpkin ice cream. Here's how I make it: Puree 2 ripened, frozen bananas with ¼ cup 100 percent canned pumpkin puree, 1 tablespoon maple syrup, and 1 teaspoon pumpkin pie spice until the mixture is completely smooth and no frozen chunks remain. If the frozen bananas are too hard to blend, add a splash of milk for easier mixing. This makes about 3 servings (½ cup each). Scoop your Pumpkin Ice Cream into small bowls and enjoy immediately as soft serve. For hard-packed ice cream, pour the mixture into a loaf pan and freeze for about 30 minutes. Top each serving with a sprinkle of chopped, toasted pecans, if desired, for a tasty crunch.

Pumpkin—fresh, canned, or frozen—is a terrific ingredient to add to any recipe, any time of day (breakfast, lunch, dinner, or dessert), year-round. But it's particularly handy when you're expecting that special someone.

4. Hot Pepper

Some like it hot . . . when it comes to their food. But there is a physical connection, too. A spicy pepper will not only help you turn up the heat in the kitchen but perhaps in the bedroom, or wherever you like getting frisky. Capsaicin, the ingredient that gives peppers their heat, stimulates your nervous system, getting your blood pumping, elevating your body temperature, increasing your heart rate, and triggering the release of feel-good hormones— kind of like what happens after sex. All of this can help boost your libido.

Capsaicin has been linked with weight loss, which can make you feel sexier in your own skin. One meta-analysis in *Appetite* suggests that regularly eating peppers could help you burn about 50 extra calories per day by helping to rev metabolism slightly.[6] This could mean a loss of about 5 pounds over the course of a year.

Whatever your preferred pepper—red chile, jalapeño, or habanero—the hotter it is, the higher the concentration of capsaicin. It seems that the more capsaicin there is, the greater the effect.[7] (Bell peppers do not contain capsaicin, though they are loaded with other beneficial compounds.) Try adding chopped hot peppers to scrambled eggs, chicken, or tuna salad or tossed green salads. Of course, hot peppers make the ideal addition to chili or tacos. If you need to, remove the seeds and membranes to tone down the heat slightly. The membrane boasts high levels of capsaicin, and the seeds—because they've been in contact with the membrane—also contain the heat-causing compound.

I love to make healthy Jalapeño Hummus Poppers: Combine hummus with chopped scallion, corn, and a pinch of cayenne pepper and ground black pepper. Spoon a generous amount of the mixture into halved, hollowed out jalapeño peppers. Carefully roll the stuffed peppers in panko bread crumbs until nicely coated. (I mix my bread crumbs with a dash of chili powder, kosher salt, and cayenne pepper.) Place them open side up on a baking sheet lined with parchment paper and pack more bread crumbs on the pepper tops. Liberally mist peppers with oil spray. Bake for 20 to 25 minutes at 350°F, until bread crumbs are browned and toasty. Let cool for a few minutes, and dig in!

Hot sauce offers similar benefits because it's made from hot peppers. Add to hummus, use as a sandwich spread, or mix into soups, stews, and omelets.

5. Pomegranate

The pomegranate has turned out to be a provocative pick in the produce aisle. Consider this fun piece of history trivia as proof: The forbidden fruit in the classic story of Adam and Eve may not have been an apple after all. According to the King James Bible, it's referred to only as "the fruit," and some religious experts believe the fruit was actually a pomegranate.

One study from the United Kingdom found that pomegranate juice increased levels of testosterone by 24 percent on average. It also boosted mood and eased anxiety (similar to performance jitters), a great combination for getting you ready for some romantic activity.[8] Research has shown that pomegranate seeds (officially called arils) help keep blood flowing freely throughout the body, including those ever-important southern regions.[9]

Whole pomegranates are delicious, but they can be discouraging if you don't know how to peel them properly because in this case, it's what's inside that counts—the seeds are the only edible part of the fruit. If you need some help with slicing, try this trick: Using a sharp knife, score a circle along the top of the fruit, just deep enough to pierce the skin, and then pop off the top. You'll see the fruit is divided into sections or compartments, similar to an orange. Next, score vertical lines down each of the sections. Gently stretch the fruit out to loosen the compartments. Turn the fruit over so the opening is facing down and place over a bowl. Using a wooden spoon, tap the bottom so the seeds drop out. Remove any white parts from the bowl and enjoy the seeds.

The seeds are tasty on their own, sprinkled over a salad, or mixed into yogurt or oatmeal. If you're going to enjoy pomegranate juice, it's a good idea to dilute it so you're cutting the calories and its natural sugar. You can mix it with water or some seltzer if you like a little fizz.

Curry Turkey Burgers with Pomegranate Seeds

MAKES 5 BURGERS AND ABOUT 1 CUP SAUCE

For the burgers
1 pound ground turkey
 (93 percent lean)
¼ cup canned pumpkin puree
½ cup bread crumbs, regular or
 panko, preferably whole grain
½ cup pomegranate seeds (about the
 amount of half a pomegranate)
2 tablespoons curry powder

1 tablespoon grated fresh ginger
 (or 1 teaspoon ground ginger)
1 teaspoon garlic powder
½ teaspoon salt
¼ teaspoon ground black pepper
5 whole-grain buns
5 large lettuce leaves
Slices of onion and tomato (optional)

For the sauce
Half an avocado
½ cup nonfat plain Greek yogurt
¼ cup canned pumpkin puree
1 tablespoon grated fresh ginger
 (or 1 teaspoon ground ginger)

1 teaspoon paprika
½ teaspoon salt
1 tablespoon honey
Dash of hot sauce (optional)

For the burgers: Combine the turkey, pumpkin, bread crumbs, pomegranate seeds, curry powder, ginger, garlic, salt, and pepper in a large bowl. Form into 5 large patties. Liberally coat a large skillet with oil spray and warm over medium heat. Cook the patties, 5 to 6 minutes per side. Before flipping the patties, mist the tops with oil spray to prevent sticking.

For the sauce: Combine the sauce ingredients in a bowl and mash with a spoon until smooth. Alternatively, you can puree in a small food processor or blender.

To assemble: Layer the bottom half of a bun with a cooked patty, piece of lettuce, dollop of sauce, and optional onion and tomato, and then top with the other half of the bun.

NUTRITIONAL INFORMATION
Per fully assembled burger (with bun and 2 tablespoons sauce)
360 calories • 24 g protein • 10 g total fat (2 g saturated fat, 8 g unsaturated fat) •
40 mg cholesterol • 42 g carbs • 3 g fiber • 9 g total sugar (7 g natural sugar, 2 g added sugar) •
640 mg sodium

Pumpkin Ginger Bread with Pomegranate Seeds

MAKES 10 SLICES

2 eggs, lightly beaten
¼ cup unsweetened almond milk (or any other preferred milk)
One 15-ounce can pumpkin puree
1 tablespoon canola oil
½ cup unsweetened applesauce
⅓ cup maple syrup
2 teaspoons vanilla extract
1 cup whole-wheat flour (or other preferred whole-grain flour)

1 cup all-purpose flour
2 teaspoons ground ginger
1 ½ teaspoons ground cinnamon
¼ teaspoon nutmeg
¼ teaspoon kosher salt
1 teaspoon baking soda
1 teaspoon baking powder
⅔ to 1 ¼ cup pomegranate seeds (use more for garnish)

Preheat the oven to 325°F. Liberally mist a 9 × 5-inch loaf pan with oil spray.

Add the eggs, milk, pumpkin, oil, applesauce, maple syrup, and vanilla to a medium mixing bowl and whisk until combined.

Add the flours, ginger, cinnamon, nutmeg, salt, baking soda, and baking powder to a large bowl and mix well. Pour the wet ingredients into the dry ingredients and stir until just combined. Gently fold in the pomegranate seeds (do not overmix).

Pour the batter into the prepared loaf pan and tap the bottom a few times on your counter to even everything out. Bake on a middle rack for 60 to 70 minutes, or until a toothpick inserted into the center comes out clean. (Sixty minutes will result in a super-moist, cake-like consistency; 65-plus minutes will still create a moist but firmer consistency. Both textures are delicious.) Let the bread cool for at least 10 minutes. Slice and garnish with optional pomegranate seeds on top.

NUTRITIONAL INFORMATION *Per slice*
180 calories • 5 g protein • 3 g total fat (0 g saturated fat, 3 g unsaturated fat) • 35 mg cholesterol • 34 g carbs • 2 g fiber • 11 g total sugar (5 g natural sugar, 6 g added sugar) • 190 mg sodium

Watermelon-Pomegranate Salad with Ginger Dressing

MAKES 4 SERVINGS AND ABOUT 1 ½ CUPS DRESSING

For the salad

4 to 8 cups arugula
½ cup pomegranate seeds
2 cups cubed watermelon
1 cucumber, chopped
½ red onion, finely chopped

3 mint sprigs, finely chopped (about 1 ½ tablespoons)
¼ cup peanuts
½ avocado, thinly sliced

For the dressing

⅓ cup canola or grapeseed oil
¼ cup rice vinegar
¼ cup reduced-sodium soy sauce
1 teaspoon toasted sesame oil
3 medium carrots, peeled and roughly chopped (about 15 baby carrots)
1 tablespoon lime juice
1 tablespoon honey

2 tablespoons peeled and roughly chopped fresh ginger
2 garlic cloves, roughly chopped (or ¼ teaspoon garlic powder)
¼ teaspoon salt (or more to taste)
¼ teaspoon ground black pepper (or more to taste)

Add the arugula to a large bowl. If starting with a whole pomegranate, see page 213 for the best method for retrieving seeds. Mix in the pomegranate seeds and all the other salad ingredients (except the avocado).

To make the dressing, put all the dressing ingredients in a high-powered blender or food processer and puree. If you don't have a high-powered blender, microwave the chopped carrots for about 5 minutes to soften them up before adding into an everyday blender. Divide the salad among plates, add the avocado, and toss with ginger dressing. Store leftover dressing in a closed container in the fridge for up to a week.

NUTRITIONAL INFORMATION *Per serving of salad with 2 tablespoons dressing*
230 calories • 5 g protein • 15 g total fat (2 g saturated fat, 13 g unsaturated fat) • 0 mg cholesterol • 23 g carbs • 5 g fiber • 13 g total sugar (12 g natural sugar, 1 g added sugar) • 195 mg sodium

5 FOODS TO PREVENT MUSCLE CRAMPS

A muscle cramp can strike anywhere at any time. These sharp and unpredictable spasms commonly occur in the middle of an intense workout, or shortly thereafter. But they can also strike when you're sitting at your desk or, believe it or not, when you're dead asleep in the middle of an amazing dream (you know, the one that involves you and your favorite celeb sitting on the beach with a delicious cocktail in hand). In fact, up to 60 percent of adults experience this nightmare—being woken from a dream with a painful ache in their calf.

The sudden, involuntary contraction, often referred to as a charley horse, is usually not serious, but it can be agonizing and it's most definitely inconvenient, lasting a few seconds to as long as a few minutes. Most cramps strike the leg—in particular, the calf muscle—though they can affect other muscles as well, including those in the foot or arm.

As common as cramps are, we don't know the exact cause. In many cases, the culprit can't be determined. Experts have suggested that possible triggers include muscle overuse or fatigue, nerve dysfunction, dehydration, a side effect to certain medications, and maintaining the same position for an extended period of time. An imbalance of electrolytes may also play a role.

What experts know for sure: Muscle cramps tend to become more common with age. Pregnant women are more likely to suffer from spasms in the legs, as are athletes and people with certain conditions, like diabetes and thyroid or nerve disorders.

Staying properly hydrated—aiming to drink roughly half your body weight in ounces daily—may be one refreshing fix. You will need more water if you live in warmer climates and if you're very active. Also, incorporating some gentle stretching before any kind of exercise and before bed may help keep muscles limber. Finally, certain foods may also help curb cramping.

Note: If muscle cramping becomes severe, or if you have sudden weakness or a loss of sensation, be sure to see a doctor, as this may be a sign of something more serious.

1. Bananas

Want to keep muscle cramps in check? Go bananas! One medium banana has nearly 425 mg of potassium, a mineral that plays a role in muscle contraction and function. When you don't get enough potassium in your diet, your muscles cramp. Therefore, hitting your daily goal of about 4,700 mg is key. Unfortunately only about 3 percent of Americans meet the mark.[1] Bananas provide a small amount of magnesium, another key mineral that helps with muscle function.

I love bananas because they're super convenient. You can easily stash them in your bag for a quick snack. You can blend them into virtually any fruit smoothie to enhance its creaminess, natural sweetness, and, of course, potassium content. I'm world famous (well, at least in my house) for my "healthified" chocolate milkshakes: Combine a ¾-cup scoop of light chocolate ice cream with ½ cup unsweetened vanilla almond milk, 1 teaspoon cocoa powder, and ½ of a ripe banana.

Here's a quick secret: Don't toss away overripe, brown, spotty bananas. Simply peel them, cover in plastic wrap, and stash in the freezer for future recipes, like smoothies and pancakes. They're also terrific blended into muffin and cookie batters as a natural sweetener.

I regularly make one-ingredient Banana "Nice" Cream: Peel 4 ripened bananas (the riper, the better), cut into 1-inch rounds, and freeze for at least 3 hours. Blend in a food processor until smooth. (If the bananas have been in the freezer for longer than a day, it's best to let them thaw for about 5 to 10 minutes before pureeing. If the bananas are still too hard to blend, add a splash of milk.) You can enjoy this treat on its own or mix in some almond butter and dark chocolate chips. Or use it to create Nice Cream sandwiches—simply scoop some between two chocolate graham crackers, cover in plastic wrap, and freeze until the banana ice cream firms.

While almost everyone loves a PB & Banana sandwich—you get bonus points for AB & Banana, since almonds also help with muscle cramps. Replace the sugary jelly or jam with sliced bananas and enjoy it open-faced. Another creative snack is Peanut (or Almond) Butter & Banana Sushi: Cut a banana into thick, sushi-like slices and roll them in nut butter. Top with a thin strawberry slice or finely chopped strawberries, like sprinkles.

2. Milk

Milk: It does a muscle good. As you know, it's a great source of bone-building calcium, but the mineral may also help prevent painful muscle spasms. In fact, one of the symptoms of being calcium deficient is muscle cramps, so make sure you get enough (1,000 mg per day for men, ages 50 to 70, and women through age 50; and 1,200 mg per day for women 51 and older) for strong bones and healthy muscles.

Milk contains vitamin D, calcium's bone-building bestie, which may help with spontaneous and painful contractions. And it chips in a healthy helping of potassium (about 370 mg per 1 cup on average) and magnesium (27 mg per cup). Magnesium helps transport calcium and potassium to our cells, a process important for nerve impulse conduction and muscle contraction. When we miss the mark on magnesium, one of the symptoms is muscle cramps. Magnesium supplementation is a somewhat debated treatment for cramps, with some studies suggesting it works and others suggesting it doesn't. It has been shown to have some success helping pregnant women who suffer from cramps. My advice? When these nutrients come packaged in an ultra-healthy food like milk or yogurt, it's worth a shot because it might just prove to be the delicious fix that works for you.

Depending upon the timing of your cramps, you can enjoy a glass of milk before bed or before or after a workout. Try incorporating milk into a slew of tasty meals and snacks. Blend it up with some fresh or frozen fruit (like a cramp-crushing banana) to make a refreshing smoothie or with some cocoa for a soothing cup of hot chocolate. Enjoy a bowl of whole-grain cereal with milk or try mixing it into some oatmeal. For a super food fix, add some sliced bananas and almonds.

Soy, almond, cashew, rice, and coconut milk are good options if you're trying to avoid dairy. Many are fortified with calcium and vitamin D in amounts similar to cow's milk. However, soy milk is typically the only one packed with potassium (in a similar amount to cow's milk). The potassium in other milk alternatives can vary, but it's typically less than half of that in cow's milk. Cashew and coconut milk do not contain significant amounts of magnesium, and almond milk provides just a small amount since most brands contain more water than almonds. Soy, rice, and cow's milk contain *some* magnesium, but the amounts can significantly differ by brand.

3. Edamame

Edamame, young green soybeans that are available either in the pod or shelled, are a great source of high-fiber vegetarian protein. Not only that, but they are loaded with potassium (more than 670 mg per 1 cup shelled) and contribute just about 100 mg each of calcium and magnesium to serve up a trio of cramp-busting minerals.

I always keep a bag of frozen edamame in the freezer for easy snacking. I buy them in the pods because it's fun finger food and helps to slow down eating, which is beneficial for digestion and weight control. You can boil, steam, or roast them. For boiling, simply dump the frozen pods in a large pot of boiling water for about 3 minutes, drain off the liquid, add a sprinkling of salt, and enjoy. (You can also microwave them for an even easier prep.)

For roasting, heat the oven to 375°F. Spread thawed, shell-on edamame out on a baking sheet and liberally mist with oil spray. Sprinkle with preferred seasonings (you can kick up the heat with chili powder and cumin, flavor them up with ginger and garlic, or go with the basic salt and ground black pepper). Cook until the pods start to brown (flipping them over halfway through to roast both sides), about 15 to 20 minutes total.

A 2-cup serving of edamame in the shell (or a 1-cup serving without the shell) is about 200 calories while providing 20 grams of protein and 12 grams of fiber. I stash both versions and add the little green gems to salads, pasta dishes, and stir-fries for a boost of goodness. Edamame makes an excellent side—or even main dish—when tossed with brown rice or quinoa, veggies such as bell peppers, carrots, mushrooms and scallions, a little soy sauce, toasted sesame oil, and rice wine vinegar.

Looking to try something new? If you're a fellow hummus lover, try my edamame rendition: Combine 1 cup shelled edamame (frozen, thawed), 1/3 cup water, 3 tablespoons rice vinegar, 2 tablespoons tahini (sesame seed paste), 2 tablespoons extra-virgin olive oil, 1 minced garlic clove, and 1/2 teaspoon kosher salt in a food processor and process until smooth. Season with ground black pepper and additional salt to taste. Use as a dip for veggies like broccoli florets, bell pepper sticks, celery, and more. A delicious twist on a classic.

4. Almonds

Almonds are a delicious defense against cramps: They're rich in magnesium, potassium, and calcium. They contain about 75 mg per ounce each of calcium and magnesium and 200 mg of potassium. These minerals all play a potential role in warding off muscle cramps, as being short in any one may trigger the painful spasms. And although the research on taming dreaded cramps is still inconclusive, enjoying a food that delivers the trio of super nutrients is certainly a pain-free step in the right direction. What's more, almonds are portable, readily available, and don't require refrigeration.

For fending off cramps, aim for a daily Rx of one ounce or a handful of almonds each day. Enjoy them at snack time or whip up a DIY trail mix by mixing ¼ cup of almonds with whole-grain cereal and a dash of dried fruit. As with all nuts, almonds are calorie dense (about 160 calories per 1 oz or ¼ cup), so if you're watching your weight, you can't go . . . well . . . nuts.

Of course, there are more out-of-the-box ideas that are just as tasty. Try crushing almonds and using them as a coating for fish or chicken dishes or slicing or chopping almonds and adding them to muffins or fro-yo. Also consider using almond flour (blend it in with other flours, like regular all-purpose flour, whole-wheat flour, or oat flour) in baked goods, including muffins, cookies, and pies. Because of the higher fat content, you tend to get a little more browning and a delicious flavor.

You can also make your own batch of cocoa almonds: In a large mixing bowl, beat 1 large egg white and 1 teaspoon vanilla extract until frothy. Add 2 cups raw almonds to the bowl and toss to coat thoroughly. In a separate bowl, combine 3 tablespoons cocoa powder, ⅛ teaspoon kosher salt, and 2 tablespoons sugar. Sprinkle over the almonds and toss to coat completely. Spread the almonds in an even layer on a baking sheet lined with parchment paper and bake at 275°F for 25 minutes on the middle oven rack. Using a spatula, flip the almonds over in small batches and bake 15 minutes longer. This makes 8 delicious servings (about 1 ounce/23 almonds per serving).

5. Cantaloupe

Cramping up? Have a ball—a melon ball. Cantaloupe contains 90 percent water, making it a refreshing and hydrating selection. There are only a few fruit options that offer more water, so it's a super selection in the produce aisle.

Another produce perk: Cantaloupe is packed with potassium—there's more than 470 mg per cup and most of us can easily gobble down 2 cups of this refreshingly sweet and juicy melon. As mentioned, potassium is a mineral necessary for muscle contraction and function. It's also an electrolyte that helps regulate the flow of fluids and nutrients to all our body's cells. The mouthwatering melon also contains a dash of magnesium—all for just 60 calories per cup (or about ¼ of a medium melon or 3 small wedges).

Cut cantaloupe into cubes or get fancy with a melon baller and serve it as a refreshing fruit salad along with breakfast. You can also slice it in half and fill the center with calcium-rich low-fat cottage cheese for a filling snack or a light lunch. Sprinkle on chopped almonds for another hit of cramp-fighting power. Or use small melon chunks to add a bit of sweetness to a green salad. It's delicious diced and mixed into salsa or blended into smoothies.

I like to stick cantaloupe balls on skewers along with grapes and watermelon and freeze—my kids are huge fans of my Fruit-Freeze Kebabs. They're a creative treat for a backyard party or summer barbecue.

Or try whipping up a bowl of chilled cantaloupe soup: Toss peeled, diced cantaloupe into a food processor with a bit of plain Greek yogurt, lemon juice, ginger, a little honey, and some fresh chopped mint and blend until smooth. Chill, serve, and slurp it up.

Banana Almond Bread

MAKES 12 SLICES

4 to 5 ripe bananas, chopped and mashed
1/4 cup nonfat plain Greek yogurt
3 tablespoons butter, melted
2 eggs
1/4 cup almond milk
(or any other preferred milk)
1 teaspoon vanilla extract

1 1/2 cups whole-grain flour
1/2 cup almond flour
1/2 cup sugar
1 teaspoon ground cinnamon
1 teaspoon baking soda
1/2 teaspoon baking powder
1/2 teaspoon kosher salt
1/2 cup chopped almonds

Preheat the oven to 350°F.

Mist a 9 × 5-inch loaf pan with oil spray.

Combine the wet ingredients (bananas, yogurt, butter, eggs, milk, and vanilla) in a large bowl.

Combine the dry ingredients (flours, sugar, cinnamon, baking soda, baking powder, salt, and almonds) in a separate bowl.

Add the wet ingredients to the dry ingredients and stir until the mixture is thoroughly combined. Pour the batter into the prepared loaf pan, tapping a few times on the counter to distribute evenly.

Bake the bread in the oven for 65 to 75 minutes, or until a toothpick inserted into the center comes out clean.

Remove from the oven and allow the bread to cool in the pan for about 15 minutes, loosen the edges, and then remove the loaf to cool completely on a plate or platter.

Serve immediately or wrap tightly and store in the fridge for up to a week. Alternatively, you can stash in the freezer for up to three months.

NUTRITIONAL INFORMATION *Per 1-inch slice*
190 calories • 5 g protein • 7 g total fat (2 g saturated fat, 5 g unsaturated fat) • 30 mg cholesterol • 29 g carbs • 4 g fiber • 13 g total sugar (5 g natural sugar, 8 g added sugar) • 180 mg sodium

NO BUTTER? NO PROBLEM! Follow the same recipe and replace the butter with the same amount of unsweetened applesauce, pumpkin puree, or canola oil.

Almond Butter Banana Pops

MAKES ABOUT 9 POPS

3 large ripe bananas
½ cup almond butter
½ cup unsweetened vanilla almond milk (or any other preferred milk)
1 tablespoon honey
½ teaspoon cinnamon

½ to 1 cup cantaloupe cubes (from about ¼ of a melon)
2 to 3 tablespoons almond butter (optional for garnish)
2 to 3 tablespoons chopped almonds (optional for garnish)

Add all the ingredients (with the exception of optional garnishes) to a blender and puree until smooth. Pour the mixture into a set of standard ice pop molds using a ⅓ cup of the mixture per pop and freeze for 5 to 6 hours, or until firm and solid.

For an optional garnish, place almond butter in a bowl wide enough to fit the pop. Microwave for about 20 to 30 seconds or until it becomes smooth and runny. Dip the pops into almond butter and lay them on a baking sheet covered with parchment paper. Sprinkle with chopped toasted almonds, if desired. Refreeze or enjoy immediately.

NUTRITION INFORMATION *Per pop**
130 calories • 4 g protein • 8 g total fat (1 g saturated fat, 7 g unsaturated fat) • 0 mg cholesterol • 13 g carbs • 2 g fiber • 7 g total sugar (5 g natural sugar, 2 g added sugar) • 45 mg sodium

*Note: If using optional garnishes, add 30 calories, 1 g protein, and 1 g fiber per pop.

Edamame Lettuce Wraps with Almond Butter Sauce

MAKES 28 WRAPS

Edamame Lettuce Wraps

1 to 2 heads butterhead lettuce, leaves
   separated and patted dry
2 cups shelled edamame beans,
   cooked and cooled (fresh or frozen)
1 red pepper, diced
1 cup shredded carrots

2 cups shredded purple/red cabbage
½ cup chopped fresh cilantro
⅓ cup chopped almonds,
   plus more for garnish
1 lime, wedged

Almond Butter Sauce

½ cup almond butter
½ cup almond milk (or any other
   preferred milk)
2 tablespoons reduced-sodium
   soy sauce

2 tablespoons honey
2 teaspoons ground ginger
1 teaspoon sriracha sauce (optional)

Lay out the lettuce leaves on a platter.

Mix the edamame, red pepper, carrots, and cabbage in a large bowl. Then, place about ¼ cup vegetable mixture onto each lettuce leaf.

To prepare the Almond Butter Sauce, combine all the ingredients in a saucepan. Warm over low to medium heat, stirring occasionally, until smooth and creamy. Alternatively, you can warm the sauce in the microwave, stirring every 30 seconds, until the almond butter is fully incorporated into the sauce and everything is well combined. Let cool.

Drizzle the sauce generously over each vegetable wrap and top with cilantro and chopped almonds. Garnish with lime wedges.

NUTRITIONAL INFORMATION *Per 4 wraps with 1 tablespoon sauce on each*
240 calories • 11 g protein • 14 g total fat (1 g saturated fat, 13 g unsaturated) • 0 mg cholesterol •
20 g carbs • 6 g fiber • 9 g total sugar (5 g natural sugar, 4 g added sugar) • 260 mg sodium

5 FOODS TO
STRENGTHEN
BRITTLE NAILS

It's often said that the eyes are the window to the soul, but your fingernails may just be the window to your health. Prime example: Dry, brittle, cracking nails can be an indication that you're suffering from a vitamin deficiency or a medical issue like a thyroid problem or osteopenia (a condition in which bone density is low but not low enough to be considered osteoporosis). Or it could be a sign that you get too many manicures or do too much housework (that's my excuse this week for skipping the dishes). And in some cases, it can simply be a result of aging.

Let's talk about a healthy nail. Fingernails grow at a rate of about 3 millimeters per month, with a complete replacement of the nail happening in six to nine months. Nails are made of a protein called keratin, and healthy nails need to be hydrated (Vaseline, Aquaphor, or a Eucerin-type product will do the trick). In fact, when the amount of water in nails is reduced to less than 16 percent, they become brittle.

Brittle nails, or *onychorrhexis*, is basically just fragile and dry nail plates. It affects 60 million people, and women are more likely to suffer than men.[1] Typically, it affects the first three fingernails, and nail-biting (*onychophagia* is the scientific term) puts you at an increased risk for the condition.

So how can you protect yourself? Wearing waterproof gloves (ideally, lined with cotton) to keep nails dry whenever you do the dishes or any other household task that involves water is key. Ironically, water is drying—nails are porous and water can get into small spaces and cause cracks once the nails dry. Not to mention, soaps and detergents can be tough on your nails. Rehydrating nails with a topical moisturizer when they're exposed to water can help, as can keeping nails short and filed to prevent any snags or easy breaks.

The following foods have been shown to help strengthen nails. But be patient. It can take time to see the results, so keep on the path of healthy eating and eventually, you'll, um, nail it.

1. Eggs

When it comes to nail health, it's biotin for the win. The B vitamin (B_7) can be found in a variety of foods, but egg yolks are a particularly rich source. You need 30 micrograms (mcg) of the vitamin daily (breastfeeding women need 35 mcg per day), and you'll score a third of your goal—10 mcg—with just a single whole egg.

Several studies show that biotin helps with brittle nails and brittle nail syndrome, a chronic condition of splitting, peeling, and surface layering in the nails as well as a loss of flexibility on the surface of the nail so it breaks easily and the edges fray.[2] In one study, biotin improved the thickness of nails by 25 percent and reduced splitting compared to a control group.[3]

Of course, eggs are a go-to breakfast food and there are so many ways to prepare them, including scrambled, poached, hard-boiled, and sunny side up, in addition to in omelets and breakfast burritos.

Don't have time to prepare eggs in the morning? No problem! Try this quick and simple trick: Mist an oversize mug with oil spray, add 1 whole egg and 2 to 3 egg whites and whisk. (I prefer to mix 1 whole egg with a few egg whites to dilute calories and saturated fat, which are both concentrated in the yolk along with beneficial biotin.) Microwave for 45 seconds, add preferred seasonings and optional cheese, and then gently stir to mix throughout. Microwave for another 45 to 60 seconds (or until it's set), remove, and dig in.

You can also enjoy them for a snack—I'm a huge fan of hard-boiled eggs because they're quick, easy, and protein-packed, so they're satisfying and have staying power. You can also have eggs for lunch. Toss them into salads for an extra hit of nutrients or whip up a scrumptious egg salad sandwich. At the Bauer house, we're famous for having breakfast for dinner—we frequently whip up vegetable-packed omelets and frittatas and wear our PJs at the dinner table. Fuzzy slippers optional!

2. Cauliflower

Talk about cauliflower power. This cruciferous veggie is another good source of biotin, with as much as 4 mcg per cup. Biotin has been shown to help strengthen nails in a multitude of smaller studies. Not only that, but it's a head (pun intended) above other foods when it comes to vitamin C. You'll get more than 50 mg in 1 cup of chopped cauliflower. (The daily goal for C is 75 mg a day for women; 90 mg a day for men.) Research suggests that people who are deficient in the immune-boosting vitamin may suffer from thin, soft nails that break easily.[4] Also, vitamin C helps boost iron absorption.[5] Because iron deficiency can be associated with dry, brittle nails, getting more vitamin C in your diet could help boost nail health.

You can eat cauliflower as is. When it is raw, it makes a delish crudité dipper or crunchy snack. It's also an easy side—steamed, boiled, or roasted and seasoned up with your favorite spices—with almost any main entrée, such as fish, chicken, or pork.

That being said, I like to get a little more creative. I'm completely obsessed with using it as a low-carb replacement for comfort foods. Cauliflower plays a starring role in my mashed potatoes; I regularly use a 50-50 mix (50 percent spuds and 50 percent steamed, mashed cauli) or go 100 percent mashed cauliflower, seasoning it up with light cream cheese, broth, and spices. You can make cauliflower vegan "steaks": Cut 1 head of cauliflower into 1-inch-thick slices, brush both sides of each slice with olive oil, add a sprinkling of salt and ground black pepper, then place the slices on a heated grill and cook for about 5 minutes per side. Remove from the grill, coat each side with barbecue sauce, and place back on the grill for about 3 to 5 more minutes per side. (Alternatively, you can roast your "steaks" at 400°F for about 30 minutes, flipping them about halfway through.)

You can easily make cauliflower "rice" by pulsing florets in the food processor or by grating them with a handheld gadget. Use this lower-carb "rice" as a base for your favorite stir-fry dishes, risotto, or even paella. I also use cauliflower to make low-carb bread and crust for delicious and healthier renditions of Bauer family faves like grilled cheese sandwiches, pizza, and quiche.

3. Crab

It's okay to be crabby. The crustacean contains the mineral zinc, an essential trace element (just like biotin) that serves many important functions in the body. It helps with wound healing, the immune system, and metabolism—and research suggests that a deficiency in zinc may lead to brittle nails.[6]

Keep in mind that the body can't store zinc, so we have to get it through our diet on a regular basis. Women 19 years and older need 8 mg daily; men and pregnant women over this age need 11 mg; and breastfeeding moms need 12 mg. Crab delivers almost 9 mg of zinc per 4 ounces cooked; that's 43 percent of your daily goal. Red meat, poultry, and other shellfish are also good sources. In fact, oysters are a real standout for zinc, but crab nabbed the top spot because it tends to be more universal, easier to cook with, and more accessible in restaurants and at grocery stores.

But buyer beware: It's very easy to buy imitation crab meat, a blend of starch and various fish parts and species, including the white fish surimi, which is then ground into a paste and shaped to resemble a crab leg. Think of it as the hot dog of the sea. Although it might look and taste somewhat similar to the real deal, it's significantly lower in zinc and other minerals (including iron, magnesium, and potassium), as well as protein. And it's not gluten-free, for those who are trying to avoid gluten.

Go for real crab meat and add it to dips, use it as a topping on your favorite green salad, mix it into warm pasta entrées or cold pasta salad, or use it to make "baked" crab cakes or to whip up a delish crab casserole. And I'd be remiss not to mention how much I love a Maryland soft-shell crab fest. I also enjoy getting to work on hard-shell crabs, with all the requisite tools, including crackers, pickers, and mallets . . . and yes, even the bib! I love a chilled crab cocktail, crab enchiladas, and tomato and crab soup.

You can also try your hand at whipping up avocado toast with crab. Mash an avocado with the back of a fork and season with a dash of salt and pepper. Spread some of the mashed avocado on whole-grain toast, sprinkle on crab meat, squeeze fresh lemon on top, and add the seasonings of your choice. It's super delicious.

4. Pork Tenderloin

Another food that's rich in zinc is pork. Research suggests that people with zinc deficiencies may suffer with brittle nails, and getting adequate amounts of zinc may help. Of all the various cuts of pork, I chose to feature pork tenderloin because it's a lean and healthful pick. It offers almost 3.5 mg of zinc per 4 ounces cooked and contains only about 210 calories, with minimal amounts of saturated fat. In fact, the nutrition profile of pork tenderloin is similar to that of skinless chicken and turkey breast, and it offers a nice change of pace if you're stuck in a poultry rut. Pork tenderloin also contains iron, more than 1.5 mg per 4 ounces. (An iron deficiency can also contribute to brittle nails.)

Whip up a delectable dry rub using the seasonings you love best. You could try a mix of oregano, cumin, coriander, and thyme or go spicy with garlic powder, mustard powder, dried ginger, red pepper flakes, cayenne pepper, and smoked paprika. Or coat your pork tenderloin with a combo of Parm and panko. Create your own homemade concoction. Then simply roast it in the oven at 425°F for 20 to 35 minutes per 1 to 1½ pounds or grill for the same amount of time.

I use pork tenderloin to make skewers: Cut the meat into thin strips, thread them onto wooden skewers that have been presoaked in water, and season with salt, ground pepper, and other spices. Cook in a skillet coated with oil spray over medium-high heat for about 5 minutes per side. Then serve with a spicy peanut butter sauce (½ cup peanut butter, ¼ cup broth, ¼ cup water, 2 tablespoons soy sauce, and optional sriracha). You can serve the skewers with whatever sauce you prefer (barbecue works well too) and enjoy them as an appetizer or a meal.

You can use pork tenderloin to make tacos or pulled pork sandwiches (cook the meat in the slow cooker and then shred), or simply roast the pork. It helps to sear it first—brown it on all sides on the stove before popping it in the oven—to lock in the juices. Then flavor it up with your favorite seasonings and cook until done. Serve it with a side veggie and salad and you're all set.

A lot of people rely on the color test when cooking pork—making sure it's fully white with no signs of pink. Instead, I rely on my meat thermometer to cook it until it hits an internal temperature of 145°F, avoiding overcooking.

5. Green Beans

Green beans may be a member of the common bean family, but they are anything but common. The standard Thanksgiving side dish is a good source of dietary silicon, a trace element that plays a key role in connective tissue, which includes nails. They contain about 11 mg per 1 cup (while this is significant, there is no daily requirement set for silicon). In one study, researchers analyzed a variety of foods and found that absorption of silicon was among the highest for green beans (44 percent of the dose).[7] As a bonus, it also includes a bit of zinc.

Canned, frozen, or fresh green beans are all good options, so choose whatever works best for you. Frozen and canned are often as nutritious as fresh because they're packaged at their peak. If choosing canned varieties, opt for low-salt versions if you're watching your sodium (or rinse them well), and avoid any that are creamed or in a sauce to keep calories, sodium, and sugar in check. You can enjoy them steamed, baked, in a casserole, tossed in a stir-fry, or flavored up with your favorite seasonings. They're super versatile.

I like to top steamed, tender-crisp green beans with sautéed shallots and toasted slivered almonds and drizzle on a squeeze of fresh lemon with salt and pepper. You can also microwave or steam fresh green beans and then add them to a skillet with sautéed garlic and onion. Add some sesame oil and reduced-sodium soy sauce, transfer to a serving dish, and sprinkle with whole-grain bread crumbs and sesame seeds.

For a cold spin, try a fresh green bean and tomato salad. After blanching or boiling the green beans for about 2 minutes, drain and chill them in a bowl of ice water. Cut 2 large tomatoes into wedges and set aside. Whisk together the juice of 1 lemon, 1 tablespoon extra-virgin olive oil, 1 tablespoon fresh dill, salt, and pepper. Add the green beans and tomatoes to a large bowl and toss with the dressing. So simple and scrumptious.

Cauliflower "Fried" Rice

MAKES 4 SERVINGS

3 large eggs, lightly beaten
Salt to taste
½ yellow onion, finely diced
1 bunch scallions, diced, whites and
   greens separated
2 cups diced or chopped fresh green
   beans (one 10-ounce package)
1 large red bell pepper, finely diced
2 garlic cloves, minced (or ¼ teaspoon
   garlic powder)

½ to 1 cup shelled edamame (optional)
½ cup peas (optional)
½ cup finely diced carrots (optional)
7 to 8 cups uncooked cauliflower rice
   (about 24 ounces)
1 tablespoon sesame oil
4 tablespoons reduced-sodium soy
   sauce (or more to taste)
Hot sauce (optional)
Red pepper flakes (optional)

Liberally coat a large skillet with oil spray and warm over medium heat. Add the eggs and cook until firm. Season with salt and chop into small pieces with a spatula or wooden spoon. Set aside.

Reapply oil spray to the skillet and add the onion, scallions (whites only), green beans, bell pepper, garlic, and optional veggies (edamame, peas, and carrots). Sauté for about 4 to 5 minutes until soft.

Add the cauliflower rice to the skillet, along with the sesame oil and soy sauce. Mix, cover, and cook approximately 8 minutes, stirring frequently, until the cauliflower is slightly crispy on the outside but tender on the inside.

Add the egg and mix thoroughly. Remove from the heat and mix in the scallion greens. Taste and add more soy sauce, if desired. If you like it spicy, serve with hot sauce and crushed red pepper flakes.

NUTRITIONAL INFORMATION *Per serving (about 2 cups)*
180 calories • 12 g protein • 7 g total fat (1.5 g saturated fat, 5.5 g unsaturated fats) • 125 mg cholesterol • 21 g carbs • 3 g fiber • 10 g total sugar (10 g natural sugar, 0 g added sugar) • 500 mg sodium

Pulled Pork Sandwich

MAKES 18 SANDWICHES

For the pulled pork
2 yellow or Vidalia onions, thinly sliced
3 pounds pork tenderloin, cut into 2 to
   3 large pieces
2 ¼ cups barbecue sauce
2 tablespoons Worcestershire sauce

1 teaspoon paprika
½ teaspoon garlic powder
½ teaspoon salt
½ teaspoon ground black pepper

For each sandwich
1 whole-grain bun
2 heaping tablespoons store-bought or
   homemade coleslaw

1 egg, sunny side up
Steamed green beans (on the side)

Liberally coat a large skillet with oil spray. Sauté sliced onions until browned and caramelized, about 8 minutes over low-medium heat, stirring occasionally.

Place the pork tenderloin in the bottom of a slow cooker.

Mix the remaining pulled-pork ingredients in a small bowl. Pour the mixture over the pork in the slow cooker, add the sautéed onions, and stir to coat the pork completely. Cover and secure the lid. Cook on high for 4 hours or low for 7 to 8 hours.

When you lift the cover, the inside will be very watery. This is normal. Carefully lift out the pork, place it on a plate, and shred with two forks. Place all of the shredded pork back into the slow cooker and combine with the liquid and mix until all the liquid is absorbed. Season with additional salt and pepper to taste.

To assemble each sandwich, place ½-cup scoop of pork on a lightly toasted whole-grain bun, top with coleslaw and sunny-side up egg. Cover with the top half of the bun. Serve with steamed green beans (another nail-boosting food) on the side.

NUTRITIONAL INFORMATION *Per sandwich*
330 calories • 29 g protein • 11 g total fat (3 g saturated fat, 8 g unsaturated fat) • 315 mg cholesterol • 27 g carbs • 2 g fiber • 11 g total sugar (11 g natural sugar, 0 g added sugar) • 900 mg sodium

Crab Dip with Veggies

MAKES ABOUT 3 ½ CUPS

One 15-ounce can cannellini beans,
    drained and rinsed
8 ounces lump crab meat, canned
    or fresh
¼ cup grated Asiago cheese
    (or Parmesan)
6 tablespoons nonfat plain
    Greek yogurt
6 tablespoons reduced-fat cream
    cheese, room temperature
2 tablespoons chopped fresh chives
    or scallions

2 teaspoons lemon juice
2 tablespoons chopped fresh dill
    or 2 teaspoons dried dill
⅛ teaspoon kosher salt
    (or more to taste)
⅛ teaspoon ground black pepper
    (or more to taste)
Green beans (on the side)
Cauliflower florets (on the side)

Add beans into a large mixing bowl and mash about half with the back of a fork. Add the crab, cheese, yogurt, cream cheese, chives, lemon juice, dill, salt, and pepper, and mix well to combine everything. Season with additional salt, pepper, and herbs to taste. Serve the dip with fresh green beans and cauliflower florets (raw or blanched).

NUTRITIONAL INFORMATION *Per 2 tablespoons*
35 calories • 3 g protein • 1.5 g total fat (0.5 g saturated fat, 1 g unsaturated fat) • 15 mg cholesterol • 3 g carbs • 1 g fiber • 0 g total sugar • 90 mg sodium

CONVERSION CHARTS

The recipes in this book use the standard United States method for measuring liquid and dry or solid ingredients (teaspoons, tablespoons, and cups). The following charts are provided to help cooks outside the U.S. successfully use these recipes. All equivalents are approximate.

Standard Cup	Fine Powder (e.g., flour)	Grain (e.g., rice)	Granular (e.g., sugar)	Liquid Solids (e.g., butter)	Liquid (e.g., milk)
1	140 g	150 g	190 g	200 g	240 ml
¾	105 g	113 g	143 g	150 g	180 ml
⅔	93 g	100 g	125 g	133 g	160 ml
½	70 g	75 g	95 g	100 g	120 ml
⅓	47 g	50 g	63 g	67 g	80 ml
¼	35 g	38 g	48 g	50 g	60 ml
⅛	18 g	19 g	24 g	25 g	30 ml

Useful Equivalents for Liquid Ingredients by Volume				
¼ tsp				1 ml
½ tsp				2 ml
1 tsp				5 ml
3 tsp	1 tbsp		½ fl oz	15 ml
	2 tbsp	⅛ cup	1 fl oz	30 ml
	4 tbsp	¼ cup	2 fl oz	60 ml
	5⅓ tbsp	⅓ cup	3 fl oz	80 ml
	8 tbsp	½ cup	4 fl oz	120 ml
	10⅔ tbsp	⅔ cup	5 fl oz	160 ml
	12 tbsp	¾ cup	6 fl oz	180 ml
	16 tbsp	1 cup	8 fl oz	240 ml
	1 pt	2 cups	16 fl oz	480 ml
	1 qt	4 cups	32 fl oz	960 ml
			33 fl oz	1000 ml	1 l

Useful Equivalents for Dry Ingredients by Weight		
(To convert ounces to grams, multiply the number of ounces by 30.)		
1 oz	1/16 lb	30 g
4 oz	1/4 lb	120 g
8 oz	1/2 lb	240 g
12 oz	3/4 lb	360 g
16 oz	1 lb	480 g

Useful Equivalents for Cooking/Oven Temperatures			
Process	Fahrenheit	Celsius	Gas Mark
Freeze Water	32° F	0° C	
Room Temperature	68° F	20° C	
Boil Water	212° F	100° C	
Bake	325° F	160° C	3
	350° F	180° C	4
	375° F	190° C	5
	400° F	200° C	6
	425° F	220° C	7
	450° F	230° C	8
Broil			Grill

Useful Equivalents for Length				
(To convert inches to centimeters, multiply the number of inches by 2.5.)				
1 in			2.5 cm	
6 in	1/2 ft		15 cm	
12 in	1 ft		30 cm	
36 in	3 ft	1 yd	90 cm	
40 in			100 cm	1 m

ENDNOTES

5 Foods to Minimize Belly Fat

1. The Endocrine Society, "Successful weight loss with dieting is linked to vitamin D levels," ScienceDaily, June 12, 2009. https://www.sciencedaily.com/releases/2009/06/090611142524.htm; Major et al, "Supplementation with calcium + vitamin D enhances the beneficial effect of weight loss on plasma lipid and lipoprotein concentrations," *American Journal of Clinical Nutrition* 85, no. 1 (January 2007): 54–59. http://ajcn.nutrition.org/content/85/1/54.full

2. Josse et al, "Increased consumption of dairy foods and protein during diet- and exercise-induced weight loss promotes fat mass loss and lean mass gain in overweight and obese premenopausal women," *The Journal of Nutrition* 141, no. 9 (September 2011): 1626–1634. doi:10.3945/jn.111.141028

3. Bush et al, "Dietary calcium intake is associated with less gain in intra-abdominal adipose tissue over 1 yr," *Obesity* 18, no. 11 (November 2010): 2101–2104. Published online March 4, 2010. doi:10.1038/oby.2010.39

4. Kobyliak et al, "Probiotics in prevention and treatment of obesity: A critical view," *Nutrition and Metabolism* 13, no. 1 (February 20, 2016). doi:10.1186/s12986-016-0067-0

5. Cook et al, "Vegetable consumption is linked to decreased visceral and liver fat and improved insulin resistance in overweight Latino youth," *Journal of the Academy of Nutrition and Dietetics* 114, no. 11 (November 2014): 1776–83. doi:10.1016/j.jand.2014.01.017

6. Joanne Slavin, "Fiber and prebiotics: Mechanisms and health benefits," *Nutrients* 5, no. 4 (April 2013): 1417–1435. doi:10.3390/nu5041417; Sofia Kolida and Glenn R. Gibson, "Prebiotic capacity of inulin-type fructans," *The Journal of Nutrition* 137, no. 11 (November 1, 2007): 2503S–2506S. https://doi.org/10.1093/jn/137.11.2503S

5 Foods to Boost Energy

1. Jang et al, "Luteolin inhibits microglia and alters hippo-campal dependent spatial working memory in aged mice," *The Journal of Nutrition* 140, no. 10 (October 1, 2010): 1892–98. https://academic.oup.com/jn/article/140/10/1892/4600364#111457580

2. Helen S. Driver and Sheila R. Taylor, "Exercise and sleep," *Sleep Medicine Reviews* 4, no. 4 (August 2000): 387–402. https://www.ncbi.nlm.nih.gov/pubmed/12531177

3. Armstrong et al, "Mild dehydration affects mood in healthy young women," *Journal of Nutrition* 142, no. 2 (February 2012): 382–8. doi:10.3945/jn.111.142000

4. Wu et al, "Resveratrol protects against physical fatigue and improves exercise performance in mice," *Molecules* 18, no. 4 (April 2013): 4689–4702. doi:10.3390/molecules18044689

5. Verdon et al, "Iron supplementation for unexplained fatigue in non-anaemic women: Double blind randomised placebo controlled trial," *BMJ* 326 (May 2003): 1124. http://www.bmj.com/content/326/7399/1124

6. Madhavan Naira and Little Flower Augustine, "Food synergies for improving bioavailability of micronutrients from plant foods," *Food Chemistry 238*, no. 1 (January 2018): 180–185. https://doi.org/10.1016/j.foodchem.2016.09.115

7. Nechuta et al, "Soy food intake after diagnosis of breast cancer and survival: An in-depth analysis of combined evidence from cohort studies of US and Chinese women," *American Journal of Clinical Nutrition* 96, no. 1 (May 30, 2012): 123–132. doi:10.3945/ajcn.112.035972

8. Zick et al, "Fatigue reduction diet in breast cancer survivors: A pilot randomized clinical trial," *Breast Cancer Research and Treatment* 161, no. 2 (January 2017): 299–310. doi:10.1007/s10549-016-4070-y

9. Dae-Ik Kim and Kil-Soo Kim, "Walnut extract exhibits anti-fatigue action via improvement of exercise tolerance in mice," *Laboratory Animal Research* 29, no. 4 (December 2013): 190–5. https://www.ncbi.nlm.nih.gov/pubmed/24396383

10. Maes et al, "In chronic fatigue syndrome, the decreased levels of omega-3 poly-unsaturated fatty acids are related to lowered serum zinc and defects in T cell activation," *Neuro Endocrinology Letters* 26, no. 6 (December 2005): 745-51. https://www.ncbi.nlm.nih.gov/pubmed/16380690

5 Foods to Ease Anxiety and Stress

1. Kiecolt-Glaser et al, "Omega-3 supplementation lowers inflammation and anxiety in medical students: A randomized controlled trial," *Brain, Behavior, and Immunity* 25, no. 8 (November 2011): 1725–34. doi:10.1016/j.bbi.2011.07.229

2. de Oliveira et al, "Effects of oral vitamin C supplementation on anxiety in students: A double-blind, randomized, placebo-controlled trial," *Pakistan Journal of Biological Sciences* 18, no. 1 (January 2015): 11–8. https://www.ncbi.nlm.nih.gov/pubmed/26353411

3. Hsiao et al, "The association between baseline subjective anxiety rating and changes in cardiac autonomic nervous activity in response to tryptophan depletion in healthy volunteers," *Medicine* 95, no. 19 (May 2016). https://www.ncbi.nlm.nih.gov/pmc/articles/PMC4902487/pdf/medi-95-e3498.pdf

4. Hudson et al, "Protein-source tryptophan as an efficacious treatment for social anxiety disorder: A pilot study," *Canadian Journal of Physiology and Pharmacology* 85, no. 9 (2007): 928–932. doi:10.1139/Y07-082

5. Brody et al, "A randomized controlled trial of high dose ascorbic acid for reduction of blood pressure, cortisol, and subjective responses to psychological stress," *Psychopharmacology* 159, no. 3 (January 2002): 319–24. https://www.ncbi.nlm.nih.gov/pubmed/11862365

6. Amsterdam et al, "A randomized, double-blind, placebo-controlled trial of oral Matricaria recutita (chamomile) extract therapy for generalized anxiety disorder," *Journal of Clinical Psychopharmacology* 29, no. 4 (August 2009): 378–82. doi:10.1097/JCP.0b013e3181ac935c

5 Foods to Banish Bloating

1. Lacy et al, "Pathophysiology, evaluation, and treatment of bloating: Hope, hype, or hot air?" *Gastroenterology & Hepatology* 7, no. 11 (November 2011): 729. https://www.ncbi.nlm.nih.gov/pmc/articles/PMC3264926/pdf/GH-07-729.pdf

2. Cash et al, "A novel delivery system of peppermint oil is an effective therapy for irritable bowel syndrome symptoms," *Digestive Diseases and Sciences* 61, no. 2 (February 2016): 560–71. doi:10.1007/s10620-015-3858-7

3. Diane L. McKay and Jeffrey B. Blumberg, "A review of the bioactivity and potential health benefits of peppermint tea (Mentha piperita L.)," *Phytotherapy Research* 20, no. 8 (August 2006): 619–33. https://www.ncbi.nlm.nih.gov/pubmed/16767798

5 Foods to Cure a Hangover

1. C. J. Peter Eriksson, "The role of acetaldehyde in the actions of alcohol (update 2000)," *Alcoholism: Clinical and Experimental Research* 25, no. s1 (May 2001): 15S–32S. https://www.ncbi.nlm.nih.gov/pubmed/11391045

2. https://www.acs.org/content/acs/en/pressroom/newsreleases/2013/april/on-yak-a-mein-soup-aka-old -sober.html

3. Khan et al, "Alcohol-induced hangover. A double-blind comparison of pyritinol and placebo in preventing hangover symptoms," *Quarterly Journal on Studies of Alcohol* 34, no. 4 (December 1973): 1195–201. https:// www.ncbi.nlm.nih.gov/pubmed/4588294; http://annals.org/aim/fullarticle/713513/alcohol-hangover

4. Kim et al, "Ameliorating effects of Mango (Mangifera indica L.) fruit on plasma ethanol level in a mouse model assessed with H-NMR based metabolic profiling," *Journal of Clinical Biochemistry and Nutrition* 48, no. 3 (May 2011): 214–21. doi:10.3164/jcbn.10-96

5. Ibid.

5 Foods to Combat Colds and Flu

1. Rennard et al, "Chicken soup inhibits neutrophil chemotaxis in vitro," *Chest* 118, no. 4 (October 2000): 1150-7. https://www.ncbi.nlm.nih.gov/pubmed/11035691

2. Harri Hemilä and Elizabeth Chalker, "Vitamin C for preventing and treating the common cold," *Cochrane Database of Systematic Reviews*. Published online January 31, 2013. doi:10.1002/14651858 .CD000980.pub4

3. Wu et al, "Dietary supplementation with white button mushroom enhances natural killer cell activity in C57BL/6 mice," *Journal of Nutrition* 137, no. 6 (June 2007): 1472–1477. http://jn.nutrition.org/ content/137/6/1472.abstract

4. Livny et al, "Beta-carotene bioavailability from differently processed carrot meals in human ileostomy volunteers," *European Journal of Nutrition* 42, no. 6 (December 2003): 338–45. https://www.ncbi.nlm .nih.gov/pubmed/14673607

5 Foods to Lift Brain Fog

1. Devore et al, "Dietary intakes of berries and flavonoids in relation to cognitive decline," *Annals of Neurology* 72, no. 1 (July 2012): 135–43. doi:10.1002/ana.23594

2. Arendash et al, "Caffeine protects Alzheimer's mice against cognitive impairment and reduces brain beta-amyloid production," *Neuroscience* 142, no. 4 (November 3, 2006): 941–952. https://www.ncbi.nlm. nih.gov/pubmed/16938404

3. Carrie H.S. Ruxton, "The impact of caffeine on mood, cognitive function, performance and hydration: A review of benefits and risks," *Nutrition Bulletin* 33 (first published February 13, 2008): 15–25. http:// onlinelibrary.wiley.com/doi/10.1111/j.1467-3010.2007.00665.x/full#b19

4. Crichton et al, "Chocolate intake is associated with better cognitive function: The Maine–Syracuse Longitudinal Study," *Appetite* 100 (May 1, 2016): 126–32. doi:10.1016/j.appet.2016.02.010

5. Andrew Scholey and Lauren Owen, "Effects of chocolate on cognitive function and mood: A systematic review," *Nutrition Reviews* 71, no. 10 (October 2013): 665–81. doi:10.1111/nure.12065

6. Cynthia Blanton, "Improvements in iron status and cognitive function in young women consuming beef or non-beef lunches," *Nutrients* 6, no. 1 (December 27, 2013): 90–110.

7. Zhao et al, "Inhibition of pattern recognition receptor-mediated inflammation by bioactive phytochemicals: A review of recent research," *Nutrition Reviews* 69, no. 6 (June 2011): 310–320. doi:10.1111/j.1753-4887.2011.00394.x

5 Foods to Ease Aches and Pains

1. Institute of Medicine Report: *Relieving Pain in America: A Blueprint for Transforming Prevention, Care, Education, and Research* (Washington, D.C.: The National Academies Press, 2011). https://doi.org/10.17226/13172

2. Black et al, "Ginger (*Zingiber officinale*) reduces muscle pain caused by eccentric exercise," *The Journal of Pain* 11, no. 9 (September 2010): 894–903. doi: 10.1016/j.jpain.2009.12.013

3. James et al, "Efficacy of turmeric extracts and curcumin for alleviating the symptoms of joint arthritis: A systematic review and meta analysis of randomized clinical trials," *Journal of Medicinal Food* 19, no. 8 (August 1, 2016): 717–729. doi:10.1089/jmf.2016.3705

4. Darshan S. Kelley, Yuriko Adkins, and Kevin D. Laugero, "A Review of the Health Benefits of Cherries" *Nutrients* 10 (2018): 368. doi:10.3390/nu10030368, https://www.ncbi.nlm.nih.gov/pmc/articles/PMC5872786/pdf/nutrients-10-00368.pdf

5. Connolly et al, "Efficacy of a tart cherry juice blend in preventing the symptoms of muscle damage," *British Journal of Sports Medicine* 40, no. 8 (2006):679–683; Kuehl et al, "Efficacy of a tart cherry juice in reducing muscle pain during running: a randomized controlled trial," *Journal of the International Society of Sports Nutrition* 7, no. 17 (2010). https://doi.org/10.1186/1550-2783-7-17; Howatson et al, "Influence of tart cherry juice on indices of recovery following marathon running," *Scandinavian Journal of Medicine & Science in Sports* 20, no. 6 (December 2010): 843–852. doi: 10.1111/j.1600-0838.2009.01005.x

6. Vitale et al, "Tart cherry juice in athletes: A literature review and commentary," *Current Sports Medicine Reports* 16, no. 4 (July/August 2017): 230–239. doi:10.1249/JSR.0000000000000385

7. Lisa Parkinson and Russell Keast, "Oleocanthal, a phenolic derived from virgin olive oil: A review of the beneficial effects on inflammatory disease," *International Journal of Molecular Sciences* 15, no. 7 (July 2014): 12323–12334. doi:10.3390/ijms150712323

8. Misra et al, "Vitamin K deficiency is associated with incident knee osteoarthritis," *American Journal of Medicine* 126, no. 3 (March 2013): 243–248. doi:10.1016/j.amjmed.2012.10.011

9. Davidson et al, "Sulforaphane represses matrix-degrading proteases and protects cartilage from destruction in vitro and in vivo," *Arthritis & Rheumatology* 65, no. 12 (December 2013): 3130–3140. doi:10.1002/art.38133

5 Foods to Reduce Wrinkles

1. Jouni Uitto, "The role of elastin and collagen in cutaneous aging: intrinsic aging versus photoexposure," *Journal of Drugs in Dermatology* 7, no. 2 (February 2008): s12–6. https://www.ncbi.nlm.nih.gov/pubmed/18404866

2. Fielding et al, "Increases in plasma lycopene concentration after consumption of tomatoes cooked with olive oil," *Asia Pacific Journal of Clinical Nutrition* 14, no. 2 (January 2005): 131–6. https://www.ncbi.nlm.nih.gov/pubmed/15927929

3. Riwan et al, "Tomato paste rich in lycopene protects against cutaneous photodamage in humans in vivo: a randomized controlled trial," *British Journal of Dermatology* 164, no. 1 (January 2011): 154–62. doi:10.1111/j.1365-2133.2010.10057.x

4. Cooperstone et al, "Tomatoes protect against development of UV-induced keratinocyte carcinoma via metabolomic alterations," *Scientific Reports* 7, article no. 5106 (2017). doi:10.1038/s41598-017-05568-7

5. Dewanto et al, "Thermal processing enhances the nutritional value of tomatoes by increasing total antioxidant activity," *Journal of Agricultural and Food Chemistry* 50, no. 10 (April 17, 2002): 3010–3014. doi:10.1021/jf0115589

6. Hakim et al, "Fat intake and risk of squamous cell carcinoma of the skin," *Nutrition and Cancer* 36, no. 2 (2002): 155–62. https://www.ncbi.nlm.nih.gov/pubmed/10890025

7. Soyun Cho, "The role of functional foods in cutaneous anti-aging," *Journal of Lifestyle Medicine* 4, no. 1 (March 2014): 8–16. doi: 10.15280/jlm.2014.4.1.8

8. Clarke et al, "Green tea catechins and their metabolites in human skin before and after exposure to ultraviolet radiation," *The Journal of Nutritional Biochemistry* 27, (January 2016): 203–210; Megow et al, "A Randomized Controlled Trial of Green Tea Beverages on the in vivo Radical Scavenging Activity in Human Skin," *Skin Pharmacology and Physiology* 30, no. 5 (2017): 225–233. doi: 10.1159/000477355. Epub 2017 Jul 20; Chen et al, "Anti-skin-aging effect of epigallocatechin gallate by regulating epidermal growth factor receptor pathway on aging mouse model induced by d-Galactose," *Mechanisms of Ageing and Development* 164 (June 2017):1–7. doi: 10.1016/j.mad.2017.03.007. Epub 2017 Mar 24.

9. Cosgrove et al, "Dietary nutrient intakes and skin-aging appearance among middle-aged American women," *American Journal of Clinical Nutrition* 86, no. 4 (October 2007): 1225–1231. http://ajcn.nutrition.org/content/86/4/1225.long

5 Foods to Lower Cholesterol

1. Ha et al, "Effect of dietary pulse intake on established therapeutic lipid targets for cardiovascular risk reduction: A systematic review and meta-analysis of randomized controlled trials," *CMAJ* 190, no. 8 (first published April 7, 2014). doi:10.1503/cmaj.131727

5 Foods to Relieve Seasonal Allergies

1. de Batlle et al, "Mediterranean diet is associated with reduced asthma and rhinitis in Mexican children," *Allergy* 63, no. 10 (October 2008): 1310–6. doi:10.1111/j.1398-9995.2008.01722.x

2. Castro-Rodriguez et al, "Olive oil during pregnancy is associated with reduced wheezing during the first year of life of the offspring," *Pediatric Pulmonology* 45, no. 4 (April 2010): 395–402. http://onlinelibrary.wiley.com/doi/10.1002/ppul.21205/full

3. Bonura et al, "Hydroxytyrosol modulates Par j 1-induced IL-10 production by PBMCs in healthy subjects," *Immunobiology* 221, no. 12 (December 2016): 1374–1377. doi:10.1016/j.imbio.2016.07.009

4. Sihai Wu and Dajiang Xiao, "Effect of curcumin on nasal symptoms and airflow in patients with perennial allergic rhinitis," *Annals of Allergy, Asthma & Immunology* 117, no. 6 (December 2016): 697–702. https://www.ncbi.nlm.nih.gov/pubmed/27789120

5. Kashiwabara et al, "Suppression of neuropeptide production by quercetin in allergic rhinitis model rats," *BMC Complementary and Alternative Medicine* (May 20, 2016). doi:10.1186/s12906-016-1123-z

6. Mlcek et al, "Quercetin and its anti-allergic immune response," *Molecules* 21, no. 5 (2016): 623. doi:10.3390/molecules21050623

5 Foods to Prevent Headaches and Migraines

1. Burch et al, "The prevalence and burden of migraine and severe headache in the United States: updated statistics from government health surveillance studies," *Headache: The Journal of Head and Face Pain* 55, no. 1 (January 2015): 21–34. doi:10.1111/head.12482

2. Alexander Mauskop and Jasmine Varughese, "Why all migraine patients should be treated with magnesium," *Journal of Neural Transmission* (Vienna) 119, no. 5 (May 2012): 575–9. doi:10.1007/s00702-012-0790-2

3. http://www.sciencedirect.com/topics/medicine-and-dentistry/flax

4. Harel et al, "Supplementation with omega-3 polyunsaturated fatty acids in the management of recurrent migraines in adolescents," *Journal of Adolescent Health* 31, no. 2 (August 2002): 154–61. https://www.ncbi.nlm.nih.gov/pubmed/12127385; Ramsden et al, "Targeted alteration of dietary n-3 and n-6 fatty acids for the treatment of chronic headaches: A randomized trial," *Pain* 154, no. 11 (November 2013): 2441–51. doi:10.1016/j.pain.2013.07.028

5. Maghbooli et al, "Comparison between the efficacy of ginger and sumatriptan in the ablative treatment of the common migraine," *Phytotherapy Research* 28, no. 3 (March 2014): 412–5. doi:10.1002/ptr.4996

5 Foods to Alleviate Gas

1. Kevin Whelan, "Probiotics and prebiotics in the management of irritable bowel syndrome: a review of recent clinical trials and systematic reviews," *Current Opinion in Clinical Nutrition and Metabolic Care* 14, no. 6 (November 2011): 581–587. https://www.ncbi.nlm.nih.gov/pubmed/21892075

2. Steven R. Hertzler and Shannon M. Clancy, "Kefir improves lactose digestion and tolerance in adults with lactose maldigestion," *Journal of the American Dietetic Association* 103, no. 5 (May 2003): 582–7. https://www.ncbi.nlm.nih.gov/pubmed/12728216

3. Rathish Nair and Sumitra Chanda, "Antibacterial activities of some medicinal plants of the western region of India," *Turkish Journal of Biology* 31 (2007): 231–6.

4. Fazela et al, "Effects of *Anethum graveolens* L. (Dill) essential oil on the intensity of retained intestinal gas, flatulence and pain after cesarean section: A randomized, double-blind placebo-controlled trial," *Journal of Herbal Medicine* 8 (June 2017): 8–13. https://doi.org/10.1016/j.hermed.2017.01.002

5. Agah et al, "Cumin extract for symptom control in patients with irritable bowel syndrome: A case series," *Middle East Journal of Digestive Diseases* 5, no. 4 (October 2013): 217–222. https://www.ncbi.nlm.nih.gov/pmc/articles/PMC3990147/

6. Vejdani et al, "The efficacy of an herbal medicine, Carmint, on the relief of abdominal pain and bloating in patients with irritable bowel syndrome: A pilot study," *Digestive Diseases and Sciences* 51, no. 8 (August 2006): 1501–7. doi:10.1007/s10620-006-9079-3

7. Ibid.

5 Foods to Enhance Dull, Dry Hair

1. Zuzanna Goluch-Koniuszy, "Nutrition of women with hair loss problem during the period of menopause," *Przegląd Menopauzalny (Menopause Review)* 15, no. 1 (March 2016): 56–61. doi:10.5114/pm.2016.58776

2. Edith M. Carlisle, "Silicon as an essential element for the chick," *Science* 178, no. 4061 (January 1972): 619–21. doi:10.1126/science.178.4061.619; Klaus Schwarz and David B. Milne, "Growth-promoting effects of silicon in rats," *Nature* 239, no. 5371 (November 1972): 333–4. doi:10.1038/239333a0

3. Ravin Jugdaohsingh, "Silicon and bone health," *Journal of Nutrition, Health, and Aging* 11, no. 2 (March–April 2007): 99–110. https://www.ncbi.nlm.nih.gov/pubmed/17435952

5 Foods to Fight PMS

1. Hylan et al, "The impact of premenstrual symptomatology on functioning and treatment-seeking behavior: experience from the United States, United Kingdom, and France," *Journal of Women's Health & Gender Based Medicine* 8, no. 8 (October 1999): 1043–52. https://www.ncbi.nlm.nih.gov/pubmed/10565662

2. https://medlineplus.gov/premenstrualsyndrome.html; https://www.mayoclinic.org/diseases-conditions/premenstrual-syndrome/basics/definition/con-20020003

3. Bertone-Johnson et al, "Calcium and vitamin D intake and risk of incident premenstrual syndrome," *Archives of Internal Medicine* 165, no. 11 (June 13, 2005): 1246–52. https://www.ncbi.nlm.nih.gov/pubmed/15956003

4. Tartagni et al, "Vitamin D supplementation for premenstrual syndrome-related mood disorders in adolescents with severe hypovitaminosis D," *Journal of Pediatric and Adolescent Gynecology* 29, no. 4 (August 2016): 357–61. doi:10.1016/j.jpag.2015.12.006

5. Shobeiri et al, "Effect of calcium on premenstrual syndrome: A double-blind randomized clinical trial," *Obstetrics & Gynecology Science* 60, no. 1 (January 2017): 100–105. doi:10.5468/ogs.2017.60.1.100

6. Quaranta et al, "Pilot study of the efficacy and safety of a modified-release magnesium 250 mg tablet (Sincromag) for the treatment of premenstrual syndrome," *Clinical Drug Investigation* 27, no. 1 (2007): 51–8. https://www.ncbi.nlm.nih.gov/pubmed/22069417; De Souza et al, "A synergistic effect of a daily supplement for 1 month of 200 mg magnesium plus 50 mg vitamin B6 for the relief of anxiety-related premenstrual symptoms: A randomized, double-blind, crossover study," *Journal of Women's Health & Gender Based Medicine* 9, no. 2 (March 2000): 131–9. https://www.ncbi.nlm.nih.gov/pubmed/10746516; Fathizadeh et al, "Evaluating the effect of magnesium and magnesium plus vitamin B6 supplement on the severity of premenstrual syndrome," *Iranian Journal of Nursing and Midwifery Research* 15, Suppl. 1 (December 2010): 401–5. https://www.ncbi.nlm.nih.gov/pubmed/22069417

7. Saeedian Kia et al, "The association between the risk of premenstrual syndrome and vitamin D, calcium, and magnesium status among university students: A case control study," *Health Promotion Perspectives* 5, no. 3 (2015): 225–230. doi:10.15171/hpp.2015.027

8. Ataollahi et al, "The effect of wheat germ extract on premenstrual syndrome symptoms," *Iranian Journal of Pharmaceutical Research* 14, no. 1 (Winter 2015): 159–166. https://www.ncbi.nlm.nih.gov/pmc/articles/PMC4277629/

5 Foods to Lower High Blood Pressure

1. National Institute for Health and Care Excellence (NICE), "Hypertension: The clinical management of primary hypertension in adults: Update of clinical guidelines 18 and 34," NICE Clinical Guidelines, No. 127 (August 2011). https://www.ncbi.nlm.nih.gov/books/NBK83262/

2. Ried et al, "Effect of cocoa on blood pressure," Cochrane Database of Systematic Reviews (August 15, 2012). doi:10.1002/14651858.CD008893.pub2

5 Foods to Battle Bad Breath

1. Bahadır Uğur Aylıkcı and Hakan Çolak, "Halitosis: From diagnosis to management," *Journal of Natural Science, Biology and Medicine* 4, no. 1 (January–June 2013): 14–23. doi:10.4103/0976-9668.107255

2. Outhouse et al, "Tongue scraping for treating halitosis," Cochrane Database of Systematic Reviews (April 19, 2006). https://www.ncbi.nlm.nih.gov/pubmed/16625641; Pedrazzi et al, "Interventions for managing halitosis," Cochrane Database of Systematic Reviews (First published May 25, 2016). http://onlinelibrary.wiley.com/doi/10.1002/14651858.CD012213/full

3. Yaegaki et al, "Standardization of clinical protocols in oral malodor research," *Journal of Breath Research* 6, no. 1 (March 2012): 017101. doi:10.1088/1752-7155/6/1/017101

4. Ryan Munch and Sheryl A. Barring, "Deodorization of garlic breath volatiles by food and food components," *Journal of Food Science* 79, no. 4 (April 2014): C526–33. doi:10.1111/1750-3841.12394

5. Lodhia et al, "Effect of green tea on volatile sulfur compounds in mouth air," *Journal of Nutritional Science and Vitaminology* (Tokyo) 54, no. 1 (February 2008): 89–94. https://www.ncbi.nlm.nih.gov/pubmed/18388413

6. Ryan Munch and Sheryl A. Barring, "Deodorization of garlic breath volatiles by food and food components," *Journal of Food Science* 79, no. 4 (April 2014): C526–33. doi:10.1111/1750-3841.12394

7. Osamu Negishi and Yukiko Negishi, "Enzymatic deodorization with raw fruits, vegetables and mushrooms," *Food Science and Technology Research* 5, no. 2 (1999): 176–180. https://www.jstage.jst.go.jp/article/fstr/5/2/5_2_176/_pdf/-char/en

8. Wälti et al, "The effect of a chewing-intensive, high-fiber diet on oral halitosis: A clinical controlled study," *Swiss Dental Journal* 126, no. 9 (2016): 782–795. https://www.sso.ch/fileadmin/upload_sso/2_Zahnaerzte/2_SDJ/SDJ_2016/SDJ_Pubmed_2016/sdj-2016-09-01.pdf

9. Ibid.

10. Hur et al, "Reduction of mouth malodour and volatile sulphur compounds in intensive care patients using an essential oil mouthwash," *Phytotherapy Research* 21, no. 7 (July 2007): 641–3. https://www.ncbi.nlm.nih.gov/pubmed/17380550?dopt=Abstract

11. Castada et al, "Deodorization of garlic odor by spearmint, peppermint, and chocolate mint leaves and rosmarinic acid," *LWT – Food Science and Technology* 84 (October 2017): 160–167. http://www.sciencedirect.com/science/journal/00236438/84/supp/C

12. Ryan Munch and Sheryl A. Barring, "Deodorization of garlic breath volatiles by food and food components," *Journal of Food Science* 79, no. 4 (April 2014): C526–33. doi:10.1111/1750-3841.12394

13. Ibid.

5 Foods to Boost Libido

1. Rosen et al, "Correlates of sexually related personal distress in women with low sexual desire," *Journal of Sexual Medicine* 6, no. 6 (June 2009): 1549–60. doi: 10.1111/j.1743-6109.2009.01252.x

2. Riaz et al, "Protective role of ginger on lead induced derangement in plasma testosterone and luteinizing hormone levels of male Sprague Dawley rats," *Journal of Ayub Medical College, Abbottabad: JAMC* 23, no. 4 (October–December 2011): 24–7. https://www.ncbi.nlm.nih.gov/pubmed/23472404; Ghlissi et al, "Antioxidant and androgenic effects of dietary ginger on reproductive function of male diabetic rats," *International Journal of Food Sciences and Nutrition* 64, no. 8 (December 2013): 974–8. doi:10.3109/09637486.2013.812618; Waleed Abid Al-Kadir Mares and Wisam S. Najam, "The effect of ginger on semen parameters and serum FSH, LH & testosterone of infertile men," *Tikrit Medical Journal* 18, no. 2 (2012): 322–329. https://www.iasj.net/iasj?func=fulltext&aId=71548

3. http://today.tamu.edu/2008/07/01/watermelon-may-have-viagra-like-effect/

4. Susan Mayor, "Meta-analysis shows difference between antidepressants and placebo is only significant in severe depression," *BMJ* 336 (2008): 466. https://doi.org/10.1136/bmj.39503.656852.DB

5. Alan R. Hirsch, M.D., F.A.C.P., and Jason J. Gruss, "Human male sexual response to olfactory stimuli," Smell & Taste Treatment and Research Foundation, Chicago (March 3, 2014). http://aanos.org/human-male-sexual-response-to-olfactory-stimuli/

6. Whiting et al, "Capsaicinoids and capsinoids. A potential role for weight management? A systematic review of the evidence," *Appetite* 59, no. 2 (October 2012): 341–8. doi:10.1016/j.appet.2012.05.015

7. Bègue et al, "Some like it hot: Testosterone predicts laboratory eating behavior of spicy food," *Physiology & Behavior* 139 (December 2015): 375–7. doi:10.1016/j.physbeh.2014.11.061

8. Emad Al-Dujaili and Nacer Smail, "Pomegranate juice intake enhances salivary testosterone levels and improves mood and well being in healthy men and women," *Endocrine Abstracts* (March 2012). http://www.endocrine-abstracts.org/ea/0028/ea0028p313.htm

9. Zhao et al, "Fruits for prevention and treatment of cardiovascular diseases," *Nutrients* 9, no. 6 (June 2017): 598. doi:10.3390/nu9060598

5 Foods to Prevent Muscle Cramps

1. Bailey et al, "Estimating sodium and potassium intakes and their ratio in the American diet: Data from the 2011–2012 NHANES," *Journal of Nutrition* 146, no. 4 (April 2016): 745–750. https://www.ncbi.nlm.nih .gov/pmc/articles/PMC4807641/

5 Foods to Strengthen Brittle Nails

1. Hochman set al, "Brittle nails: response to daily biotin supplementation," *Cutis* 51 (April 1993): 303-5. https://www.ncbi.nlm.nih.gov/pubmed/8477615
2. Michael W. Cashman and Steven Brett Sloan, "Nutrition and nail disease," *Clinics in Dermatology* 28, no. 4 (July–August 2010): 420–5. https://www.ncbi.nlm.nih.gov/pubmed/20620759
3. Colombo et al, "Treatment of brittle fingernails and onychoschizia with biotin: scanning electron microscopy," *Journal of the American Academy of Dermatology* 23, no. 6, part 1 (December 1990): 1127–32. https://www.ncbi.nlm.nih.gov/pubmed/2273113
4. Michael W. Cashman and Steven Brett Sloan, "Nutrition and nail disease," *Clinics in Dermatology* 28, no. 4 (July–August 2010): 420–5. https://www.ncbi.nlm.nih.gov/pubmed/20620759
5. Madhavan Naira and Little Flower Augustine, "Food synergies for improving bioavailability of micronutrients from plant foods," *Food Chemistry* 238, no. 1 (January 2018): 180–185. https://doi .org/10.1016/j.foodchem.2016.09.115
6. Michael W. Cashman and Steven Brett Sloan, "Nutrition and nail disease," *Clinics in Dermatology* 28, no. 4 (July–August 2010): 420–5. https://www.ncbi.nlm.nih.gov/pubmed/20620759
7. Sripanyakorn et al, "The comparative absorption of silicon from different foods and food supplements," *British Journal of Nutrition* 102, no. 6 (September 2009): 825–834. doi:10.1017/S0007114509311757

INDEX

ACKNOWLEDGMENTS

It takes a village. My village is filled with smart, passionate, and driven individuals who make the world a healthier place. I'm continuously inspired and forever grateful.

This book couldn't have happened without my editorial director, Donna Fennessy, who meticulously vets through endless research, while helping me translate scientific findings into delicious and user-friendly information. Donna has lived and breathed this book for the past year with unparalleled expertise, analytical rigor, and unwavering dedication. Her impeccable judgment helped shape this book into an invaluable and realistic resource that I hope will ignite thoughtful conversation around the power of food. Donna is not only an esteemed colleague, she has become a cherished best friend and confidant, whom I love with all my heart.

Special thanks to my lead nutritionist Rebecca Jay Formanm, R.D.N., who lent her careful eye and enthusiastic support 24/7. Throughout the writing process, Rebecca reviewed countless chapter drafts and scientific literature and provided insightful feedback with her signature attention to detail. While I appreciate Rebecca's intellect and work ethic every single day, I'm most grateful for her kindhearted spirit and genuine friendship.

To Ryan Nord, Jane Dystel, and Miriam Goderich, for always having my back and supporting my vision.

To my entire NBC *TODAY* family who allows me the privilege of nourishing hungry Americans with sound information. Thank you for believing in my message and enabling millions of people to live healthier, happier, and more fulfilling lives.

To the Hay House Publishing group, in particular, Reid Tracy and Patty Gift, for green-lighting this important project; my extraordinary (and patient) editor, Lisa Cheng; and Richelle Fredson, Lindsay McGinty, and Tricia Breidenthal. Infinite thanks to Lucy Schaeffer for the stunning food and lifestyle photography; to Leslie Orlandini for your outstanding food styling magic; to

Paige Hicks for beautiful props; and to my glam squad, Danielle Terry and Matthew Green, for making me look *almost* as good as the food.

Heartfelt thanks to my dear friend Sheryl Sandberg for continuously inspiring me to think big and make a meaningful impact.

Huge appreciation to Jami Kandel, who has been a dynamic force on so many of my adventures. And special thanks to Katie Maloney and Jordan Solomon for listening, for advising, and for making things happen.

Deepest gratitude to Tara Deal Rochford and Dana Fleisher, two talented R.D.N.'s and culinary whizzes who spent endless hours in the kitchen creating and testing recipes. To Erica Ilton for sharing your unrivaled wisdom on gastrointestinal health. **And to Melissa Gallanter, Jaclyn Schneider, Ginger Cochran, Carl Bender, Brooke Evans, Hailey Gorski, Molly Knudsen, Tara Lorimer, and Danielle Ziegelstein.**

To my *Nourish Snacks* family, for lending me your opinions and your taste buds whenever I need them.

A boisterous shout out—filled with high fives and hugs—to my ginormous loving family (including Debra, Steve, Ben, Noah, Becca, Chloe, Jenny, Casey, Pam, Dan, Charlie, Cooper, Granger, Elena, Glenn, Trey, Billie, Levi, Otis, Mia, Jason, Annabelle, Zachary, Bailey, Nancy, Jon, Camron, Pam, Kaheo, Madeline, Marci, Rob, Pamela, Brandon, Dave, and Beth) for always being willing to sample whatever I put in front of you.

To my mom and dad, Ellen and Artie Schloss; my other mom and dad, Carol and Victor Bauer; my husband, Ian; and three kids, Jesse, Cole, and Ayden Jane; and my favorite crumb catcher, Gatsby . . . you are my heart.

ABOUT THE AUTHOR

Joy Bauer, M.S., R.D.N., C.D.N., is one of the nation's leading health authorities. She is the health and nutrition expert for NBC's *TODAY* show and the host of *Health + Happiness*. She is also the founder of Nourish Snacks, a monthly columnist for *Woman's Day* magazine, and the official nutritionist for the New York City Ballet. Joy is the creator of JoyBauer.com and the author of 12 best-selling books. Her book *From Junk Food to Joy Food* is based on her popular *TODAY* show series, in which viewers challenge Joy to turn indulgent foods into delicious lightened-up fare for the honor of the coveted "two carrots up." This book is also the inspiration behind Joy's latest PBS special.

Previously, Joy was the Director of Nutrition and Fitness for the Department of Pediatric Cardiology at Mount Sinai Medical Center in New York City, as well as the clinical dietitian for their neurosurgical team. One of Joy's most rewarding experiences was creating and implementing "Heart Smart Kids," a health program for underprivileged children living in Harlem. Prior to making the jump to media, she taught Anatomy & Physiology and Sports Nutrition at NYU's School of Continuing Education while working to build what would soon become the largest private nutrition center in the United States.

Passionate about delivering scientifically sound, realistic information to millions of people, Joy has received countless awards, including the National Media Excellence Award from two of the most esteemed nutrition organizations, the Academy of Nutrition and Dietetics and the American Society of Nutrition Science.

When she's not dishing out health info or sharing delicious recipes on TV, you'll find Joy making a mess in her kitchen or spending quality time at home with her husband, three kids, and furry friend, Gatsby.

Hay House Titles of Related Interest

YOU CAN HEAL YOUR LIFE, the movie, starring Louise Hay & Friends
(available as a 1-DVD program, an expanded 2-DVD set, and an online streaming video)
Learn more at www.hayhouse.com/louise-movie

THE SHIFT, the movie, starring Dr. Wayne W. Dyer
(available as a 1-DVD program, an expanded 2-DVD set, and an online streaming video)
Learn more at www.hayhouse.com/the-shift-movie

. . .

ALCHEMY OF HERBS: Transform Everyday Ingredients into Foods and Remedies That Heal, by Rosalee de la Forêt

CULTURED FOOD IN A JAR: 100+ Probiotic Recipes to Inspire and Change Your Life, by Donna Schwenk

EATERNITY: More than 150 Deliciously Easy Vegan Recipes for a Long, Healthy, Satisfied, Joyful Life, by Jason Wrobel

All of the above are available at your local bookstore,
or may be ordered by contacting Hay House (see next page).

. . .

We hope you enjoyed this Hay House book. If you'd like to receive our online catalog featuring additional information on Hay House books and products, or if you'd like to find out more about the Hay Foundation, please contact:

Hay House, Inc., P.O. Box 5100, Carlsbad, CA 92018-5100
(760) 431-7695 or (800) 654-5126
(760) 431-6948 (fax) or (800) 650-5115 (fax)
www.hayhouse.com® • www.hayfoundation.org

———

Published in Australia by:
Hay House Australia Pty. Ltd., 18/36 Ralph St., Alexandria NSW 2015
Phone: 612-9669-4299 • *Fax:* 612-9669-4144 • www.hayhouse.com.au

Published in the United Kingdom by:
Hay House UK, Ltd., Astley House, 33 Notting Hill Gate, London W11 3JQ
Phone: 44-20-3675-2450 • *Fax:* 44-20-3675-2451 • www.hayhouse.co.uk

Published in India by: Hay House Publishers India,
Muskaan Complex, Plot No. 3, B-2, Vasant Kunj, New Delhi 110 070
Phone: 91-11-4176-1620 • *Fax:* 91-11-4176-1630 • www.hayhouse.co.in

———

Access New Knowledge.
Anytime. Anywhere.

Learn and evolve at your own pace
with the world's leading experts.

www.hayhouseU.com

More JOY in your life!

Hungry for more?

Visit JOYBAUER.COM
for delicious recipes and healthy
lifestyle tips.

Free e-newsletters
from Hay House, the Ultimate
Resource for Inspiration

Be the first to know about Hay House's free downloads, special offers, giveaways, contests, and more!

Get exclusive excerpts from our latest releases and videos from *Hay House Present Moments*.

Our *Digital Products Newsletter* is the perfect way to stay up-to-date on our latest discounted eBooks, featured mobile apps, and Live Online and On Demand events.

Learn with real benefits! *HayHouseU.com* is your source for the most innovative online courses from the world's leading personal growth experts. Be the first to know about new online courses and to receive exclusive discounts.

Enjoy uplifting personal stories, how-to articles, and healing advice, along with videos and empowering quotes, within *Heal Your Life*.

Have an inspirational story to tell and a passion for writing? Sharpen your writing skills with insider tips from *Your Writing Life*.

Sign Up Now!

Get inspired, educate yourself, get a complimentary gift, and share the wisdom!

Visit www.hayhouse.com/newsletters to sign up today!

radio for your soul®

HAY HOUSE
online learning

Hay House Podcasts
Bring Fresh, Free Inspiration Each Week!

Hay House proudly offers a selection of life-changing audio content via our most popular podcasts!

Hay House Meditations Podcast

Features your favorite Hay House authors guiding you through meditations designed to help you relax and rejuvenate. Take their words into your soul and cruise through the week!

Dr. Wayne W. Dyer Podcast

Discover the timeless wisdom of Dr. Wayne W. Dyer, world-renowned spiritual teacher and affectionately known as "the father of motivation". Each week brings some of the best selections from the 10-year span of Dr. Dyer's talk show on HayHouseRadio.com.

Hay House World Summit Podcast

Over 1 million people from 217 countries and territories participate in the massive online event known as the Hay House World Summit. This podcast offers weekly mini-lessons from World Summits past as a taste of what you can hear during the annual event, which occurs each May.

Hay House Radio Podcast

Listen to some of the best moments from HayHouseRadio.com, featuring expert authors such as Dr. Christiane Northrup, Anthony William, Caroline Myss, James Van Praagh, and Doreen Virtue discussing topics such as health, self-healing, motivation, spirituality, positive psychology, and personal development.

Hay House Live Podcast

Enjoy a selection of insightful and inspiring lectures from Hay House Live, an exciting event series that features Hay House authors and leading experts in the fields of alternative health, nutrition, intuitive medicine, success, and more! Feel the electricity of our authors engaging with a live audience, and get motivated to live your best life possible!

Find Hay House podcasts on iTunes, or visit www.HayHouse.com/podcasts for more info.